Television

The Public Sphere and National Identity

Monroe E. Price

CLARENDON PRESS · OXFORD

OXFORD
UNIVERSITY PRESS
Great Clarendon Street, Oxford OX2 6DP

Oxford University Press is a department of the University of Oxford.
It furthers the University's objective of excellence in research, scholarship,
and education by publishing worldwide in

Oxford New York
Athens Auckland Bangkok Bogotá Buenos Aires Calcutta
Cape Town Chennai Dar es Salaam Delhi Florence Hong Kong Istanbul
Karachi Kuala Lumpur Madrid Melbourne Mexico City Mumbai
Nairobi Paris São Paulo Shanghai Singapore Taipei Tokyo Toronto Warsaw
and associated companies in Berlin Ibadan

Oxford is a registered trade mark of Oxford University Press
in the UK and in certain other countries

Published in the United States
by Oxford University Press Inc., New York

Reprinted 2000

ISBN 0-19-818362-3
ISBN 0-19-818338-0 (Pbk.)

Printed in Great Britain
on acid-free paper by
Bookcraft (Bath) Short Run Books
Midsomer Norton

Acknowledgements

WHILE writing this book I was fortunate to be a member of the Commission on Radio and Television Policy, established by President Jimmy Carter, bringing together people interested in television from both the United States and the former Soviet Union. Research in the United Kingdom, Russia, Ukraine, and the United States was made possible by a grant from the John and Mary R. Markle Foundation and Lloyd Morrissett, its president, who saw promise in this undertaking. I acknowledge the special contribution of Edith Bjornson, the Markle Foundation's senior program officer, who has steadfastly supported efforts to enrich public discussion of media policy.

During my research I have also benefited from support from the Eurasia Foundation, the Ford Foundation, and the Jacob Burns Institute for Advanced Legal Studies and the Howard Squadron Center on Law, Media and Society at Yeshiva University's Benjamin N. Cardozo School of Law. I was fortunate to be a Visiting Fellow at the Centre for Socio-Legal Studies at Wolfson College, Oxford, where this work originated, and a frequent and welcomed guest at the Institute for International Communications in London, the Institute for Information Law at the University of Amsterdam, the Media Studies Department there, and the Institute for Constitutional and Legal Policy at the Central European University in Budapest.

Part Two of the book was enriched by my work as editor of the Post Soviet Media Law and Policy Newsletter, and in that enterprise I gained enormously from a close association with Professor Peter Krug, University of Oklahoma, Aleksei Simon of the Glasnost Defense Foundation and Andrei Richter, Moscow State University. Chapter 4 of the manuscript reflects two earlier publications: an article entitled 'The Market for Loyalties: Electronic Media and the Global Competition for Allegiances', which appeared in volume 104 of the *Yale Law Journal*, and the 1994 *InterMedia* Prize Essay, published in volume 25 of *InterMedia* (October–November 1994). Gary Greenstein was my loyal and careful editor at the *Yale Law Journal* and *InterMedia*'s Rex Winsbury made valuable comments as well. Charles Firestone, director of the Communications and Society Program of the Aspen Institute, constant resource and friend, has co-travelled many of the roads described in the book. Mavis Maclean, stalwart member of Oxford's Socio-Legal Studies Centre, was a guiding and encouraging light for this book, as she has been for so many works of others. I also wish to thank my colleagues at the Benjamin N. Cardozo School of Law, especially Professor Arthur Jacobson and Dean Frank Macchiarola, for their support.

My thanks to Professor Andras Sajo, Central European University, Professor Eric Barendt, University College, London, Professor Robert Entman at North Carolina State University, and Professor Krug, each of whom commented on the manuscript in detail. Ad Van Loon, Legal Expert of the Audiovisual Observatory in Strasbourg, was a willing guide to intricacies of Dutch, Belgian, and European law. Dr Aimée Brown Price, fresh from her exploration of the work of Puvis de Chavannes, gave trenchant, perceptive, and loving comments, all of which enriched the final manuscript. Asher G. B. Price, Gabriel E. Price, and Joshua M. Price, each in his own startling way, made important contributions and criticisms. Suzannah Kennedy, Renée Burmeister, Blake Stimson, Douglas Turnbull, and Mia Higgins aided me as research assistants. At Oxford University Press, my thanks to Andrew Lockett, Vicki Reeve, and Hilary Walford, not the least for coping with the vagaries of transcontinental spelling and cross-cultural syntactical variations.

Contents

Part One

Loyalty and Identity

1 The Nation-State and Global Media

THE electronic media pervade our daily being, and yet we hardly have a grip on what radio and television mean to the political geography of modern life. Imagery affects loyalties: that has always been known. What has been less clear is that the structure and capacity of communications and the fate of governments are inextricably intertwined. Throughout the world, the organization of broadcasting and the dissemination of television programmes are changing and often radically. The millions of images that float through the public mind help determine the very nature of national allegiances, attitudes towards place, family, government, and state. No wonder that in all locales—developed or undeveloped, democracy or dictatorship, transition society or not—the question of the structuring and future regulation of media is so important.

In the late 1940s, during his post-war search for a new utopia, the poet W. H. Auden longed for an 'ideal open society [that] . . . would know no physical, economic or cultural frontiers'.[1] Today, the open society that knows no physical or cultural frontiers is upon us, or at least appears to be through its media version. Satellites drive signals within their own 'footprints', regardless of borders. Everywhere, historic images of collective identities are shifting. Seventy years of a power-oriented, strongly directed Soviet Union, with a committed policy of controlling imagery, were insufficient to prevent the very badges of loyalty from being turned against those who propagated them. Czechoslovakia dissolved in the whisper of an election. The set of imposed identities that was Yugoslavia was insufficient, alone, to maintain unity among those with long-nurtured bitter hatreds. The sign—without force—proved incapable of maintaining a polity. Images may sustain the idea of a people, but they are not sufficient to maintain the bonds of a state far beyond the convenience of its citizenry. Still, communal symbols reinforce cohesion, affect the duration and nature of any particular hegemony, and, therefore, have a central place in the idea of the state.

Nation after nation has learnt the modern impossibility of maintaining a monopoly over imagery, but the effort to do so persists. The open society—one that, in Auden's words, knows no cultural or physical frontiers—is difficult to achieve, partly because democratic values, without concrete loyalties, leave the apparatus of public life too weakened. The task, then, is to determine how the state can generate, sustain, or encourage narratives to communal well-being and remain true to democratic values. If the state cannot undertake these tasks satisfactorily, the question becomes one of state survival.[2] The focus in this book is on those instruments for communication that have been employed primarily to undergird the established order, though they have also been used, at times, effectively to undermine it. Radio and television have been generators of mass public imagery, inscribed with special powers. Who runs broadcasting, how it is organized, what images are permitted to pass through towers and transmitters—all these questions have been the subject of almost a century of debate. But radio and television are only an example, only a segment, of the general subject of images in society. When we think about the impact of these media, it must be in the context of the collection of symbols and signals that compose society and constitute its stimuli. Those who worry about curriculum in the schools are cousins to those who fret about the appropriate level of dignity for the flag. Those who are concerned about images of race and depictions of women are cousins to those who are concerned about violence and obscenity and those who fight over the appropriate means of funding and encouraging the visual arts. Advocates of public-service television have this much in common with their opponents: both groups see the importance of imagery in altering the nature of community. Throughout, the search is on for the proper phrasing of public debate over impact, social limits, and the effects of new technology.

This plethora of changing signals, floating, then raining from space, poses impressive problems of belonging, identification, nationalism, and community. Each nation thinks it is important to teach its own history to its children. Monuments constructed in public squares are important for more than their time. They are temples of remembrance, building loyalties for the future. A national public debate about the flag—its desecration and reverence—can still raise passions with those on both sides feeling themselves patriotic. Even in a world exploding with information, there is a role for a government-funded public broadcasting system that will enrich and help to define and reflect the national identity. And the struggle over the content of the curriculum in public education and in college still flares with an explosive brightness that indicates what the participants consider to be at stake.

There is little consensus about these issues: about the content of public space and the government's responsibility over the images that appear on the television screen. For most of this century, especially in the United States, the role of government in regulating broadcasting was predicated on the scarcity of opportunities for individuals and firms to send forth their ideas and programmes. Bursts of technological change have undermined these assumptions, but not necessarily eliminated the social ills that they addressed. In other parts of the world, it has been not the move from scarcity to abundance, but transformations in the idea of the state (often, itself, related to technological change), that have led to a similar need for re-examination.

Beginnings and Consolidation

The first half-century of broadcasting—the period from 1915 to the mid-1960s—was the era, generally, of the nation in control of its radio and then its television structures. That was the time of pioneering and of consolidation; it was a period that ended at the introduction of the satellite and in the morning of cable television. It was a half-century marked by events that in many ways emphasized the political and cultural needs of the state. The mentality of the first generation of broadcasters was affected by the sense of national identity that emerged in the wake of the First World War. The first director of programmes of the British Broadcasting Company, for example, started his radio tenure collecting and editing, for his government, intercepted wireless propaganda of the Central Powers.[3] For each of the major Western powers, modern communications were part of a tendency towards centralization and an emphasis of national over regional influences. The bureaucracy almost everywhere matured in the protectionist and isolationist mood of the Depression. Their successors were more cosmopolitan, but not by much. For them, the instructors in the need for strong state identity were the antagonisms of the Second World War and the harsh separateness of the Cold War. Even in the United States, where the division between government and the press is so highly valued, it was a matter of pride that executives could move back and forth from the Voice of America to the private networks. It is little wonder, in a period so condemned to the importance of borders, that national concerns over the shaping of imagery would be so pronounced.

Radio, actually, had an essentially non-national birth. Almost by definition, radio waves are not respecters of national boundaries. And, as a technology, the first application of radio was to conquer boundaries, to reach out, for navigational safety, beyond borders, through transmissions from ship to shore.[4] Conceptually, the earliest audience uses of radio were of little significance in terms of the government's substantive interest in content. From the outset, music, a cross-cultural commodity, was a mainstay. And programmes existed to sell equipment, not for any other purpose, covert or expressed. Given this infancy, radio could have been considered a mechanism precisely to cut across national lines, to reach an audience of hobbyists and crystal-set makers irrespective of state identity.

And yet, the international or transnational use of radio was not to be its major characteristic. Shortly after its ship-to-shore beginnings, the struggle was to contain radio within national borders, to provide that its growth would occur within the protective and insular supervision of the government. Where possible, there would be strong limits on the intrusion of signals from one country to another. Policing this process came to be a chief function of international broadcasting organizations, a function echoed, fifty years later, during the early days of satellite communications.[5] In Canada, by the late 1920s, the first fears were being expressed of over-dependence on US programming and of competition for frequencies from the United States.[6] The drum roll for national consciousness was often phrased in terms of the 'public trust' or the 'public service'. This was the moment—a flash that vanished—of unrequited insight by Herbert Hoover, then Secretary of Commerce, who was charged with the initial regulatory responsibilities. Hoover argued that radio should not be considered 'merely as a business carried on for private gain, for private advertisement, or for the entertainment of the curious. It is to be considered as a public concern, impressed with a public trust, and to be considered primarily from the standpoint of public interest.'[7] In 1923 the Sykes Committee, established by the British government, stated that 'the control of such a potential power over public opinion and the life of the nation ought to remain with the State'.[8]

The almost immediate government reaction to threats from transnational broadcasting was the subject of a brilliant little book on the early history of the BBC by the famous economist R. H. Coase.[9]

In 1925 an 'unauthorized' radio service, using the Eiffel Tower in Paris as its transmission point, broadcast an English-language programme directed to the United Kingdom, with advertising from a London department-store chain, hoping to build a British audience. Immediately, British government and broadcasting interests sought to limit the competition. By the early 1930s there was a vigorous business in English-language broadcasting, supported by British advertisers, emanating from France and directed at British listeners. To protect the national broadcasting monopoly (and the arrangements with the newspaper industry that were involved), it became government policy to suppress foreign commercial broadcasting in English.[10]

The US experience is often contrasted with that of the British, and, in many ways, the traditions are quite separate and distinct. Neither US industry nor Congress sought the emergence of a powerful national public-service entity with a monopoly over audience and a state charter. Still, the history of broadcasting in the United States is the history of frequency allocation by government and licensing by the government as well, a history that underscored the state-organized nature of the medium.[11] By treaty with Mexico and Canada, the United States sought to minimize the number of television signals originating outside its borders that were directed at American audiences. Foreign ownership was limited. Powerful radio entities—'clear channels'—were licensed that could reach across a huge expanse of the then-forty-eight states and served to redefine internal identities. The establishment of the clear channels was a domestic version of the international debate over patterns of signal transmission and patterns of cultures. Government licensing contained substantive content restrictions for the licensees. The very act of licensing and the threat that a licence would not be renewed assured that the bond between broadcaster and state would be a close one.

In one country after another, the state first came into the picture to help in the structuring of the industry, to regulate entry, to limit competition. And, once in, the state stayed as a substantial factor in determining the role of the broadcast media in the society. Radio became instrumental as a forum for explanation, for patriotism, for mobilization, and for maintaining morale in the Second World War. In Germany and Italy the potential of radio and film for instilling a mad loyalty to the state was soon being perfected. This preoccupation with the power of radio became the norm, not the exception. Afterwards, radio, and then television, remained a tool not only in building the new society and providing reinforcement for national attitudes, but in projecting competing official views around the world. As Eli Noam has written, 'the single and unified nation-state, the main unit of governance around the globe, was matched and served by its national monopoly communications network, usually owned and operated by the state as a public service, like the road system'.[12] These bonds were strong in the Soviet Union and in post-war Central and Eastern Europe, where the state and broadcasting were the same, or, much to the same effect, were both under the control of the Communist Party. Radio, and then television, were direct, unequivocal instruments of state policy in totalitarian and authoritarian regimes—'engineers of the soul', to adapt a phrase used by Stalin with respect to the function of the arts. Control of these tools of mass information and persuasion was central to the idea of a commanding state. Not only was broadcasting an instrument of the state, but the government media had exclusive use of the airwaves. To the extent that there was purposive, or even accidental spillover of signals across borders, jamming was an active policy to enforce the monopoly voice.[13]

At the end of this first half-century of broadcasting, while the policies of the countries of Western Europe were often far more benign and more plural than those of the East, radio and television were still, by and large, strongly connected to the state. In France, by the mid-1970s, the ORTF was a scandalous handmaiden of the government, with new directors-general appointed with each election. In England, to be sure, there was a tradition of independence and a structure that largely immunized the BBC from the influence of the government of the day. In many ways, the BBC was *sui generis*. But even there, except within the sacred precincts of the true believers, it was argued that the BBC was part of the establishment of the state. A growing critical movement suggested that the vaunted independence disguised deep hegemonic relations between the ruling élite and those in control. Anthony Smith has captured this well, writing about the BBC's 'protective view of society and its institutions'. It had been the practice, not only in Britain, but throughout Europe, to discern, from time to time, 'those practices and institutions which comprise the settled external order which it deems its duty not to disturb'.[14]

Government officials throughout the world have used their power to influence the direction of broadcasting to support particular conceptions of the state and national identity. These efforts have ranged from censorship or specific directions as to what stories to cover and what could not be said to structural interventions. Both those in control of the state and those in charge of broadcasting have had strong ideas about the role that the media could play in altering or reinforcing proper habits of speech. For decades, the BBC was an instrument of elocution enhancement, a blanket of propriety, with the specific intent of influencing the way a population conducted itself. In some settings radio and television language was the language of empire, present or past: Russian throughout the Soviet Union; French in francophonic Africa; English in the Celtic lands. The history of language and broadcasting itself is a useful study of the relationship of state-making to the media.

Broadcasting and Propaganda

In the United States, the relationship between radio and government in the Second World War as a means of unifying the home front was an example of this not always pernicious tendency.[15] More notorious was the period of McCarthyism; for that was a time in which the leverage of state power was used to identify and purge the expression of themes, of stories, and of news approaches allegedly hostile to the dominant view of American culture. In the celebration of the American free market of ideas, one tends to forget how searing, how thorough, and how lasting the impact of McCarthyism was. Unambiguous signals emanating from congressional hearings placed an ideological frame around the programmes that were broadcast.[16] Reinforced by these pressures, radio and television stations in the 1950s purged their rolls of commentators, script-writers, and actors who were suspected of Communist sympathies.[17]

As basic a question as the award of frequencies—internal boundaries of the air—has always reflected particular notions of the nature of the state. In the United States, the Congress, as early as 1927, directed the then Federal Radio Commission (FRC) to construct a system that provided equitable distribution of licences among areas; the nation was divided into zones with one FRC commissioner representing each zone. The successor agency (the Federal Communications Commission (FCC)) established the policy that, if possible, every community would have its own station, even if that meant that there were fewer national services or that a less efficient comprehensive allocation would result.[18] In France, in England, and in most of Western Europe, almost all frequencies were held centrally, and this was particularly true of television. In Canada, from the 1920s forward, the structure and administration of broadcasting became a fulcrum for the persistent struggle between a 'national' Canada and its diverse parts. Allocating frequency between broadcasting and competing uses was another pointer, for it might disclose the extent to which the government considered it important to have multiple voices in the society, some of which might not always be subject to control. Using frequency sparingly, providing only for a limited number of signals, is a less visible form of control. Government could determine, as it sought to do in South Africa, whether the polluting quality of television would be permitted at all; when colour television could be introduced; or, as in France in the late 1960s, whether television should be permitted at dinner-time. It was, almost everywhere, a government decision whether the medium could be used to show advertising and alter the advance of consumerism in the society.

Still other examples of the state and national identity relate to the family of activities called propaganda, which, among other things, constitutes the positive use of television and radio to enforce ideas of nationhood. Even those Western democracies that have the strongest constitutional prohibitions on censorship recognized how important and how necessary propaganda had become in the twentieth century. We remember and revere the stirring speeches of Winston Churchill in the Second World War, but we should not forget that they were part of concerted, substantial, and effective efforts in each warring state to win hearts and minds, to maintain and strengthen loyalties.

Crises are the test of utility, and the role of radio and television in times of national strain is of such force that no leader is willing to leave the direction of the most effective means of mass persuasion solely to chance. That is why the television tower is still among the first objectives of revolutionaries, why control of imagery remains so important in war and other crises. But it is not only a matter of crisis. The fireside chats of Franklin D. Roosevelt are a pleasant token of sustained White House shaping of public attitudes—a capability now so bureaucratized and institutionalized that the White House has had a Director of Communications and 'spin control' becomes a euphemism for the science of creating national narratives. By ritualizing and sometimes creating great national events, such as those informal talks between President and people, the coronation of the Queen, the inauguration of the President, the first moonwalk, or the funeral of John F. Kennedy, government use of radio and television has played, and continues to play, a vital part in establishing the new mythologies of the state in modern times.[19]

It is because of this long and intimate history of the state's relationship to the broadcast media that the belief persists that the state can continue to affect the content of radio and television. Interest groups expect that government officials can use their power to influence television to represent a particular vision of the good society. Those who object to violence and obscenity in the United States have prevailed on Congress to force rules that limit indecency and programmes that might be deleterious for children. Those who think that less dominant ethnic groups within the United States should be better represented on the screen have consistently lobbied for government pressure to obtain change. Portrayal of women, portrayal of business, portrayal of gays, portrayal of the elderly, portrayal of Democrats and Republicans, portrayal of Native Americans, or of those for or against abortion have all been the subject of inquiry and, sometimes, action by the Federal Communications Commission. And this is the case in the United States, where, because of the First Amendment, the relationship between state and broadcaster is thought to be the weakest, where the broadcaster is most protected by law (indeed, by the Constitution) from over-zealous interference in the broadcaster's depiction of society.

Transformation and Globalization

I have already tried to show how, during the entire historical period from the introduction of radio until the 1960s, there was virtually universal determination to maintain control of broadcasting, generally speaking, within national boundaries. If one looked at the world's radio and television systems, an essential, almost ever-present feature would be their rootedness in a single place and their exclusive relation to that place. That was the constant. There were exceptions, and exceptions of great importance: in the congested pattern of territoriality of Europe, and elsewhere (the United States–Canada border, for example), there was unavoidable spillover of signals. And in times of conflict—and as the modern tools of propaganda were well learnt—the use of broadcasting as an instrument of ideological persuasion, to be used against an enemy, became more and more an everyday practice.[20] For the great empires, even the empires of freedom, having radio follow the flag became a tradition. But these exceptions (and the purposeful foundation of Radio Luxemburg) were technological, screened-off changelings: short wave for access to international and foreign signals, highly directed broadcasts for purposes of ideological conversion,[21] and the accidents of the cross between border and technology.

If the idea of 'home', of a bond between the nation and broadcasting, was the common theme, the seeming difference was in the mode of financing. Governments varied as to whether advertising-supported programming would be permitted, whether broadcasting would be a private undertaking with a minimum or absence of government subsidy, public airwaves aside. During this long period, most Western nations were wrestling with the way in which their broadcasting systems should be structured within these alternative nodes in the light of domestic ideologies, public needs, and technological change.[22] Those writing about diversity, public service, and cultural values focused on these differences and their impact on programming. From the perspective of the moment, the disparities among the various national solutions were of extraordinary significance. The gulf between the BBC, free of advertising pressure, and American commercial television, filled with advertising and non-reliant on subsidy, seemed enormous. Yet, in retrospect—from the television of the future—it will be the similarities, not the differences, say between the United Kingdom and the United States, that will begin to emerge. What will be significant is the capacity the state had to shape broadcasting; informally or formally to have it incorporate, reflect, and shape the community's identity.

For, as the first half century of broadcasting came to a close, there were already strong signs that the state-based primacy of first radio and then television was under attack. Radio Luxemburg was a constant counterpoint to the vaunted supremacy of the national broadcasters, the ethereal threat that commercial broadcasting, appealing to popular tastes, could someday overwhelm the European state-based systems.[23] Much later, the significant creativity of pirate radio—adventurous young broadcasters of the 1960s, using the protection of international waters for zany and triumphantly boisterous successes—also demonstrated the potential weaknesses of the broadcasting behemoths. Mischievous and entrepreneurial modernists, they saw a market opportunity in the BBC's conservative policy towards popular culture. It was the boundary itself that was the basis for arguing immunity and the capacity to compete. After a long battle, the pirates were routed, but the BBC (and public-service broadcasting in the Netherlands and beyond) was forever altered, the idea of competition had been firmly planted, and popular music programming in the United Kingdom was revolutionized.[24]

Apart from the directed intrusion by novel forms of transmission, some scholars were arguing that national dominance over their media, the very capacity to tie the media to local identities, was being overwhelmed by a sea of programming flowing from the United States. Herbert Schiller, a Marxist sociologist from the University of California at San Diego, wrote an aggressive and influential book which claimed that a purposive cultural imperialism, jointly sponsored by American television producers and the US government, was responsible for the weakening of national media structures around the world, whether in Europe or in less-developed areas.[25] A generation of research sprang up to disprove the Schiller thesis, and the Schiller thesis no longer holds the sway it once did.[26] Perhaps this post-Schillerian avalanche demonstrated that the United States was not a purposive villain. But the work reinforced the notion that programme flows and programme influences from various external sources—US and otherwise—were increasing markedly, and programme offerings on television outlets in widely disparate settings were getting to look more and more alike.[27]

In this first round of changes—changes in the programme market—the structures of broadcasting remained relatively constant, but the content began to be less national in its composition. In this transformation, American-made programming flowed, in an accelerated pattern of growth, to a wide variety of national systems all across the globe. The reasons range from the power of monopsony buyers, to lower costs, to greater ease in physical distribution, to the development of a European, and then a world taste for things American, to the Schillerian charges of US manipulation of the market to advance imperialistic, capitalistic tendencies.[28] The important point is that the national character of broadcast services began, for the first time, to be put in serious doubt.

The old order, shaken by these global programming interrelationships, this movement towards sameness, was threatened anew at the turn of the 1970s by a technological wonder. Broadcasting had always been an industry of turmoil and change: consider the shifts from radio to television, from black and white to colour; from light entertainment to influential cultural force; from supplemental source of information to controlling news presence. But now there would be a change which would substantially erode the local nature of broadcasting regulation and tear at the capacity of the state to determine content. The coming of the satellite began physically to undermine the national character of state television. Notions of space, time, and distance—always key to the profile of communications technologies—seemed to be altering even more rapidly than before. Satellite and cable, together, have placed into question notions of scarcity that seemed to legitimate state monopolies and state licensing schemes. These changes would reduce the state's capacity to use broadcasting to reinforce the current public and political order.

Cable television alone did not seem so much of a threat to the national hegemony. True, there was the potential for a larger number of channels into each home, with an implicit threat to the national channels in European settings. But the pace of cable's introduction, its technology, its relationship to government—all these seemed well within the control of the state. The US FCC, in the early 1970s, considered it within its authority to determine what signals cable television could carry (and therefore how much of a threat it would be to existing broadcasters), to divide the market for programmes so that only certain films or sports events would be carried exclusively on cable, and to require the blacking-out of programmes that conflicted with local broadcast carriers.[29] Similarly, European and other governments maintained control of what they thought were the key decisions concerning the entry and growth of cable television.

The synergy between communications satellites and the new technologies brought a new era into being. The introduction of satellites meant that new networks could efficiently be established which conveniently elided national lines for the distribution of programmes. And it was primarily because of the new retailers—the cable television systems with their newly available shelf space—that satellites could find an earth-based economic outlet of sufficient magnitude. The emblem of the new order was the specific satellite that could broadcast direct to the home, a technology created in the early 1970s that would someday mean that a producer in one country could, through a specially configured satellite, send information and programming directly to households in another, bypassing not only the national television service, but even the cable systems constructed under national control.

Of a sudden, it appeared that the powerful images of television would be receivable without the check of a nation-based gatekeeper.

The entry of this technology was not so rapid as anticipated, but the psychological impact of its potential altered the way governments and broadcasters thought about the delivery of imagery. There would be no intermediary, no entity, no corporate giant, no government-controlled funnel through whom the signal would come. Before the direct-broadcast satellite—with the exception of terrestrial spillover and the jammable largely short-wave propaganda services such as the BBC World Service and the Voice of America—almost all information could be said to go through a national intermediary: mail through the post, radio and television programming through the local licensees, even books through local bookstores. Now, there was the possibility that television (primarily, but radio as well) would become truly global.

Immediately, government tribunals were established to determine how to cope with this potential technological breakthrough, one which was seen as inconsistent with historical broadcast structures. In the United Nations, in the International Telecommunication Union (ITU)[30] and in other international settings, governments sought a set of rules that would place responsibility on the state from which a programme service, destined for a direct-broadcast satellite, would emanate. That government, it was argued, should ensure that satellite signals were not purposely directed at areas in which the local government had not given its consent. Failing that, the government of a signal's origin should ensure that no programming sent forth should break commonly set international standards (with restrictions on advertising and on content). Finally, these debates were given expression in an international resolution, establishing standards for direct-broadcast satellite emissions. The United States abstained.

Defining the Future

Much is at stake in the transition from the national to the global—most important, perhaps, the continued capacity of the state to engage in the ancient task of nation-building. 'National television' cannot be understood without a clearer definition for 'national identity'. Rather than rely on essentialist meanings of the term (what it is *really* to be French or German or Hungarian), a more functional, though less aesthetically satisfying approach is necessary. 'National identity' becomes any given set of language practices, myths, stories, and beliefs propagated to justify a dominant group in maintaining power, or to justify a competing group in replacing them or shifting power among them.

These elements of national identity are usually bound up in arguments asserting that the common interests, history, and customs binding the residents of a nation-state far outweigh any conflicts among them. Central to the struggle for power among groups within the nation-state is deployment of the symbols and rhetoric of national identity: my coalition and its values embody the national identity better than others.

Broadcasting approaches, in its use and transformation, other tools of nationhood. One can consider by analogy the close relationship between established religions and national identity. Dominant, sometimes established, churches, like dominant, established broadcasters, set forth the framework of national identity, of prefiguring the state's claim to legitimacy, supporting it with a set of moral precepts, providing a history and a vision of the future.[31] As an example, the Church of England has been a profoundly important element in the national identity of the United Kingdom (and the Commonwealth), Islam is the centrepiece of national identity in the fundamentalist republics; and Judaism is interwoven with the national identity of Israel.

Broadcasting encompasses the narrative force of economic ideologies as foundations of identity. The making of economic systems into civic religions, and therefore centrepieces of national identity, has been a strong twentieth-century phenomenon. The loyalty due to religion became the requirement of Communism; by reflex, a similar set of loyalties has become true for 'the market economies' or capitalism. Ideology, in this sense, has become an element in national identity; or, where ideology has been the justification for power, then ideology has been grafted into identity. And broadcasting, even today, is an instrument for the carriage and promotion of these competing ideas of the good.

Since this book is about government structuring of broadcast systems, some sense of limitation of this term is necessary. Government structuring refers to the specific efforts by governments to determine the ownership, management, and content of systems for the distribution of television signals and the associated aspects concerning the production of programmes. Few governments are *laissez-faire* in this regard. Even vaunted efforts to 'deregulate' may be merely the allocation of market share, in terms of power or sway of ideology, from one group to another. Government restructuring of broadcasting reflects many other aspects of government policy: attitudes towards education, towards language, towards minority cultures, towards religion, towards internal concepts of federalism, and towards ideas of citizenship and participation.

Deregulation, globalism, and the lack of criticism of government may oddly coalesce: the emphasis on market forces can reduce the function of television and radio as *the press*, as a critic of the state. Heroic private networks and great public-service broadcasters have been praised (with a bit of golden-age romanticism) precisely because they can pose threats to a complacent status quo. Ironically, by subjecting these organizations to greater market forces, however, television programming develops a new form of neutrality; its managers become co-administrators of the global culture of consumption. Transformed, broadcasting no longer has the same politically subversive potential; if subversive, it is so in a new way, sapped of what was potentially its explicitly critical perspective. Globalization becomes virtually synonymous with a tendency toward depoliticization, part of an effort by the state to diminish the potency of the media to disturb the status quo.[32]

A New Typology

As a result of all these changes,[33] technological and political, a new typology, a new way of looking at broadcasting structures begins to emerge, away from national boundaries, away from the old categories of public-service versus market-driven systems. The old categories persist, but seem increasingly weak and unusable. Styles of ownership and forms of financial support become more and more similar across national settings. And, while debates continue about the transformation of local terrestrial broadcasters (the future of the BBC, for example), the dramatic possibilities lie in reconceptualizing the nature of the audience across national lines.

Traditional national approaches to regulating television imagery must adjust to those transformations that Ithiel de Sola Pool presciently called 'technologies of freedom'.[34] Rather than thinking of broadcasting entities as primarily 'public' or 'private', our mental categories have a new divide: global broadcasting enterprises, regional (supranational) broadcasting enterprises, and, then, a residual category of broadcasting entities that work primarily within traditional borders, often more locally than before. It has already become almost impossible, consistent with maintaining democratic values and following international norms, to determine means of 'protecting' domestic audiences, or dividing markets through government supervised restraints. In the new environment, the confounding question is determining what constitutes, in American terminology, the public interest in the global-communications era and how that public interest implicates the state. If the broadcasting structures of the past have been so closely tied to national identity, the question will arise what kind of identity is associated with a transnational communications period. Additionally, the shift will be to considering what supranational structures, if any, can be constituted as a match for the transnational programme providers.

Global broadcasting generally implies the search for a transnational—perhaps even intercontinental—virtually universal audience. Implicit in our aspiration for the global, inherent in its muscular challenge, is a television largely unmediated by any state, or any government entity, including a public broadcasting authority.[35] The new generation of producers and reconstructed broadcasters—the great multinationals—have the possibly illusory goal of reaching audiences regardless of locality and without negotiating with governments to reach their audiences. Globalism, in this definition, depends not just on the reach of the producer but on the power of the state. Only if the state has little control over the capacity of the signal to be received or exercises no such control is a scheme of spreading narratives considered global. Signals can become global because they are selected by 'the market'. A clearer way of defining unmediated global television is to confine it to that set of signals beyond the control of the receiving state.

To say that the programming is global does not mean that it comes from nowhere, or has no cultural impact. Deciphering its impact is already a small industry. It is becoming important to determine how the global menu of programming gets developed; what constitutes the relationship between the global menu and the national; what means are or ought to be available to improve the global menu, to make it more responsive to audiences, more efficient in terms of choices available, and more sensitive to intensity of interest on the part of the consumer.

The counterpart to 'global' imagery is broadcasting that must pass through the skein of governmental authority. 'National' radio and television involve some combination of the furtherance of state power and of a state-defined national identity. The proliferation of new nation-states, or newly assertive nation-states, underscores a need to re-examine what is meant by national television, and how national television functions in an era of greater globalism and pressures towards regionalism as well. National television, in this definition, implies a television (and broadcasting structure) that has some implicit or explicit obligation to reinforce the community that constitutes the state, whether it is one or more 'nationalities', and is seen as an instrument of the state to shape the image it holds within the populace. The case for a television service with obligations other than to the market will ultimately rest on the need for reinforcement of the idea of community, the strengthening of democratic values and the idea of the state. But because this is a strong role, it may be hard to mount in a state divided as to the nature of its sovereignty or the set of images associated with the relationship between community and state.[36]

These are hardly neat categories. The point, rather, is that emerging broadcasting patterns are not congruent with the borders of existing countries and have the potential to undermine them and build new loyalties. The new patterns can be accidentally or purposefully redefining. Broadcasting to the Basques in Spain and France, straddling borders, or to Palestinians in Jordan, Israel, and contested territories, provides examples. But broadcasting policies are also arranged to help support the integrity of a group of states or substantial portions of states. Europe is a region in that sense, and its Broadcasting Directive is an effort to use television and radio to undergird a European culture and identity. Without hyperbole, it could be said that the history of US broadcasting involved the creation of a more homogeneous United States out of its culturally dissimilar and previously antagonistic parts. Canada's history of mediation between a national whole and decentralized diversity is similarly reflected in creating the reality of a region through the media.[37] What is important is whether, as technology alters the space for the delivery of television signals, regional governing mechanisms emerge or are adapted to supplement or displace the now less-significant state.

Trying to determine the correct conceptual way of thinking about radio and television structures in this moment of change is far from an idle task. Massive changes in political thought and political boundaries make the invention of new broadcasting structures a matter of great political and economic importance. In the West, the transformations have been technology driven, largely influenced by the expansion of channel capacity. In Central and Eastern Europe and the republics of the former Soviet Union the political shift—towards the market, away from statism—determines that every broadcasting system there is in transition.[38] Both in the West and in the transition societies, fundamental problems exist that bring planning for change to a stalemate. New parliaments seek to determine which combination of models to adopt, both among the public-service and private, wholly market-based structures. To the extent that 'state' television is considered an option, there are difficulties in defining what the state should be for these purposes, how to finance cultural and political dreams, and the relationship that should exist between the state and the furtherance of particular national or cultural goals. Since the operative categories are shifting, there is the classic problem of policy-makers engaging in meaningless conflict over outmoded outcomes and failing to take advantage of the opportunities clearly enough to think through the broadcasting structures that will inevitably evolve. In other words, policy-makers may be working primarily with the vocabulary of the old axis (state/private) while the context in which they are operating requires decisions that recognize the new (global/national/regional).

The continued role and function of the state in its relationship to the media, during these times of change, are a vitally important puzzle. The future of the state itself may be at stake. The transformation of the media has consequences for the internal workings of democratic societies and for current patterns of world influence and dominion. This book deals with the vocabulary of that change. In Part One I examine two possible justifications for continued state intervention: reinforcing national identity and building a civil society that sustains institutions of democracy. Part Two plays out these ideas in the context of transition societies, particularly in Central and Eastern Europe and the former Soviet Union. In Part Three I turn to the United States and the problems of speech, identity, and communications policy in a society where discussion is framed by the First Amendment. The goal is to help develop a novel jurisprudence for these times: a constitutional mode of thinking of the relationship of a democratic state to the media of its citizenry. There is, in all of this, a relationship between geopolitical remapping and the transformation of television structures, part of an ongoing evolution of the link between community and communications technology.

2 The Public Sphere

GOVERNMENT and media are yoked, often tragically, in the architecture of the democratic process. When the curtain went up on post-Soviet society, experts from the West—academics and technicians from political parties—swarmed into the transition states to draft new media laws as part of the shoring-up of the machinery of change. Among their very first steps was the recommendation of specific rules to govern access to the media during elections.[1] If democracy was the objective, then its theatrical conventions (how candidates get access to television time, who performs the moderating task, whether debates are mandated) had to be performed well. These experts soon recognized that law and regulation affect not only media's role in elections, but the entire relationship between broadcasting structures, the modern state, and democratic values. State intervention to establish the infrastructure of modern political life is universal, even though that fact is often denied. What renders the project tragic is the difficulty of properly designing and executing the role of the state so as to render it compatible with the exercise of freedom. For all the brave talk of separating press from the government, issues of state and media are deeply intertwined; and in that intertwining rest the most subtle questions of enhancing opportunities for speech without abridging fundamental freedoms.

A short account of a 1992 Washington DC conference illustrates the core tension between fostering public debate and over-regulating the media. On this occasion, a group of pundits met under the auspices of the American Enterprise Institute for a discussion on the global impact of US popular culture.[2] They exhibited an anguished consciousness and substantial discomfiture over the impact of American programming—broadly conceived—on the flowering of democracy in the post-Communist transition societies. Around the table, almost all—scholars, broadcasters, journalists—were satisfied to conclude that American popular culture coupled with electronic media had been instrumental in encouraging the process of political change in Eastern Europe and the former Soviet Union. The cautious consensus led, however, to a set of worries. Continued and accelerated waves of American culture could be hostile to the development of strong democratic institutions in the future. The point was not to inculcate 'family values' or avoid the impact of violence on the character of the young. At issue was a series of questions about the healthy growth of a democratic society. Many of the panelists were concerned that filling the foreign public space with *Wheel of Fortune* and the throbbing and distracting siren songs of MTV might subvert or inhibit the building of democratic practices. The job of being a citizen in a transitional society would be tough and gruelling, demanding full attention to the structure of government and society. An overly zealous commercial culture, they worried, would pre-empt the development of an adequately functional political culture.

Then-commissioner of the Federal Communications Commission, Ervin Duggan, was typical in his views. Willing to agree that the impact of American media on Central and Eastern Europe, thus far, had been largely positive, he saw the future as much hazier. A deregulator, though sometimes a reluctant one, at home, Duggan had fears about the effects of unregulated broadcasting on democracy abroad. American policy should reinforce and undergird the new democratic governments and societies and help them find the strength to counter the evils of the material flowing into their boundaries. Like many on the panel, he espoused the view that, for a transitional society to make the crossing to a secure democracy, civic practices would have to be reinvented and a population re-educated. Moderation, patience, and the avoidance of undue cynicism would be necessary aspects of the political and cultural climate. Television culture, with its emphasis on instant gratification, iconoclastic attitudes towards authority, and substitution of consumerism for civic pride, could, and probably would, undermine the process of building democratic institutions. Even a former champion of unbridled free speech, Eugene Pell, once president of Radio Free Europe, concluded that the transitional societies had gone from total restriction to untrammelled licence and mellifluously implied that some trammelling might be suitable.

The theme of danger in the transmission of American culture was by no means new, nor was it particularly new that the cautions were sounded not by European Marxists but by a group of American neo-conservatives. Important was the conclusion that the process of building democratic institutions can be derailed if a proper environment for the fostering of democratic values is not encouraged. The export of American popular culture was to be applauded if it destabilized regimes unfriendly to democratic values; implicitly, the response should be different if it were the progress towards democracy that was being undermined.

The group was asking an instrumental question about the abundance of entertainment messages, the new openness, the permeability of borders. Assuming the US interest was in the building of democratic institutions, how should its 'soft power', its popular culture, be deployed in the post-Cold War era. Could or should the United States encourage greater restraint and censorship in the transition societies? Could, or should, the United States, as putative generator of these images, institute more controls at home? Would it be enough to have such institutions as a revamped Voice of America or Radio Free Europe try to counterbalance or supplement the impact of American popular culture? What would be the motivation for the United States to invest in such a cultural export?

For any society that seeks to achieve a substantial degree of democratic participation, the structure of the communications systems is integrated with the functioning of the political system. That is why it is particularly vital to have meaningful public debate about any law that alters the relationship among principal elements of communications systems and between government and the private systems of communication, or even the balance of power between the makers and distributors of information.[3] While it is right to be concerned about censorship, not every government intervention in the structure of broadcasting and telecommunications is wrongful. In every society, from the United States across Europe through Central Asia and beyond, government is called upon to act as mediator, as legitimator, as allocator in constructing the internal system of communication. The true need is to develop a logic that allows for some other grid of evaluation, measuring the health of the society in terms other than whether broadcasting is governed by the market, or the state is acting as a censor.

At stake, from a speech perspective, is the essence of a modern democratic state. In the American context, the reigning First Amendment metaphor vaunts the 'market-place of ideas', and much scholarship is about the rules that ensure that a market-place exists. The prevailing US theory of a free press assumes that a largely unrestricted market-place of speech will take care of the problem of supporting a democratic society; such an unencumbered press is sufficient as well as necessary, it is assumed, to protect the citizenry from coercive government. Pure advocates of a free press see even public-service broadcasters—PBS in the United States, the BBC in Great Britain, and others—as mere correctives to ill-defined imperfections of the market. If the market could just work better (it is argued), by providing more channels, for example, then government intervention would be unnecessary, according to those who hold this theory most dear. But the measure of an effective democracy is not only adherence to verified rules of the game—who can speak and when—but also to the substance of discourse and debate: the quality of speech and political life. Within that framework one might determine what role, if any, the state should assume.

Habermas and Democratic Society

To distil these questions and place them in a theoretical framework, it is useful to turn to the concept of the 'public sphere', as it has evolved in passionate debate among political scientists and philosophers, drawing on the work of Jurgen Habermas.[4] The Habermasian construct of a public sphere is a technique for evaluating speech practices and media structures to measure progress towards a democratic society. The public sphere, most centrally, is a zone for discourse which serves as a locus for the exploration of ideas and the crystallization of a public view. In Habermas's original description, the public sphere should be free of restrictions—not only from government, but from the great and overbearing forces of the economy—so that the exploration of issues, the development of points of view, have a certain authenticity. The key opinions of the public are, as it were, forged in the public sphere. The public sphere, in this classic aspiration, is a zone in which there is sufficient access to information so that rational discourse and the pursuit of beneficial general norms is made more likely. The public sphere is a set of activities in which the authority of pre-existing status attributes—such as wealth, family, and ethnicity—lose their sway in the distribution of civic authority. Argumentation based on assumed laws of nature comes to have more influence. The public sphere is neither a fiction, nor a mere debating society. It is a locus—though not a physical place—where debate has consequences.

The distinguishing characteristic, perhaps the signature for Habermas, is that the conclusions reached in a properly working public sphere must actually have a limiting impact on the state.

Accounts of the historical evolution of the public sphere, though much disputed, illuminate its significance for modern democratic society and its relationship to media. Students of the emergence of liberal democracy in the eighteenth century pore over the preconditions of change, sometimes with the hope of recreating those conditions today. In England, according to the most favourable reports, a small, select group of middle-class citizens had, it is said, the luxury and resources to create a rich, complex, politically sophisticated civil society in which the instruments of discourse—newspapers, books, salons, debating societies—were used to create a social order largely independent of both Church and State. Another characteristic was the openness of this discourse to all, in the same way that the market is open to all. Every citizen, in the very limited eighteenth-century meaning of the term, could, in theory, participate in the public sphere. And participants in this public sphere 'obeyed the rules of rational discourse, political views and decisions being open, not to the play of power, but to that of argument based upon evidence, and because its concern was not private interest but the public good'.[5]

Habermas, later in his work, gave a grand name—the Ideal Speech Situation—to the operation of the public sphere: 'every time we speak we are making four validity claims: to comprehensibility, truth, appropriateness and sincerity.'[6] Ideal speech is inconsistent with an intention to distort, or to use overweening power or wealth purposely to manipulate. The ideal speech situation is hardly the norm, though its assumptions permeate aspects of European broadcast legislation. The elements are a condition to which a journalistic or speech community can aspire, a set of measures by which one can evaluate any particular society or a structure of telecommunications.[7] The health of the public sphere is related to the respect for the elements of ideal speech by those who use it. Or, put differently, a medium cannot be considered truly a participant in the public sphere if those who habitually use it do not, in their speech, abide by a high standard of truth, comprehensibility, appropriateness, and sincerity.

There is a temptation to compare, unfavourably, the eighteenth century to the twentieth, to infer from the calamities and disorder of the present scene an impossible culture for the maintenance or restoration of the public sphere. Habermas himself despaired, seeing the collapse of the eighteenth-century liberal world into the twentieth-century social-welfare, mass-democracy, commercialized state. The citizenry is no longer an exclusive, passionately rational collection of people. The public sphere, as a broad field for communication, has lost the coherence furnished by a relatively high standard of education. Instead, public debate is more consistently a locus only for harsh competition among political groups, with political agendas and a kind of force that originates in powers different from reason itself. 'Laws which obviously have come about under the "pressure of the street" can scarcely still be understood as arising from the consensus of private individuals engaged in public discussion. They correspond in a more or less unconcealed manner to the compromise of conflicting private interests.'[8]

Assessing the role of the modern media in the making of a contemporary public sphere means re-examining its specific conditions as guidelines to the danger of its impairment. For example, an important quality is accessibility to citizens, with relatively low entry costs and relatively equal opportunities. A system in which costs to participate are bid way up and entry is scarce and difficult will, therefore, be a poor version of the public sphere. The zone of contemporary discourse, by ideal public-sphere standards, is distorted, if not mutilated, by imbalances of access, wealth, and power, The force of advertising, the power of public relations, the transformation of entire systems of the sponsorship of speech—all this affects the ideal of the public-sphere model. And, of course, since the golden age of Habermas's imagination, the state has become a strong participant in what once constituted the public sphere: sometimes as the authoritarian or totalitarian monopolist of speech, but always in the details, as controller of spectrum, manager of satellites, subsidizer of newsprint, subsidizer of libraries, censor, or controller of some of the means of communication. 'Thus, the space between civil society and the state which had been opened up by the creation of the Public Sphere was squeezed shut between these two [the economy and the state] increasingly collaborative behemoths.' No longer is there—if there ever was—a 'space for a rational and universalistic politics distinct from both the economy and the state'.[9] One consequence of these historical developments is that, in a way different from the classic understanding of Habermas, government becomes an implementer of the public sphere, not a 'separate dimension of social life'.[10]

Radio and television, as vehicles for discussion, do not fit easily into the mechanical niceties of Habermas's ideal-speech situation. Almost from the beginning, radio was a vehicle of entertainment, a toy, a soother, or organizer of the masses rather than a locus for rational discourse among individuals focused on the public welfare. Radio was not necessarily the descendant of the newspaper (more so the vaudeville and the music hall), though it claims that mantle of succession today. Too little in its history suggests the conditions of the public sphere, one of equality of access and of reasoned distance. The new technologies immediately became too useful a set of tools for the sale of goods (or of ideas) for them to be conceptualized as a neutral forum for public discourse. Indeed, there is something about the emergence and history of radio (and later television) that is almost antithetical to the idealized notions of the public sphere.

And yet, no account of the public sphere in the twentieth century would be complete without addressing radio and television. Over time, the electronic media have become so pervasive, so linked not only to political institutions, but to the machinery of debate and decision, so seized with importance, that they suffuse and overwhelm other aspects of public discussion. If anything, a persistent (if latent) sense of the need to construct a public sphere has undergirded the continuous though often ineffective attention spent on moulding the technological and legal impact of the electronic media on democratic institutions. If a public sphere is essential to a democracy, and the electronic media control the quality of the public sphere, the architecture of the media is of utmost importance.

Ulrich Preuss has discussed the current German understanding of this point: 'in modern complex societies, freedom has to be organised, and . . . it is the state which has to promote the realisation of individual freedoms by creating the appropriate institutional schemes.' The flourishing of civil society depends not only on basic rights of individuals, but on the nourishing of the public sphere 'in which all relevant opinions, values, interests, perspectives can be and in fact will be expressed'. Because an ideal pluralist public sphere 'is not likely to emerge spontaneously', it is necessary for the fundamental laws of society to place a duty on instruments of mass communications to further pluralism and public discourse.

While the immediate impulse has been to think that an ideal broadcasting system is at the core of a healthy public sphere in modern society, that is not necessarily the case. Given alternate, serious, enveloping modes of discussion, the electronic media could recede into their commercial fantasy. There have been societies where the coffee house has been the centrepiece of democratic discourse. Now the prediction, on all sides, is that it is the information highway, the public sphere *du jour* which will wholly revolutionize the nature of discourse. The point, perhaps, is that it is not just radio and television, and not just books and newspapers, that are revelatory of the vitality of the public sphere. It is through an interrelationship among all the mechanisms of communication that a particular public sphere emerges. To conclude that broadcasting dominates the public sphere is to avoid the process of analysis that sheds light on how debate is conducted and how the media relate to debate in any particular setting. Laws that focus on one medium, especially at a time of such rapidly changing technology, cannot gauge or affect adequately the composition and nature of the functioning of civil society.

Also, the possibility must be considered that radio and television are positively destructive of the public sphere. In some settings, broadcasting has become, at best, irrelevant to the operation of a democratic society and, at worst, so implicated in the harmful transformation of culture that the possibility of recuperation for an effectively institutionalized public sphere is dim indeed. Instead of a culture of rational discourse, a culture governed largely by the market-place emerges, culture as private interest to be bought and sold rather than as collective negotiation of common, public interest. So overwhelmed is the society by the use of common space as a means for the sale of goods that 'individual response becomes distracted, passive and uncritical, easily manipulable through advertising techniques and political propaganda'.[11]

Radio and television, in this telling, undermine democratic society. More expansive media, with more outlets, more channels, greater availability of information and entertainment, would not necessarily be better, even if 'more' automatically serves up some version of greater diversity.

> If the general public . . . neither can nor will reason critically because its 'organs'—the mass media—have been structurally transformed . . . such that their critical thrust is blunted, then neither the increased range and effectiveness of the media nor even the multiplication of chances to have access to them would make much difference.[12]

Broadcasting and 'the Audience'

There is no quick and accurate test of the situation of broadcasting as contributing to or detracting from the public sphere. One that is particularly telling, especially true to the prerequisites of Habermas, is the identity of the citizen, the individual in the rhetoric of the medium. Specifically, the account that matters is the transformation of citizenry, in the conception of the medium, from 'public' to 'audience'. The ideal public sphere is a group of citizens talking among themselves, forming an opinion, fashioning, and using a reserved space for mutual discourse that allows for an independent coalition critical of the state.

Broadcasting often creates the illusion of a public sphere. The political talk show reflecting critically on the actions of government, call-in radio, the man-on-the-street interview, the person-next-door as news anchor: these are techniques to import the memory and fantasy of public discourse into the everyday life of broadcasting.[13] But in the ideal public sphere the reader or viewer is an engaged participant; in the simulated model, the audience takes part in the debate only vicariously, only as spectators. The reader or viewer can be viewed as a market share to be delivered to advertisers, or the process can be one of transition and education where the broadcasting process provides viewers with training to take their place in the political system.

Walter Benjamin's concern about art in the age of mechanical reproduction applies to democracy as well. In an era of talk shows, broadcasting inflicts mechanical reproduction on the aesthetics of debate. Now, the televised town meeting has the aura of the real, and the physical enterprise itself is the reproduction, the ersatz staging. Raboy and Dagenais could have been speaking of CNN:

> Henceforth, all discussion of what the world's rulers do is organised through the spectacle, through the unilateral and unidirectional communication via the mass media of the results of decisions that have already been made. Only that which is recognised by the spectacle has historical validity; only those consecrated by the spectacle are entitled to speak with authority. . . . those who consume the spectacle cannot act.[14]

Despite efforts to find 'the real' or 'the meaningful' in citizen engagement, the spectacle recuperates.

The passage of the citizenry from a theoretical position of critic to one of passive receptor has been well traced.[15] Ien Ang, for example, has written about the shift in both the Dutch and British context:

> Public service broadcasting's ideal-typical concept of audience does not constitute a market, but a public. This audience-as-public consists of citizens, in whose interest it presumably is to be reformed. . . . In this context, the importance of radio and television programmes lies in their potential to transfer meaningful messages rather than in their capacity as vehicles to deliver audiences to advertisers; programmes and programming matter for their symbolic content rather than as agent for economic exchange value.[16]

Ang quotes from the memoirs of Lord Reith, recalling the foundation of the public-service tradition at the BBC, 'a new national asset', an asset of the 'moral and not the material order—that which, down the years brings the compound interest of happier homes, broader culture and truer citizenship'.[17] Reith considered that he was contributing to the British idea of a liberal democratic state by uplifting the radio audience, with the long-term task of enhancing homogeneity and reinforcing a unitary notion of the society. Radio would help create a society in which a public sphere could meaningfully and broadly function. As Ang notes, 'Habitual non-stop listening or using the radio as background noise were discouraged. Instead, the audience was summoned to listen seriously and constructively . . .'. Unlike its commercial counterparts elsewhere, the Reithian BBC discouraged programme standardization and regularity, instruments which are consistently employed to build audience. The BBC even allowed irregular silent periods between programmes, a virtual guarantee, in a competitive environment, of losing an audience. The point of all this was to construct listening as a 'serious, well-controlled activity'. Ang's main point is that, in the inter-war period, the BBC's strategy for its audience was 'prescriptive not descriptive; it was preoccupied with what the audience required, not what it wanted'. Even if the BBC sought to gain knowledge of its audience, it was for sociological, not merely statistical reasons.[18]

After the Second World War the BBC no longer so forcefully sought to lead and reform, but rather subtly moved in a direction in which the goal was to 'match and anticipate' public taste.[19] By the 1960s Hugh Greene, the BBC's Director-General, put forward a new metaphor to characterize the public-service role and its relationship to its audience. The BBC would be a mirror of a changing society and culture. 'I don't care whether what is reflected in the mirror is bigotry, injustice and intolerance, or accomplishment and inspiring achievement. I only want the mirror to be honest, without any curves, and held with as steady a hand as may be.'[20] Here Ang's conclusion is useful:

The change of metaphor implies a dramatic shift of the place assigned to the audience *vis-à-vis* broadcasting in public service philosophy. Abandoned was the explicit desire to take the audience on board, as it were, and lead it in a previously determined direction—as implied in Reith's model of public service. Instead a far more neutral task was formulated: that of representing and 'registering' society's many different voices and faces. The BBC came to embrace a new conception of serving the public by taking up . . . the role . . . of middleman of all possible sectional positions and interests in an increasingly pluralist and conflict-ridden society.[21]

Ang focuses on the BBC, but there is a universality to her findings. Far more than the BBC, the commercial networks world-wide are concerned with a passive audience more than a critical public. The extraordinary interest in polling and metering and the fine art of demography and statistical analysis have a curiously anti-democratic feel to them, at least in terms of the public-sphere analysis. In familiar free-market vocabulary, audience ratings are important because success demonstrates to producers that they are 'giving people what they want'. From the perspective of the public sphere, however, the ethos of mass audience satisfaction is inconsistent with the important role of the independent public. As Jean Cohen has written:

For what makes opinion *public*, what makes its influence legitimate is the way it comes about and the broad agreement it expresses. But once propaganda techniques predominate in the media of communication, once issues are chosen and agendas are set 'from above' by small circles of the powerful and/or the rich, once public debate and critical discussion disappear from the generalized media of communication, the public opinion that is measured by opinion polls . . . cannot be considered autonomous or of any normative weight. It is simply a statistical aggregate of singly solicited and privately expressed individual opinions. . . . Such 'opinion' is, in short, no longer the product of a public debate in which peers can have an influence on one another's way of seeing things through rational argument, arrive at an agreement on key principles and therefore *legitimately* exercise influence on the powers that be.[22]

Different constructions of the viewer imply different theories of a democratic society. Reith considered the raising of common values a predicate to an informed public, rendered, thereby, more capable of performing its constitutional rights. Those, in contrast, who make a mirror of the medium are linked to 'mass democracy' and the most cheapened and industrialized view of the public. Finally, the authoritarian approach to the management of the electronic media, limiting access, for example, to the state, almost by definition excludes the possibility of the viewers, as a whole, playing a pivotal role in a democratic society.[23]

Defining Public Service

In this set of distinctions, relevant to the Habermasian guidelines, lies the difficult path to rescuing systems of public-service broadcasting from their near-universal exhaustion. It is in this context that we can reconsider the efforts of broadcasting empires so beleaguered, so often challenged technologically, politically, and financially that their very survival is in question. Within the debates over the future of the BBC, public-service broadcasting in Canada, the survival of the Dutch system, the tenuous hold of public broadcasting in the United States, and the nature of transitions throughout the world, are complex visions of the performance of democratic values.[24]

The elements that contribute to excellence in public-service broadcasting have a certain cross-cultural commonality. The keystone, often proclaimed but seldom perfectly achieved, is the development of a system that is immunized from direct government intervention, a refrain familiar as an element of Habermas's Ideal Speech Situation. Given that the public-service broadcasters are organized by government, it is hard to escape the state's heavy hand. The creative, virtually impossible, architectural challenge has been to provide structures that combine independence with accountability. In most statements of the importance of independence, freedom of expression is the objective, with the fear of censorship being the antithesis. In the discourse of the public sphere, the goals can be articulated somewhat differently. The function of independence is to encourage and nourish the formation of a 'public' that is the quintessential aspect of the public sphere. That public must, by definition, be in a zone of independence, as uninfluenced as possible by the power of government or of the economy. The media, in this sense, serve as an envelope for the jelling of views so as to have an influence on the state and to render its decisions more responsive.

Seen in this light, the entire wrapping of public-service systems can be reinterpreted. Take the brash desire of Reith, in the early days of the BBC, to insist on a monopoly for the BBC. That monopoly was not designed, in this gloss, to exclude competing voices but rather to have a higher and different motivation. A monopoly was the best way to sustain an entity, the task of which was to be in symbiotic relationship with the British public, to engage the public, to help it form an agenda, to expose it to the policy issues that the public would have to face, to become, as it were, in conjunction with its public—as opposed to government—the carrier of an external consensus.[25] The British experience is the basis for one of the many criticisms of the architecture of the American public broadcasting system: its decentralization, the result of a purposeful attempt to ensure that there was not a strong central entity that might serve to nourish a strong reciprocal 'public'.

The tangled issue of governance, an issue now plaguing broadcast design in many transition societies, is also central to a public-sphere analysis. If broadcasting is to make the appropriate kind of contribution to discourse and debate, the public-service broadcaster must be governed in a way, and with a mandate, that contributes to the proper functioning of a public sphere. Reith, anxious to demonstrate that the BBC was 'the property of the entire nation, above party dispute and commercial gain', sought a Charter under Royal Seal, as opposed to a licence from Parliament or a traditional corporate form.[26] Governance, in the German system, is crafted to identify the broadcasting organization with 'the public', not the government, through the *Grundegesetz*, a virtual Parliament of broad interest groups and citizens which are charged with the supervision of the public entity from each of the Länder. Ulrich Preuss, writing about the German structure, underscores the importance of basic rights 'for the flourishing of civil society'. Broadcasting laws in Germany have been interpreted to support 'a sphere in which all relevant opinions, values, interests, perspectives can be and in fact will be expressed'.[27] The German mode of regulating broadcasting is particularly interesting because it was imposed after the Second World War by the Occupying Forces, rather than being a system that evolved as a consequence of political compromise. The public broadcasting organizations were to be controlled neither by the state (a reaction to the Third Reich) nor by large corporations (a fear of the power of capital to include less than the full range of voices). Each public broadcasting corporation, and the ensemble of corporations together, would serve the principle of 'internal pluralism' of views; and, to assure the fostering of the public sphere, the plurality of the opinions, values, interests, and perspectives in the society would be represented in the governing board.[28]

The mode of financing public broadcasting organizations is also a determinant of how deeply felt the need has been to identify and nourish a public sphere. It is possible to have a broadcasting system, encouraging of the public sphere, that is financed directly by government, through the Legislature. But we have seen, in the United States, in France, and elsewhere, that the direct financing of public broadcasting carries with it special perils of interference. Advertising support, calibrated according to the number of people watching, tends to convert the 'public' into an 'audience', as I have tried to show. For this reason there has been a search for automatic funding devices, undertaken over a long term, that will allow the relationship between broadcasting and its public to be largely unencumbered by political and market forces.[29]

In the United States, a lonely search for automatic funding has found voice in the advocacy of an endowment to be gained from the auctioning of spectrum for private purposes or some similar self-executing tax.[30] The method used in much of Europe to accomplish immunity from government pressure has been the licence fee, in which households using television or radio have paid an annual amount (and in some cases a contribution upon the occasion of buying a receiving set). At least two factors have made the licence fee less appealing as a mode of financing: reluctance by parliaments to raise the licence fee (especially as the presumption that its citizens are viewing the public channel loses validity), and the increased costs of producing and transmitting competitive television programming. Still, the fee approach has yielded a minimal institutional sense of independence, at least at the BBC, sufficient to reinforce its national, autonomous role.[31]

Rules concerning advertising itself, varying among European systems, can be tied to public-sphere concerns. The European consensus is that, even where advertising is an acceptable form of revenue-raising, it should not be used in connection with news programmes. In some settings, the role of newspapers was strengthened by providing them with a stake in advertising revenue from broadcasting as well as from the printed press. The idea seemed to be that the revenue obtained from the production and distribution of images should be pooled to strengthen the information function of the media as a whole. Until recently, Channel 4 in the United Kingdom, charged specifically with encouraging pluralism, had a unique relationship to advertising revenue. A percentage of advertising on private broadcast stations was funnelled to Channel 4, separating programming decisions from those relating to advertising revenues. The operation of a common advertising agency for the multiple pillarized production centres in the

Netherlands is somewhat similar. In the Dutch broadcasting cases, the government of the Netherlands fought against unregulated advertising directed at the Dutch viewer, on the grounds that this interfered with the capacity of the Dutch system to preserve a pluralistic broadcasting voice.

One issue that divides European attitudes from American has to do with rights to take editorial positions and requirements to maintain objectivity and standards of factuality.[32] These differences, too, can be explained in terms of the public sphere. In the United States, a law that prohibited public broadcasting stations from engaging in the practice of stating the station's own views on an issue was struck down by the US Supreme Court as an invasion of free-speech interests.[33] In 1992 Congress awkwardly imposed obligations upon the Corporation for Public Broadcasting to enforce goals of objectivity, producing cries of intervention and censorship.[34] Throughout European broadcasting, requirements of objectivity and prohibition on editorializing by public broadcasters are common. Again, the model of the public sphere provides some insight into the difference. Public-service broadcasters are not, themselves, in the European model, 'speakers'. They exist to find and help define a public voice. There must be opinions, and they must be reflected. That is the essence of the media role. But the true 'speakers' are to be the citizenry, the public, not the broadcaster itself. In European broadcasting, objectivity has the meaning of searching out competing views of the proper running of society, acting as a forum for diversity, providing a mechanism for the coming together of a public consensus. If the media are to be respected in aiding in these democratic tasks, they must not be seen as picking and choosing, favouring one view among many. Objectivity, in that sense, is a process, not a narrow attitude towards truth.

Most important, perhaps, is the culture of the organization, how the ambitious goals of a broadcasting organization are stated and implanted in those who create its identity. The BBC was, for the longest time, like the Crown itself, apart from and above the State. The BBC, during the time of Reith at least, could be seen as similar to the Established Church, the Church of England, with a deep moral and historic obligation.[35] In Germany, there was also a post-war culture of the function of broadcasting that is significant, civic, and enforced through the Constitutional Court. The aim of the law—beyond the question of government interference—was to construct a media that ensures 'that all relevant ideas and interests and all relevant spheres of life find expression and are reported in a balanced, fair and truthful manner'. This objective 'cannot be expected from market regulation alone' and required a legal framework that permits the mass media to fulfil their functions, without external or internal misuse. Much is extraordinary about the German system, but two elements will suffice here. The German courts see the accomplishment of these civic goals as the responsibility of the public- and privately owned media, working together. And, most important, the courts have an obligation to intervene affirmatively—to force change—if the media are not fulfilling their civic purpose. Government is not only authorized to act, but obliged to act (*Schutzpflicht*) so that the pluralistic function of the media is achieved.[36]

These strong structural features are most important in terms of the messages they send to those who work within the media organizations and those who support them. An organization dedicated to goals of forming a public, encouraging the brokering of diverse views, shaping an agenda for policy, and helping society reach consensus requires a social setting in which the need for a public sphere is consistently articulated. For these goals are usually (though not always) different from objectives of maximizing audience, competing for viewers, increasing revenue, or determining the proper bundling or tiering of programmes. The very ways in which public-service entities are governed, financed, regulated, and perceived: all these help determine, though hardly conclude, whether furthering the public sphere is an internalized civic and spiritual quest, or left to the margin, a hoped-for product of market interaction.[37]

Globalization and the Public Sphere

Now we must ask how this forum for public discourse is affected or might be affected by various incidents of globalization of the media. Some might conclude that broadcasting is not a net contributor to the public sphere and that its relationship to the public sphere is so slight that globalization is an irrelevant factor. A tendency that is already so advanced as to be beyond recall is merely accelerated. The cliché of global media is that globalization creates diversity, open skies, and new speakers, and that the consequence of globalization is the enhancement of public spheres in many formerly closed societies. A third view, more mechanical, ameliorist, and liberal, would contend that the impact of globalization depends on the particular society, on the structure of discourse within it, and the response of the government and the society to the possibilities provided by transnational voices.

One can begin with the more optimistic perspective. A critical aspect of the public sphere—in the Habermas formulation—is access to information. Extraordinary differences in access to information between those in and out of power are a major flaw in this aspect of building a democratic society. One of the key consequences of globalization is to provide the appearance—and often the fact—of greater equality of access. After all, what was stunning about such satellite-driven innovators as the Cable News Network (CNN), as it made its reputation in the great crises of world change, was its impact on the flow of information into societies where imbalance of access had been a major characteristic. Even in sophisticated Western societies, CNN seemed to obtain and redistribute information to large chunks of society who received it at the same time as world leaders and their intelligence networks. It was this astonishing fact that was revolutionary, even more than the nature of the information itself. For months, CNN promoted its prowess with preening clips of press conferences in which the American Secretary of Defense or the Chair of the Joint Chiefs of Staff would say that they learnt of certain events on CNN, not from their staffs. In the failed Russian *coup* of August 1991, enough viewers in Moscow had access to signals beamed in by CNN of pictures and interviews of Boris Yeltsin and his defence of the Parliament that the standard domestic news services were no longer an exclusive source of information. In Tiananmen Square in 1989, the young rebels obtained information (not always valid) from foreign media, from media representatives, and through a new medium, the fax.

Globalization, in this sense, has the potential of creating its own public sphere, outside and, potentially, against the domain of the nation-state.[38] Here the effect of the transnational trend is at least the appearance of imposing a new cast of characters, changing (potentially diminishing or increasing) the status of national or regional leaders and introducing other actors in the drama of world transformation. A 'new world order', to use a somewhat discredited term, but a new order with an effort at reinforcing collective action, is the promise of a global public sphere. At the regional level, for example, a more effective public sphere for a United Europe requires a zone of discourse and debate which makes European policy its object and surmounts, to some extent, national tendencies and prejudices. The decision of the Council of Europe to underwrite Euronews and to take conscious steps to strengthen its audiovisual sector is justified, in part, by the desirability of such a strengthened regional consciousness. A specific, narrow public sphere undoubtedly exists that relates to the decisions of the United Nations. Under an optimistic understanding of the sphere's utility, for the United Nations to be more credible and more effective, its policy initiatives, as with those of other world bodies, must be more fully aired, open to the debate of a more broadly constituted transnational civil society.

These are the hopes and desires for the relationship between globalization and the transition to more democratic institutions. The opposite argument is that the seeming natural tendency of broadcasting—free of state ownership or regulation—is away from the public sphere, undermining serious public discourse. This was the argument of Neil Postman in his trenchant book, *Amusing Ourselves to Death*. Offered 'entertainment' or open discussion about our political institutions, it is assumed, the audience will normally flock to the former. Private competition, from the skies or from terrestrial transmitters, moves the audience even more to song and dance, drama and comedy, violence and sex, soap operas of the mind. Global tendencies accelerate the incapacity of the state to shape its electronic media, rendering it porous and largely outside national government control.

Globalism implies choice and competition. Globalism is more than expedited access to a greater library of programming through existing gatekeepers. Whatever role the state has played, globalism tends to weaken it through the enhancement of competition. The nature of global competition is to increase, markedly, the quantity of television drama programming (and the special view of reality that constitutes television news). The domestic public sphere is necessarily adversely affected. Ironically, globalism may be welcome to authoritarian governments precisely because it erodes the domestic public sphere. Traditionally, one of the first objectives of those who seek to consolidate power is to eliminate a competitive political press. But a global broadcasting system that is neutral, even apolitical, is a highly acceptable substitute. Polished global services, delivered by satellite, dilute any competitive political voice at home as much as they weaken the controlled voice of the state itself. News of events abroad are another television drama, portrayed as it evolves, not an indictment of the regime. Broadcasting is, under these assumptions, neutralized as a vital factor in the public sphere.

There is evidence for each of two perspectives—that globalism is strongly supportive of the democratic process and that globalism is hostile to it. Television will not be eliminated,[39] and globalism marches forward. The state, therefore, will be faced with the task, in the onrush of events, to determine what steps can and should be taken to mediate globalism's and television's combined and pervasive impact.

3 National and Post-National Identity

In addition to sustaining and strengthening the public sphere, government often claims a responsibility, to its citizens, to help sustain and enrich the national identity. As was true with respect to the public sphere, this government interest forces a relationship between the state and the media. In the first chapter, I defined national identity as the collection of myths, ideas, and narratives used by a dominant group or coalition to maintain power in a society. That is a fairly instrumental (and unusual) definition, but it is useful to set against the more appealing, popular, and less cynical uses of the term. The common invocation of national identity forwards the conviction that something is being described at a level of abstraction that all share in common above party or sectarian concern. Behind this second, more romantic view is that American-ness, German-ness, Russian-ness are all proper deeply rooted national identities and each has a unique historic essence. Institutions must be established to protect, nourish, articulate, and perpetuate such identities. Symbolic forms like flags, architecture, works of art, and treasured histories give form to these identities. The public schools, the university, the Church, and the broadcasting organizations are repositories of them as well. If the government supports these symbols and reinforces the ideas behind them, it is often assumed that it is doing so independently of sectarian political expedience.[1]

There is a third, increasingly important meaning for national identity protection, a meaning found in statutes throughout Europe and in the new transition societies. A state-protected pluralism evolves, one in which various ethnic and religious groups are protected, often through explicit legal requirement. For example, the Republic of Ireland requires its public broadcasting system to

> be responsive to the interests of the whole community, be mindful of the need for understanding and peace within the whole island of Ireland, ensure that the programmes reflect the varied elements which make up the culture

of people of the whole island of Ireland, and have special regard for the elements which distinguish that culture and in particular for the Irish language.[2]

Swedish television, by agreement between the state and the major national broadcasting service, must pay special consideration to linguistic and ethnic minorities so as to meet, 'to the extent reasonable, in quality, accessibility and variety, the differing needs and interests of the population'.

The very fact that there can be such disparate models of national identity (the instrumental, the essential, and the pluralistic) helps demonstrate why one of the most difficult questions in both the mature Western democracies and the transitional post-Communist societies is determining the proper government role in structuring and regulating the broadcast media. For those who hold to the essentialist view, a strong government interest in television (as a moulder of attitudes and opinion) is vital. If there are to be enduring, deeply felt bonds that bring a nation and a state together, then the ornaments of national identity must be nourished, exhibited, and respected. For those who hold to a pluralist definition of national identity, it is immensely important to attend to the administration of any mechanism that can overwhelm or shatter delicate multi-cultural balances. Just as there is a homogenizing, globalizing, border-obliterating trend, so there is a process of disintegration and fracturing within political cultures and nations, with subgroups moving to challenge the dominant national identity and claim cultural and even territorial rights. There are demands on the state and on the media at a time of these simultaneous centripetal and centrifugal forces. To be sure, it is not television alone that creates and maintains cohesion (or mediates the process of change and evolution), but it can be television that contributes, significantly, to its dreadful and destructive absence.

It is the instrumental definition which is most troublesome yet most alluring. National identity can easily become a camouflage for a series of controls that occupy the creative space and deny the opportunity for a pluralism of views and freedom of expression. National identity is too often flaunted as a means not of positive expression, but of criticism and the stifling of ideas, used to 'divert people from paying attention to malfunctioning social orders'.[3] For those who use identity claims to maintain power—and they have been many and detestable—national identity can be yet another term for the maintenance of national security. In a less complicated fashion, national identity is an umbrella for determining what speech and passion is permissible and what is not. Thus, the search for an acceptable definition of national identity is connected with the long-standing discourse about the relationship between the government and individual rights.

Definitions of national identity provide the community with a sense of who belongs and who is differentiated, what is the norm and who is the 'other'. Without too great an extension, these definitions reinforce or feed on other processes related to community, goals such as enhancing productivity, the rearing of the young, valuing and protecting the customs and habits of the population as a whole. In a totalitarian society, the connection is obvious: the totality of the state is expressed in its monopoly of the images of meaning, the signs on walls, the design of buildings, the nature of acceptable art, the content of the media. In the modern democracies, questions of national identity are far more complicated: they are not tied so resolutely to a strong single identity claim, but, at least in principle, are built on constant conflict, contest, and coalition. Disputes over the nature of the common identity are not always about the flag or the obvious symbols of national consciousness. They can be about race, history, gender, and violence. Questions about the social role of the media give voice to many aspects of these unarticulated disputes over the shaping of the national identity.

Much of the impulse to censor, much of what constitutes concern with the mix of images on television, much of the debate over the international flow of programming—all this is related to concerns over 'national identity'. The banners of tradition that, collected, compose a national identity figure centrally in the relationship between the state and broadcasting (whether private or public); simultaneously, the power to shape and maintain national identities is undermined by increased globalism in the flow of imagery. In that contradiction lies one of the principal dramas of thinking about radio, television, and the future.

It is, therefore, not surprising to see national identity so often related to regulation of the media. National-identity concerns are, for example, the grounds for the great exceptions to the human-rights documents concerning freedom to receive and impart information: the International Covenant on Political and Civil Rights and the European Convention on Human Rights. Potential assaults on its national identity are also a ground for complaint by a receiving member state under the Television Without Frontiers Broadcasting Directive. In the final stages of the Uruguay Round aimed at concluding a General

Agreement on Tariffs and Trade, a significant aspect was the European Union's effort to defend its audiovisual sector from what it deemed to be the cultural invasion of US productions. The principal legislative foundation was the Directive's mandate that the television channels of member states broadcast a majority of European programming. Thus, despite the fervour for the transnational right to receive and impart information, there are often exceptions or assaults on what could be considered hallowed aspects of national identity.

Force and Image

A world view in which there is a separation of nation and state can easily be imagined; but the twentieth century has been supportive of the position that national ideals should have outlets in the organization of governments and states. To celebrate the union of nation and state, elements of history must be selected, adorned, even invented. Memory becomes as important a boundary as river or mountain or artificial line. Memory then turns into industry. Symbols must be reiterated, incorporated into teaching materials, protected against dissolution. A national identity must be defended against those who assault it, particularly if that identity is the justification for the state. Indeed, the close of the 1980s and the start of the 1990s quite suddenly became a living, gruelling incarnation of this debate, with the search for the relationship between state and nation bursting from the academic conferences to street fire and chaos.

What changes, over time, is not whether the state engages in the processes of constructing or supporting an identity; rather, what changes is the combination of force and image, technology and prevailing ideology. Changes in communications technology both enhance and destroy the power of the state to have an impact upon concepts of national identity. Shifts toward the free-market conceptions of the role of the state in relation to broadcasting have made the nature of state intervention more problematic. The megaphone of the state can be more powerful, though its potential competition, similarly armed, can be even more devastating. And this is what brings the definitions of national identity together. What they share is the assumption that what we call 'the state' is a combination of power, values, and imagery and that the state has always had some role, and usually a substantial one, in shaping and confining the most important imagery —namely, the imagery of loyalty. For the romantic, this process is what has given meaning to human existence, particularly in times of deprivation; it has been a source of important values, of religion, and of inspiration. For the cynic, this aspect of the state has too often been a sham, hiding the processes of control under the aesthetic of community.

European law, far more than American, has been sympathetic to national identity claims.[4] The differences between the European and US approaches may, in themselves, be an aspect of identity. The twentieth century, for Europeans, has been one of radically shifting political allegiances, altered maps, provisional governments, and violent struggles for loyalty and permanence. For the United States, the prevailing account has been one of stability, cohesion, ascension, unity, and steady expansion. The portrait has come into question, but its broad acceptance for so many decades helps determine the definition of the state and its functions. A consequence is that, for most American legal scholars, the focus has been almost wholly on condemning the role of government as censor, and not at all on the ways in which actions of the state might enhance a liberal democratic culture.

Proponents of 'the public interest', especially where that has implications for the building of a common theme, have been supplanted by proponents for privatization, deregulation, and the unencumbered working of a market-place that has little role for government as actor.[5] This is not to deny that, even in the United States, the public manufacture of contributions to the imagery remains strong; but the explicit tradition, especially in regard to the media, is antagonistic to government involvement. Because the protection of free speech and the reinforcement of national identities have not been adequately harmonized in American thought, the complexities of the government role in structuring the media and in sponsoring images in society are perceived in a muddled way when communicated by Americans spreading the word abroad. The complexity of the problem, and the crux of the battle between the cynic and the romantic, arise from the relationship between censorship and the positive propagation of ideas and views by government (often through the direct or indirect control of broadcasting). The two phenomena—one negative, one arguably affirmative—are closely related. Acknowledgement of the appropriateness of the state's power to articulate its case for loyalty is needed to distinguish it from the ugly side of the censor (and from connotations of propaganda). The search for a proper definition of national identity plays this role.

Endurance and Symbolism

It is possible to conceive of a state that is no more and no less than a convenient set of arrangements to provide for the requirements of its citizens, a Switzerland of the mind. Such a theory of the state requires no myths, no romance; it is an arrangement in which efficiency, clarity, and simplicity are the key. For those who have minimal desires for state functions, who see the state as existing only for defence, security and maintenance of the roads, for example, such a simple model of the state suffices. This theory, however, does not offer any explanation about the relationship between the state and identity. It does not allow for the way the state exists as a fantasy for its constituents, the way it is a part of who we are.

The state, rampant, produces an elaborate image for its citizens and for itself, a history, uniforms for its military, books of civic lessons, commissioned art. Then, in the blink of an eye, it dies. Empires rise and fall, full of national identity at their crest and then empty and embarrassed at the moment of decline and disappearance. At each moment, attributes of identity seem essential. Even if the abiding physical needs of the population are identified, the pain of fulfilling them, the dislocation of change, and the allocation of scarce resources require a consoling vision. This is clearest in the societies in transition from authoritarian to democratic forms. Uniting pluralism and civil power in a liberal nation-state means that imagery becomes an instrument of a more accountable power authority.

In a world of wholly rational actors in states of minimal, elections would not involve appeals to national identity far beyond those necessary to nourish sensible choices on matters of material concern. But contests for power move past unemotional efficiency; so do such things as the definition of external threat, the determination of the proper mix of consumer goods and investment, or the coercion of obedience from varied internal groups. For most people, more is necessary than the articulation of the rules of the game. New national identities are necessary to overwhelm the poisons of the old. New symbols are necessary to keep hope alive during periods of economic depression and governmental chaos. Society becomes a useful instrumentality for the individuals within it, and part of that is the articulation of ideals to which the community can aspire.[6] The continued existence of states is an aspect of tragic complexity: the need for symbols to coordinate large-scale human interaction and the inevitable failure of those symbols, ultimately helping to bring down or weaken the societies they represent.

Imagery is a complement to the inevitable limitations on efficiency. The altruistic notion of the state relies on history, religion, and culture to define why the state stands for what is good, and, therefore, why it should command loyalty. Sometimes these notions are collected and bound together in the 'national history', in ideas of patriotism and citizenship, or of faith in a legal system. They may be 'Western' and 'modern', or they may be seen as underdeveloped or encapsulating heathen religions packed with superstition. The imagery that, together, constitutes the state may be believed for reasons that are provable and rational, or those that may be quasi-religious: it may be attached to a particular *ethnie* or nationality; it may or may not encase ideas which maximize the holder's welfare.

If the choice of state was like a simple matter of product or investment selection, then it would be easy to say that the state exists, in a particular form with a given set of adherents, for so long—and only so long—as the state serves the purposes of efficiency for its citizens. Secession might be made more agreeable as well, so that the transaction costs in rearraying interests would not be so high as it is now. To be sure, in a free market of travel and movement, some elements of choice of state exist in this way. But that is not the predominant fact, despite the number of refugees and asylum-seekers. The endurance of the state, and the form of its continuation, is a combination of far more abundant and complex considerations. Its capacity to govern, especially in times of crisis, is only as reliable as its capacity to enforce the orders that are issued in its name. When the state is seen as vulnerable in terms of its potential to command obedience to its orders, its days are numbered.

It is wrong to ignore the necessity and inevitability of the state's role in the manufacture and nourishment of imagery. The state (more often the nation it seeks to incorporate) becomes, among other things, what has been called by some philosophers and social scientists the 'imaginaire sociale', and by others a set of stories or inventions or imaginings. To describe the state as such is by no means to denigrate the concept (or a particular state) or to diminish its legitimacy. It recognizes the complexity of the state's continued existence and the constant need for communicating a package of ideals and accomplishments. The content of information and imagery that comes to the citizen falls within these factors, establishing the place of history, patriotism, and loyalty. Broadcasting—whether public or private, whether national or global—cannot help but affect the basket of images that constitutes the state.

National identity is related to another way of describing the organization of many societies: approximating a monopoly of force is part of the state's ambition if not definition. Ideas and ideology can be a substitute for coercion. In the rank of things, encouraging actions through belief is superior to commanding them through force or torture. This does not mean that we applaud a society that is driven to horrific acts because it is mesmerized by the charisma of its leader. Or that a society so driven is superior to one where the whip causes unhappy slaves to commit otherwise immoral acts. What a state does, how valid its established goals are, is a different question from the use of education, imagery, and narrative to encourage fidelity and cohesiveness. Still, in the range of the ordinary, the idea that citizens willingly do what might otherwise require force is appealing, even if it is the drama of national identity that causes the result. James Donald, in words attributed to a colonial administrator, recounts a story about the origins of English literary studies as a technique of government in colonial India in 1838: 'The Natives must either be kept down by a sense of our power, or they must willingly submit from a conviction that we are more wise, more just, more humane, and more anxious to improve their condition than any other rulers they could have.'[7]

Images of identity have also been the underlying bedrock for a patriotism that makes the threat of force credible. A state cannot make a durable threat against another if there is serious doubt about the loyalty of its citizens. The fright of those in government during the Vietnam years in the United States had to do with the danger of communicated weakness; a failure of consensual national identity betrayed itself in the absence of internal support for a foreign commitment.[8]

Imagined Societies

For Benedict Anderson, every nation—not yet a state—is 'an imagined political community', and what is meant by this rubric is useful in understanding the relationship between modern polities and the media. To survive the vicissitudes of political and geographical disarray, it is precisely the remembered idea of the nation that is important and that can provide the prospect of a future of regained glory. A nation, in this sense, must transcend boundaries of space and time and rest largely in the imagination. Dispersed, the members of even the smallest entity cannot rely on face-to-face contact with all their fellows. But still, 'in the minds of each lives the image of their communion'.[9] In this definition of the term, 'a nation exists when a significant number of people in a community consider themselves to form a nation, or behave as the formed one'.[10]

Anderson has written not of the era of television, but of print, not of the time of globalism, but of empire. The dangers and the opportunities that existed then exist now; if the life of a nation has the strength of the intangibility of its images and history, it also has its weaknesses. Memories cannot be destroyed the way buildings can or objects of veneration. But any particular set of shared mental images is subject to a variety of forces and influences through which it is continuously altered (and in dissimilar ways in dissimilar sites). Those who consider themselves custodians or keepers of a nation's memories are always in a contest for control. Now, more than before, the contest is both from within and without a state's borders.

These characteristics have a bearing on the attitude a state has towards broadcasting. For Anderson, a critical boundary of any nation is the idea of the 'other', the people from whom the nation is differentiated, and perhaps estranged. Any nation 'has finite, if elastic, boundaries, beyond which lie other nations. No nation imagines itself coterminous with mankind.' So it is not only the narrative concerning the treasures of the nation that must be managed and cherished. An intelligent government, custodian of national identity, will also wish to concern itself with the repertory of the external, the representation of the designated other. National-centrist parties in the states of ex-Yugoslavia, for example, used national sovereignty to shape the 'symbolic space in which people could recognise themselves'. Media, presumably under some form of state influence, played a crucial role by filling the mental vacuum 'not only with images of hatred of other nations but also with images of the "happy" future which is to arrive with national liberation'.[11] A letter-writer to the *New Yorker* in 1994 put it well:

> Federal Yugoslavia had six media monopolies—one in each republic. When the Slovenian, Croatian, and Serbian ones fell under chauvinist control, Yugoslavia's fate was sealed. In addition to the propaganda barrage of distortions and lies mounted by all three television networks, every possible measure was taken to hermetically isolate their respective captive audiences. . . . An independent Yugoslav journalist, writing on media gangsterism in the murder of Yugoslavia called television 'the cathode of evil'.[12]

The demand to seize the popular spirit and fill it with ideas of loyalty has a special poignancy when a nation has the aspirations but not the reality of statehood, or the actuality of statehood but not its full blossom. In the imagining of the community that constitutes 'the nation', there has been the dream of a collection of treasured memories, of the power to organize a state around its dreams, to obtain its vision of behaviour, language, and life through rules and the exercise of legitimate power. Thus the modern idea that communities are imagined as *sovereign*, i.e. as states, is critical to strategies towards broadcasting. Control over at least some of the instruments of imagination becomes an attribute of sovereignty. These communities are not to be mere aspirations; national culture must be accompanied with power to proclaim its patrimony and uniqueness.[13]

Formats of Identity

Narratives of national imaginings require their own art form, a space and format of relationship between audience and government that may be difficult to achieve. Icons of legitimacy change, but the context of imagery and substance of appeals to loyalty have a certain cross-cultural familiarity. There are standard elements to narratives of identity, just as there are in other kinds of dramas. These include a given history of origins, of blessedness, of chosenness, of victimness and redemption—still the basic elements of successful narratives of nationhood. The traditional task of communication is to adapt these narratives, invigorate them, alter focus, and provide new tropes of legitimacy. In France, there has been a debate, over many centuries, concerning the congealing of the state role. One example is the nineteenth-century French debate over whether art exhibitions should be government sponsored or market driven. There were proposals to have parallel modes of distribution: a private market system for the production, exhibition, and sale of images, together with a publicly financed system. In 1799, the state's role was defined, foretelling the debates over twentieth-century patronage, as follows:

> State authority can put conditions on its gifts, and in fact it ought to do so. If it encourages history painting and statuary . . . it is because these eloquent and tangible signs should especially inform the citizen, from the palace to the farm cottage . . . of public or private virtues, by either recalling fine actions or immortalising the deeds of great men.[14]

Renata Salecl, the sociologist, has abstracted new narratives of legitimacy and sought to find patterns among them in the media of

Central and Eastern Europe. Stories of the Communist period find replication in the post-Communist period. In the half-century of Communism, for many of these states, the narratives provided 'two stages' in constructing socialism: 'The terror and the sacrifices of the first stage legitimized are as a necessary moment on the path towards the future opulent society.' But this familiar narrative is echoed in the 'two stages of democracy', in which it is necessary to 'limit democracy in current society for the sake of future democracy'.[15] The economic sacrifices of shock therapy now lead the way to the abundance of the free market later. In both instances, the narrative justifies arguments for unity, against impatience, and for caution concerning the criticism of public officials.

Other patterns demonstrate emerging narratives of national identity that find their reflection in the past. The narratives of identity during the Bolshevik regime were famous for repetitious symbols of the state: the ubiquitous statues and representations of Lenin, the manufacture and promotion of heroes, the pervasive influence of programmed music and art. The post-Communist era does not always have its obvious substitutes, but in each of the transition states the search for replacing icons continues to occur. In the socialist period, as part of the redemptive mode, the media were filled with stories of economic progress, accomplishments central to projections of pride and virtue: five-year plans, great hydroelectric structures, happy collective farms. Think of the brave photographs, the soaring and muscular sculptures, the booming sounds of Shostakovich. Now, the state-regulated media of the transition societies are filled with the narratives of models of the new economic progress: conventions of foreign investors, ribbon-cuttings which announce the opening of joint ventures to manufacture Western products, the arrival of American rock stars or French officials. Pictures of the Berlin Wall coming down, in the early days, were complemented with the images of economic liberation.

A different geography of narrative takes place in Central Asia among the former Muslim republics of the Soviet Union. There, Turkey's state television and radio authority took the narrative familiar to it at home—'a vehicle to promote a common and collective agenda in the direction of modernisation'—and projected it to Turkmenistan, Kazakhstan, and elsewhere, as an advertisement for the Turkish model of development, 'to show them how a unified world of Muslim Turks can be successful if they look to the West'.[16]

The narratives of the socialist period had the luxury of monopoly, at least relatively so. Now the question is whether new accounts of national identity can compete with the popular imagery from abroad. In the early period of the transitions, these local stories found voice in the folk-songs of the past, a parade of newly vaunted ethnicity, dominion for neglected languages, the featuring of previously suppressed minorities. But these images, often amateur depictions of national identity, faced devastating competition from music videos and American motion pictures; without the buffer of efforts to eliminate competition, they could not compellingly keep an audience and succeed in the task of building loyalties. It will not be touristic reminiscences, but rather the repetitious messages of advertising, indigenous versions of Western imagery, that now, and for the future, will occupy the psychic space necessary for identity concerns. Unless other means can be found, national identity appeals will oscillate between demagogic vaunting of insularity and the state's claim to deliver the goods of the market.

How does one fit, into the theory of the state and the manufacture of national identities, the impact of transformations in communications technology? The megaphone in the village has one sense of control, while the multi-channelled satellite-distributed signal, or the world of e-mail and fax has another. Rather than think, immediately, of the most modern technology, it is worthwhile to reflect, as Anderson did, on the evolution of the old media. The growth of the newspaper and the novel in the eighteenth and nineteenth centuries had significant impact on the development of the concept of the nation. Print, like broadcasting, started with local nodes. Those who early organized the print industry sought to break through dynastic boundaries. The power of print to spread languages yielded a consciousness different from what existed before—one in which millions of people, people who had never met, began to see themselves as having a common past, a community of some sort. What occurred was the consequence of the way in which the print industry was developed as an enterprise. There was a self-contained commercial incentive for expanding language fields to publish and distribute books more efficiently—a building of an audience through the emergence of languages of print that became languages of power. The shift of publication, away from the monasteries, away from the use of manuscripts for personal small-scale delectations and towards the broad distribution of books, compelled the collection and identification of new audiences—the organization of readers.

This process—the reflection between the industry of publication and the nature and self-concept of the audience—is an intriguing one. It continues in the jockeying among today's newspapers: the search for a global audience for the *Wall Street Journal* and the *Financial Times*, how technology makes a new readership possible, and how, as a consequence, that audience redefines itself. Readers of the *Wall Street Journal* in London or New York are related as part of a community which shares the same information, sometimes with similar purposes. It was also present in the effort, successful or not, of a newspaper like the *Los Angeles Times* to expand its circulation and embrace a region, such as Orange County or Southern California, to affect the way the region sees itself—in part so that there can be symbiotic growth between the entity and its organs of publicity. In the last decade, one could see this phenomenon in the infant efforts of the oft-plagued newspaper, the *European*, to establish a readership that was not defined by national boundaries. In each case, demography and circumstance contributed to opportunity; but in seizing the opportunity the newspaper's publication then reverberates and reinforces, to the point of altering the notion of the community in which it is a part.

If print made people aware, however dimly, that there were millions of others sharing the same experience and reading the same material, television has an intensified impact—and the scale of intensity means that television is different in kind. Now people become aware of the vast number, maybe billions, in their particular 'language-field' who are assumed to be fellow viewers; to whom they are connected, in Anderson's term, in 'their particular, visible invisibility'.[17] What they might imagine is a community that is nearly universal, not limited, encompassing, and not national. Common images, powerful images, are simultaneously seen in a village in India, a beach in Saipan, an inner-city ghetto in the United States, and post-Communist Ukraine. And people know or sense that these are common images, commonly available. It is true that there are different glosses, and often different words, that accompany the images. But what is shared may be sufficient to render some significant change in the concept people have of their relationship to a given political system as opposed to their relationship with one another.

The organization and development of print—out of the exclusive domain of the church, into many hands, containing the ideas of many and disparate individuals—contributed to the relationship between print and identity. The new fixity of language helped to contribute to defined accounts of history, and usually to national histories. New definitions of the past—often invented—paved the way to enhanced and specific ideas of national consciousness. Now television changes popular notions of time itself and hierarchy and, as a consequence, popular notions of history. People may come to think of their leaders as equals, as accessible, as immediately accountable. Without the distance that characterized former systems of communication, people consider it more possible to have immediate change. The suddenness of communications may, in the more developed societies, become an essential element of identity.

Already, memory is closely intertwined with both photography and film. For a generation educated through television, the idea of history will be increasingly grainy (or very clear) pictures from archives, which are arranged, packaged, and rearranged. The American Civil War will be remembered through the productions of public television, the assassination of Czarist nobility prior to the Russian Revolution through film replayed on the tube. Video plays tricks of time. If tape does not yellow and fade, time will seem more collapsed. History becomes a collection of magnetized stored digits that can be mixed and played in different sequences. The existence of the amateur motion picture footage, together with the infinite opportunities for its replaying on television, cause the John F. Kennedy assassination to be remembered in a sense fundamentally different from Lincoln's.

A final point in comparing television with its predecessors is that print capitalism created languages-of-power: certain languages gained in status and the spread of particular languages contributed to shifts in power. As part of his study of the effect of print on the formation of communities, Benedict Anderson makes a Darwinian point. As with organic evolution, stronger languages survived and supported greater power bases while other languages faded—with implications for the communities they nourished. Too facile comparisons can be made about the spread of television languages. One could count the audience for English-language programming and consider its impact on local-language viability. The preoccupation of France with the survival of its language and culture in the face of imported American culture owes much to similar concerns.

But it may be that what we think of as the content of television is, in fact, the very development of a new *kind* of language—read or interpreted in new *kinds* of imagined communities. Language here means not a series of words, but rather a vocabulary of images and a syntax of forms. There is the language of news presentation, or the pattern of stories covered, or the inflections of the news presenters. One way to approach this new form of language is to determine whether any of the new global channels are developing a different voice—not an extension of a pre-existing one; not a global version of a national station, but one that has some non-identifiable source—not American, not British—but news, perhaps, from nowhere.

Viewing CNN, at least in the early 1990s, one was presented with three possible voices: 'becoming global', providing a home identity for tired business executives in hotels across the globe, or exploiting the notion (already exploited by Hollywood) that the United States is everyone's second imagined community. One could look at MTV for an additional set of clues, closer to a global channel with a new video language, perhaps closer to the idea of some new place. Global television produces a vocabulary and syntax of consumer imagery which becomes a language of non-loyalties, inherently subversive of existing orders. The language of consumer sovereignty suggests a power to shape existence that does not depend on the state. This is the case not because of any specific or isolated message, but because of the redefining nature of the language itself.

The audience, lying on their local couches, will increasingly not think themselves passive. Viewers will have the power to choose programmes (not merely a network or service), the opportunity to select from a vast library, and the power to meld all offerings into a zapped combination, a grazing among elements. All this contributes to an illusory sense of the triumph of the individual, a triumph over the state as well as a triumph over torpor. Baudrillard puts it more poetically, redefining boundaries of knowing and being as derivatives of

> private telematics; in a new technological moment, each individual sees himself promoted to the controls of a hypothetical machine, isolated in a position of perfect sovereignty, at an infinite distance from his original universe; that is to say, in the same position as the astronaut in his bubble, existing in a state of weightlessness which compels the individual to remain in perpetual orbital flight and to maintain sufficient speed in zero gravity to avoid crashing into his planet of origin.[18]

Clashing Civilizations

The need for narratives and imagery remains, even though their content and means of distribution are transformed. The issue is not whether there will be new narratives, but who will create them successfully and with what respect for democratic values and what adheres to common good. Particularly in periods of transition, there is the search for those narratives that yield cohesion and stability. Anciently, the monarch as centrepiece provided a ready-made focus for the narratives of divine right and the consequent power of the state. A modern state, with its cavalcade of leaders and the imperfections of democratic processes, has more difficulty marshalling the legitimating narratives unless pluralism, democratic values, and market-oriented economic theories themselves can remain compelling legends of cohesion and promise.

Thinking about globalization and democratic values presupposes a range of technology, but that range is always in the process of change. The difficulty of transportation—by road, by rail, by plane—provided communities with particular senses of themselves in relationship to neighbours, regions, other cities. Our sense of space and time is a function of communications and transportation technology. The more fluid the notion of space, the more a person may consider himself or herself part of a larger community. The capacity to reach across borders by telephone, for example, alters the definition of what constitutes a relevant community. So it will be as satellite technology, adorned by companion devices, alters signals and languages.

Modern broadcasting devices seem the perfect instruments for maintaining the imagined community, but they are, also, consummate devices for undermining the established order. The nation-state was, as Eli Noam has written, 'at tension with cross-border allegiances—whether proletarian international solidarity, rebellious youth culture, international financial capital, or ethnic minorities'. Now, however, new networks (for him the electronic capabilities as well as the satellite) weaken national cohesion, strengthening particularism and internationalizing it. 'It is difficult for a state to extend its powers beyond traditional frontiers, but it is easy for the new networks to do so.'[19] Audio cassettes, circulated from France to Iran, rendered immediate the fiery zeal of the Ayatollah, helping to unite opposition to the Shah. Radio, in the last days of the Soviet era, gave to the people of Moscow the sense that they were a community, independent, at least, and stronger, at most, than the organizers of the reactionary *coup*. For each place in Central and Eastern Europe there is yet another dramatic story of the role of radio and television in quickly establishing the legitimacy of revolution. The lesson is not necessarily the lesson of freedom: it is also the lesson of imperilled narratives and susceptible regimes.

Patterns of communications and patterns of identity have a tendency to converge. If one way of understanding the political essence of society is to examine and calibrate its internal web of message-sending,[20] then new technologies mean that the society of reference requires reinterpretation as the codes of interconnection are modified. The satellite, the most modern form of communication, echoes ancient forms of social organization, 'the older imagining, where states were defined by centres, borders were porous and indistinct, and sovereignties faded imperceptibly into one another'. Then, the technology and organization of imaginings contributed, 'paradoxically enough, [to] the ease with which pre-modern empires and kingdoms were able to sustain their rule over immensely heterogeneous, and often not even contiguous, populations for long periods of time'.[21] Now, new kingdoms, outside the established order, have a similar capability.

Who are the candidates for these new kingdoms? Sometimes they have names, in the fashion of the monarchs of old, like Murdoch or Disney, or, more gruesomely, Maxwell. These are familiar temptations, with a familiar global lure. The possibility gives way to a global competition, as, currently, among the BBC, CNN, NBC Superchannel, and Murdoch, to establish a kingdom of news. These are not kingdoms, however, that can sustain power over far-flung peoples, replacing the current order. There is no national identity of Murdoch, no flag or loyalty to Disney. The contest of imagery is more likely to be found in the next generation of global tensions, not among nation-states, but rather between clashing civilizations, defined by history, language, ethnicity, and religion.[22] Seizure of the instruments of imagery, as much as weapons of destruction, will be a threat of the twenty-first century.

The nature of the global drama, the role of the programmes and narratives poured through the skies as a technique of the new era, may have been best captured—or inferred from its opposite—by the gifted Polish journalist and author Ryszard Kapuściński. He was writing about Iran and the turn to Khomeini after the Westernizing experience with the Shah, but the words have a more general truth:

> A nation trampled by despotism, degraded, forced into the role of an object, seeks shelter, seeks a place where it can dig itself in, wall itself off, be itself. This is indispensable if it is to preserve its individuality, its identity, even its

ordinariness. But a whole nation cannot emigrate, so it undertakes a migration in time rather than in space.[23]

Kapuściński was writing, here, of resistance to existing messages from the West, a 'walling-in' that must use every technique possible to screen the compelling, attractive, permeating voices from without. Screening out the new is, and will be, combined with generating images of the old. This process of rejection and projection requires the passion and total authority that is associated with theological fundamentalism united to the state. A dome of belief and privacy is necessary to protect such a culture from the pressures of outside. Yet, the high emotion and all-encompassing religious faith which inspires millions has already become a compelling, militant narrative of world-wide recruitment.[24]

What Kapuściński wrote about Iran applies, in varying degrees, to other societies which establish a wholesale campaign to control imagery. But what he concludes about these few could apply, at some time, to Romania or Ukraine or Tajikistan:

In the face of the encircling affliction and threats of reality, [the nation] goes back to a past that seems a lost paradise. It regains its security in customs so old and therefore so sacred that authority fears to combat them. This is the way a gradual rebirth of old customs, beliefs, and symbols occurs under the lid of every dictatorship—in opposition to, against the will of the dictatorship.[25]

This theory of atavism, this turn against modernity, also suggests one of the strong motivations, conscious or not, on behalf of the West, for projecting the enveloping narratives of its contemporary radio and television. There is a key here to the importance of the stories that are pumped into the transition societies and the periphery of the developed world, a key to the impact of the dramas that emanate from the dream factories of Hollywood to be delivered to the villages of the Carpathians, pub-keepers in Wales, shepherds in the Basque Country, or workers in Azerbaijan. The rhythm and music of Western radio and television become, themselves, a push towards modernity against competing forces.

It is as if, in Kapuściński's terms, a void was created by the fall of the *ancien régime*, and that void will be filled, if not by the aspirations towards the West, then by the ever-present impulse inward, often characterized as regressive. The West must fill this void, it is argued, must enable its signals to flow in so that its dramas and representations fill the space. Otherwise, darker, more sinister, nationalist, fundamentalist images may appear. And the modern global media are perfect for this task: they are efficient, endowed with abundant capacity, and technically constructed to extend zones of influence.

This global narrative of modernity, whether willed or not by other governments, becomes a substitute for the alternative recessive longing, Kapuściński's theorem of retreat from modernity towards the shelter of a nostalgic past. Underneath so much of Western altruism, in this account, is an unconscious instrumentalism, television as bearing an aggressive iconography of secular religion, individualism, and the market. With its origin abroad, the demand for individual freedom from state control can mask a concrete goal, a notion that, if consumer-oriented television is watched, if American sitcoms and dramas are popular, they will displace the narrative of inwardness and fundamentalism. The United States and the West defend or enhance their political ascendance through trade in ideas. Power follows not the flag, but the popular image. Alan Rusbridger of the *Guardian* caught this 'full surreality of the New Media World Order' in a village, an hour from New Delhi, where, adjacent to the temple of the monkey-god, Hanuman, young people chant, while the family of Yogbal Sharma zaps to MTV with its legs, lipstick, kisses, jeans, fast cars, beaches, cafés, drink, and waterfall. In the years to come, Rusbridger observes, children will have to choose whether to spend Tuesday evening singing songs to Hanuman or watching the latest Hollywood fare.[26]

Yet to think of Western radio and television, with their cornucopia of images, as the vanguard of the open society and as an antidote to their opposite is to fall subject to a kind of Potemkin's folly. Too many Westerners identify the arrival of consumer television and familiar imagery with progress in the conversion to democracy, when all it may be is a temporary and ineffective antidote to its opposite. Television's impact may be as superficial as its glossy exterior. The mesmerization and addiction of a public may have their limits where other entities that have shaped behaviour—the family, the church, the state—strongly reassert themselves. And globalism may only be the temporary vanquishing of borders by technology, awaiting the structuring of new lines of demarcation.

The existing order will not pass quietly. If the new kingdoms, those that flourish on porous borders, threaten, the existing states will do what can be done to control the flow of information, to affect reception, and to reorganize the space in which information can flow. The contradictions that exist between television as subversive and television as reinforcing will become more evident: television will be seen as the facilitator of new regimes and as the engine for the retention of power. These are contradictions inherent in concepts of national identity, underscoring the complexity of harmonizing the state's narrative with aspirations of freedom. In this pass, the instrumental definition of national-identity considerations will triumph: groups who hold or can gain power through the machinery of the state will coalesce to retain an oligopoly of allegiance. The form this takes is the market for loyalties, the subject of Chapter 4.

4 The Market for Loyalties

THE previous chapter focused on images that constitute versions of national identity, the conscious effort to provide a cohesive framework for continued state legitimacy. This 'official nationalism', as Seton-Watson has called it, is heavy-handed and difficult, in its execution, to accommodate with human rights. The effort, here, is to domesticate and bring within democratic theory the enormous effort expended by governments, everywhere, to articulate, shape, and reinforce images of the communal self. Fear of the state virtually precludes a model in which it has direct control over the media. And yet the state seems destined to play some role, at least as architect, and usually far more. The government is inevitably a speaker, but we fail to have the means to express the limits on its speech; nor can we define the boundary between government-generated imagery and the full and boisterous speech of the rest of society.

The 'market-place of ideas' has an established meaning and a history of proponents and detractors.[1] Legal metaphor of the century, that market is an active, thriving bazaar with atomized buyers and sellers free, by aspiration if not by definition, from anti-competitive conduct. Here, I invoke a different rhetoric, likewise borrowed from law and economics, inverting the language of the market to help understand the role of the state. I construct, instead of the familiar market, what may be called a market for loyalties,[2] as a closer approximation of reality. In this market, large-scale competitors for power, in a shuffle for allegiances, use media regulation to organize a cartel among themselves. Regulatory arrangements reflect a competition not only for goods, but also for minds and souls. The state seeks sufficient market power over loyalties to assure its continued existence.

Delineating a market for loyalties can help us understand legal and political responses to the gigantic, mysterious transformations now taking place in media industries as telecommunications becomes more global, confounding national borders and the reach of national legislation. The market for loyalties is a mechanism for explaining the manner in which national identities move from collections of stories to allocations of power. In the first part of the chapter, I describe the concept of a market for loyalties, focusing on the price citizens' loyalty to a nation exacts in terms of sacrifice or commitment. The second part discusses the ways in which governments thwart competitors in the market for loyalty, focusing on approaches to media law in various countries. Finally, the chapter addresses the ways in which emerging global technologies are likely to affect the market for loyalties in the future.

Defining the Market

To show how law reflects or structures a market, we might start with a slightly maverick, unprovable theory, one that is independent of the complexities of television and radio history. The theory involves the reading of the US First Amendment, in its literal form, specifically and exclusively as a prohibition on the power of Congress to abridge freedom of speech and of the press. In this argument, the Amendment—'Congress shall make no law . . . abridging the freedom of speech, or of the press'—should be read not as a mandate for unfettered speech, but as a conspiracy among existing regulators of identity in the young Republic (the states and private enforcers of moral rectitude) to prevent this creature of federation from competing with them. For all of the hallowed remembrance of a Republic of Letters in the late eighteenth century, there were severe bounds to permissible speech and conduct and harsh sanctions for breaching those bounds. The task of setting and implementing standards was hardly effaced by the adoption of the First Amendment. It was only *Congress* that could make no law abridging speech and the press.[3] To the cultural regulators like the eighteenth-century churches, the power to control speech and behaviour was sufficiently important that it would not be shared with the new central administration. The First Amendment, like other artefacts of federalism, was an allocation of authority among competitors.[4]

What is nice about this hypothetical reading is that, whether or not it is historically sound, it shows how a speech-related law (here a constitutional provision) can be reinterpreted as an effort to protect groups of interests from each other and from outsiders. In the United States and Western Europe, radio and television are increasingly a battleground for competing notions of the good with respect to race, gender, violence, and obscenity. On reflection, it is commonplace to see law and regulation deployed in the interests of one interest group or another.[5] In the so-called transition societies of Central and Eastern Europe and the former Soviet Union, even more is at issue.[6] There, often, the very existence of the state is in question, and persistent control of the media to reinforce fragile national identities is predictable. Broadcast regulatory structures, even if couched in terms of freedom of speech or tolerance of human rights, become architectural elements designed to help one or another version of national identity gain an advantage in an economy of significant political transactions.

It is easier to describe a market for goods than a market for loyalties or ideas.[7] In a market for automobiles or sugar, there are usually identifiable buyers and sellers, a market-clearing price, and a means for settling accounts. In a market for loyalties, the major 'sellers' or producers are the manufacturers of identities, classically states or governments, but others as well, interest groups and businesses, for whom myths and dreams and history can be converted into power and wealth.[8] Large and powerful interest groups fabricate their own model of national identity to render themselves more powerful. Especially at a time when there are a feast of identities competing for attention, the supply-side in the market for loyalties is disserved by reliance on reductionist terms like 'state' or 'government' or 'political party'.

The 'buyers' are citizens, subjects, nationals, consumers—individuals or their surrogates—receivers of the packages of information, propaganda, advertisements, drama, and news propounded by the media. The consumer can and does 'pay' for one set of identities or another in several ways which, together, we call 'loyalty' or 'citizenship'. But the price is not in the ordinary coin of the realm. More often, the charge for loyalties includes assuming economic burdens of the state, obeying laws, and readiness to fight in the armed services. Indeed, merely staying within the dominion of a state, where migration is an option, can constitute a form of payment for loyalty.[9] Jacques Ellul recognized these notions of loyalty and allegiance, in a somewhat exaggerated way, in describing the cost of modernity and its loyalties: the twentieth-century citizen, he wrote, is 'saddled by his government with . . . sacrifices, such as ever-increasing taxes', and increasingly, he argued, these are paid out of conviction, not overt force. The modern consumer of loyalties must 'participate in wars such as have never been seen before'.[10]

How have these 'payments' worked and been related to the production of identities? Take the form of physically remaining or actively emigrating as a demonstration of loyalty. Outmigration from the then-Soviet Union was an act that proved, in its most obvious form, an unwillingness to pay the cost of loyalty. To be sure, a state may render emigration or immigration technically and legally difficult. The heightening of allegiances, an increase in patriotism, however, may cost the state less than a policy of force or subsidy or physical maintenance of its population base. The state must decide, in a time of mobility, which technique to use (if the holding of population is desired). For the individual, the benefits of physically departing, and the alternatives of other available identities, are the opportunity costs to remaining.[11]

As Ellul pointed out, the relationship of the citizen to the fisc is another aspect of loyalty. In most modern societies, because of the complexity of social and business transactions, compliance with tax regimes has a measure of the voluntary to it. Patriotism is not necessarily a function of the extent to which a taxpayer gives the benefit of the doubt to the government. But it is true that it is a sign of trouble when a government cannot collect the taxes it duly levies. New York City charges an income tax, over and above that of the state; there are those who move to Long Island, New Jersey, and Connecticut to avoid it. Many of those who remain have, for complex reasons, no choice. But for others, there is a degree of loyalty manifested by their willingness, more or less voluntarily, to undergo the additional cost of adhesion.[12] Because of a history of exemptions, deferrals, and inequities, rates of compliance with the draft are not a perfect sign of degrees of adhesion of a community to its government. But studies of compliance or desertion or the burdens of raising an army through means other than conscription suggest that there is a cost to loyalty and that sometimes that cost is too high.[13] History is studded with cases where mass desertion has meant the end of empire; where, all of a sudden, the duty to fight for a particular cause is no longer enforceable.

The market for loyalties also operates when consumers (sometimes acting as voting citizens, sometimes as merely the mass of public opinion demonstrating their views in other ways) appear to weigh the cost of various national identities and choose among them through political action. Such sharp ideological choices are a means of revealing that a particular identity is too costly or, for other reasons, that another identity is preferred to the incumbent one. There are sophisticated calculations to be made. In elections in the transition states of the former Soviet Union, adherence to principles of 'the free market' may receive approval because of the expectation of an infusion of Western aid that may improve conditions and enhance the possibility of prosperity. A public may be measuring the material existence possible or likely during one's lifetime against a religious promise of a later reward. Consumers of competing national identities must, like those who choose among other goods that are a complex combination of barely quantifiable factors, seek to order the choices expressly or implicitly put to them. Nor must an individual hold just one national identity, or be loyal only to a single such idea. Individuals can be multilateral in their patriotism as they are promiscuous in their other product choices. They can be loyal to the land of their ancestors and the land of their current home. They can be loyal to France and to the idea of Europe. They can be primarily Parisians or cosmopolitans or Muslims or Catholics, but simultaneously be French or American. What is important from the point of view of the suppliers of identity is not whether individuals hold more than one allegiance, but rather how intensities among loyalties fluctuate and are expressed. Will people vote, or send money, or pledge their children to the armed forces to manifest their loyalty?

These sketches of buyers, sellers, and the currency of choice provide the merest outline of the market for loyalties. They should suffice, however, as an introduction to thinking of ways competitors for power, including incumbent governments, seek to affect the market's operation. It is common to think of citizens as having little choice in terms of national identity, with only a single seller (or a small, relatively undifferentiated group) with which to deal. Passports would signify the producer's tie to the consumer. Were this simple model the case, there still might be a market, but with the qualities of a totalitarian society where the cost of disloyalty is high and competition is almost always outlawed.[14] The plurality of national identities available is inherent in the definition I have already advanced: that what is grandly called national identity may be no more than the collection of myths, promises, and renderings of history that will keep one party rather than the other in power. Under this definition, even political parties which often represent differing notions of a national identity, different concepts of membership in the community, are producers in the market.

Within the framework of this market, we can look at how law is used to alter and distort loyalties, the range of effects, including effects that would, in other environments and with respect to other products, be called anti-competitive. The model helps explain why government is commonly ceded a role in the market for goods but, in the rhetoric of the Western democratic tradition, so rarely tolerated as an intervener in the market for loyalties.[15]

An economic model of media law provides insight into what government considers competition in its effort to maintain power, since these competitors are, if constitutionally possible, most likely to be taxed or proscribed or otherwise discriminated against. Here, the question is what products constitute 'substitutes' in the market for loyalties. Thus, looking at statutory, constitutional, and treaty efforts to regulate the market for loyalties, we can ask whether new packages of identity are substitutes for traditional national allegiances or whether national identities—of the traditional sort—compete only among themselves.

In this way, we can see whether the contest for loyalty can encompass the pull of religion or a global way of life represented through consumer advertising. The preoccupation that many European governments have long had with competition from private commercial broadcasters suggests that advertisers are effective competitors. To see why requires harking back to the modes of payment by the consumer of identities. Assuming, for a moment, that a citizen can express loyalty in terms of willingness to pay taxes, then the seller of the product (national identities) has either to persuade the voter to allocate a greater portion of disposable income to identity expenditures or to divert expenditures from one sort of identity to another. Taxpayers can refuse to pay taxes. People can decide that, as a consequence of their religion (whether Islam or consumerism), particular salvations are more important than the public weal, and consequently vote to divert income from the defence industries or to lower the public revenues altogether. Or citizens can determine, through voting or the articulation of public opinion, that they should spend more on local taxes and less on taxes for the federal government. Advertising can persuade individuals to consume rather than to save and invest, with consequences for particular visions of the public good. In this sense, marketers of 'pure' national identities compete with sellers of consumer goods, who are trying to impress the citizen with another identity. Here the question is how a person decides, at the margin, whether a higher or lower percentage of disposable income should go to the state (in taxes), say for education or environmental protection, or, instead, for personal goods like food or television sets and automobiles.[16]

As with the First Amendment example earlier in this chapter, in which the individual American states might not have wanted the Congress as a competitor in the task of censorship, comparative statutory analysis provides opportunities to capture how the market for loyalties is codified. In the Soviet sphere, of course, channels were traditionally few and wholly reserved for the government; here there was an ultimate barrier to entry, part of a general, expressly articulated programme to shape loyalties.[17] The emergence of British broadcasting involved the use of law to protect British commercial interests from foreign competitors. But it was also a legal expression of fear that this early transborder data flow might injure British nationhood. One of R. H. Coase's early economic analyses of law, discussed in Chapter 1, showed how national and international regulation was used to limit competition from radio signals from France and Luxemburg.[18] Today, issues of control of viewpoint access arise in the broader context of European integration. Article 10(1) of the European convention on Human Rights and Fundamental Freedoms provides that the right to freedom of expression embraces the right to receive information and ideas without regard to frontiers.[19] In 1990 the European Court of Human Rights added teeth to this provision in *Groppera Radio A.G.* v. *Switzerland*[20] and *Autronic A.G.* v. *Switzerland*.[21] In those cases, the Court ruled that Article 10 rights apply not only to the printed press but also to radio and television. Although the court acknowledged a limited right for receiving states to protect their technical licensing schemes, state-imposed barriers to transfrontier television would generally offend the principles set out in the Convention.[22] The Television Broadcasting Directive of the European Community,[23] and the virtually equivalent European Convention on Transfrontier Television of the Council of Europe,[24] reaffirmed this regional-market approach. In the 1990s the focus has shifted from the regulation of transmission across the borders of individual European states to the protection, mainly through the imposition of quotas, of European programme production from foreign attack.[25] During negotiations of the Uruguay Round of the GATT in 1993, the European Union sought to exclude film and television programming from the general lowering of trade barriers on the ground that a European cultural space ought to be preserved, strengthened, and protected from the influx of American entertainment.[26]

Regulating the Market

In Western Europe, the extent of competition for national identities within broadcasting has been finely calibrated, and, until the mid-1970s, was limited primarily to entities controlled by government or closely related to it.[27] To trace, in more specific detail, the construction of a market for loyalties and the impact on it of changing technologies, I want to turn to the Dutch example. The Netherlands has a more elegant history of statutory expression in this area than most other countries. And the impact of transformations in the organization of the media (as well as other social changes) has been more transparent. We can see how broadcasting statutes and practices were instruments for mediating among long-established rival components, stabilizing divisions in the market, and protecting them from outsiders.

The Dutch radio and television system has long been famous for its intricate recognition of specific separated perceptions of Dutch national identities. Consistent with a political philosophy that assumes 'pillarized' segments of society, Catholic, Protestant, liberal, and socialist, the Dutch have established a television system that, for a long time, gave each segment its own unencumbered opportunity to broadcast, first on radio, then on television. These groups competed for allocation of broadcast time, with awards dependent on numbers of members or adherents each group could claim. Informal sanctions, including taboos imposed by the groups themselves, rendered these pillarized broadcasting organizations powerful reinforcers of separate visions of Dutch identity, to limit, as it were, interbrand competition.

Law not only determined which groups could participate, but which could not, excluding competitors that would pose a challenge to all of them. These associations recognized that their capacity to appeal to the loyalty of their members would be threatened if commercial outsiders, unrestrained by public-interest obligations, not restricted to a relatively narrow message, had the opportunity to compete. As occurred elsewhere in Europe, pirates (broadcasters from international waters) attempted to compete outside the constraints of the legally sanctioned oligopoly. The traditional associations, draped in their commitment to historic Dutch identities, sought, with the government, to exclude the new entrants. As the Netherlands became subject to European law, this system came under attack. The government argued, in a court challenge, that these pirates—Veronica and TROS—did not ' "sufficiently address . . . society's cultural, religious or spiritual needs", as required by Article 13 of the Broadcasting Act'.[28] An administrative judgment in favour of the intruders was based on a novel statutory interpretation: that the absence of a particular religious philosophy or view about the conduct of life did not prevent an organization from fulfilling the cultural needs of society. As a temporary but ultimately doomed measure to safeguard existing competitors from further competition, the Broadcast Law was amended to require that, to obtain a licence, an association or group had to represent some point of view, some social, cultural, religious, or spiritual trend.[29]

In the era of cable, the problem of raising barriers to entry rose once again, demonstrating the impact of technology on existing market-sharing arrangements. The government-protected pillarized suppliers of particular national identities, already weakened by competition from the centrist, popular, and now legal pirates, saw new transborder competitors in cable franchises. To address these concerns, the government adopted rules precluding cable operators from carrying foreign programmes with commercial advertisements specifically directed at the Dutch market, including programmes with Dutch subtitles. Ultimately, again as a result of Dutch judicial intervention and the European Court of Justice, the new competitors, too, could not be forestalled.[30]

The Dutch situation remains complicated. In terms of the economic model, however, the history of broadcasting in the Netherlands is illuminating. Here was a place where the system was originally and explicitly designed to identify and promote alternative proponents of a national identity and to allocate markets among them. These competitors, as might well be expected, sought to exclude others who might reduce their market share. When competition occurred, it became clear that, for television watchers, commercial programming was clearly a substitute for programming that promoted a particular national identity. As society evolved in the 1960s and 1970s, demand for traditional public-service programming (provided by the pillarized groups) proved highly elastic. People could satisfy whatever need they had for a bundle of national-identity ideals elsewhere; they were not willing to pay, in terms of their calculus of quality and entertainment, in terms of time or reduced satisfaction, for the claimed virtues of their traditional association. Perhaps most important, increased competition reinforced and accelerated what is known as 'depillarization', an expectable economic response from the traditional associations: their programming no longer reflects a narrowly targeted version of a national identity and each of them seeks a broader and broader audience. Competition from abroad has altered the capacity of the state to preserve the strength of the existing competitors or to stabilize the ability of those who continue to seek to market loyalties to use the media to reinforce particular identities.[31]

Turkey provides another dramatic history of the effort to maintain control over national identity. Article 133 of the Constitution gave Turkish Radio and Television Authority (TRT), at least until mid-1993, a monopoly over broadcasting. TRT was not only monopolistic, 'it was also essentially the voice of the state, disseminating the unitary ideology and culture of Turkish republicanism and highly susceptible to government intervention'.[32] TRT was charged by statute with 'promoting the values of country, unity, republic, public order, harmony, and welfare and to strengthen the principles of Kemal Ataturk's reforms'.[33] In an environment in which there had been deep divisions about alternate national identities, TRT, as the proponent of the modern secular state, was seen as an instrument for cohesiveness. When the number of available channels was expanded in the 1980s to bring programme availability closer to world standards, the new channels were all made part of TRT. When TRT was attacked for leaning to the left and broadcasting programmes that legitimated Islamic fundamentalism—a doctrine considered hostile to the secular state—the agency's director-general was forced to resign.[34]

The first break in the monopoly came as a consequence of satellite technology and involved, much as in the Dutch case, uplinking television programmes to satellite transponders leased from Eutelsat and Intersat, and then sending them back down into Turkey. These channels were, in the fiction of the law, classified as foreign transmissions, a kind of unchallenged exception to the Constitution's monopoly. They provided opportunities for additional wealth to some associated with the government, including, among the first of these 'pirates', the President's son. According to Aksoy and Robins, satellite dishes became 'symbols of how taboos and prohibitions are being dismantled';[35] informal, squatter-type radio stations followed. Much of what occurred was tolerated by the government. The new speakers had a primarily commercial and entertainment tone which reinforced the secular mandate of the parties in power. But the proliferation of voices, the increased use of the new channels by a deported Islamic imam, and the fears of splintering within Turkey itself, led to an intense ambivalence about competition. In early 1993 the Ministry of the Interior issued a directive banning all private television and radio stations.

Within days, largely because of massive protest, the Minister exempted broadcasting via satellites from abroad. Those who favoured the government's original action argued that the closures were necessary to pave the way for a more orderly scheme for broadcasting regulation; those against argued that the decision was autocratic, based on 'the government's inclination to create a single-voiced democracy'.[36]

The Belgian experience parallels that of the Netherlands. In Belgium, reflecting the pluralistic gulf between the French-speaking and Flemish-speaking communities, the unitary system was fractured as early as 1960.[37] The Belgian Nationaal Instituut voor de Radio-Omroep, or NIR, was replaced by three public organizations: one in charge of French-language broadcasting, one in charge of Flemish or Dutch broadcasting, and the third to provide technical, administrative, and financial services to all broadcasters as well as to address the common culture and the German minority. By constitutional amendment in the early 1970s, national jurisdiction in the field of cultural policies was attributed to the more local and discrete 'Culture Councils' in Flemish-speaking Flanders and the French-speaking Walloon provinces, and broadcasting was brought within this mandate.[38] By 1977, by pact among the competitors for national identity, the opportunity for each group to reinforce loyalties more efficiently was strengthened: the central co-ordinating mechanisms were weakened or dissolved so that each community could determine the structure of its own broadcasting organization. At least formally, a strict division of markets, tightly arranged by potential competitors, had been successfully arranged.

In the 1980s the appetite for an alternative to the public-financed monopoly arose, particularly in the Flemish community. A misbegotten effort to assure an economic base for a Flemish commercial station and, presumably, to preserve and strengthen Flemish language use demonstrates the intricacy of market-sharing efforts. The Flemish business interests and political parties agreed on two principles: to survive, a Flemish station required an advertising monopoly in the community; and to assure the survival of the Flemish newspaper industry, the Flemish station should be 51 per cent owned by the Flemish newspapers established in the Flemish community. Implemented in 1987, the decree would, in addition, have allowed cable to carry European Community public-service television stations only when programmes were made in the original language of the Member State. The purpose of the rule was to prevent broadcasters, other than the Dutch, from targeting the Flemish-speaking audience in Flanders.

The European Court of Justice, based on Article 59 of the Rome Treaty (protecting the free movement in services), held the language (and other) requirements discriminatory and illegal.[39]

These examples could be duplicated by looking at statutes and practices in a wide variety of other countries, both democracies and authoritarian governments. National media legislation is commonly used to allocate markets, to establish, where possible, cartels of allegiances. In Germany, as I have already discussed, public broadcasting corporations are obliged to adhere to a rule of 'internal pluralism', enforced in terms of governing councils, the *Rundfunkrat*, in which the opinions, values, interests, and perspectives in the society must be represented.[40] The statutory idea is for broadcasting 'to mirror, as it were, the society's pluralism in the organic structure'. A 'plurality directive' is the outcome of the inter-Länder treaty entered into in 1991, which sought to assure the pluralistic character of the overall system. 'The existence of external pluralism is presumed if each of three programs produced in Germany by three different private broadcasting corporations and broadcast nation-wide can be received by more than half the population in Germany.' There are

> special state broadcasting agencies which supervise the private license holders to assure that they work towards the realization of the goal that the entirety of the three programs is pluralistic, i.e. that the total of them articulate the plurality of opinions and voice the views of the relevant political, ideological, and social forces and groups of civil society.[41]

The 'market-for-loyalties' model also helps explain why advocates for various national identities would have different attitudes towards the use of ordinary commercial advertising on television.[42] In the market for loyalties, proponents of some identities recognize the indirect supporting role that the barrage of traditional commercials, for everything from orange juice to computers, might play in connection with their own narrations of future happiness. Take, for example, a rather simple one-dimensional view of the Republican Party in the United States or the Conservative Party in the United Kingdom or the parties advocating a more rapid transition to a market-place economy in Russia. These parties may see the virtues of a citizenry saturated with the culture of advertising and consumerism as containing indirect or secondary messages of political significance. The message of the seller of toothpaste and automobiles may, almost by definition, buttress a national-identity claim that the opportunity to have maximum choice to exercise actively the right to purchase is good. We see assertions of national identity in the interstices of commercials, in their depiction of idealized home life, of opportunities to travel, or in their depiction of a certain idea of traditional family values.[43] If the images of the consumer society are supportive of the party in power, then that may be ground enough for the advocacy of an increase in advertiser-supported broadcasting.

In other instances, a ruling party may see the images of advertising and the narratives of foreign programmes as a threat both to the culture and, perhaps more centrally, to its continued power. These often foreign images (usually labelled 'American' for convenience) are then characterized as subversive in the most important sense: they persuade and advocate, virtually by the basic aspects of their story-lines, a view of the individual that is wholly at odds with the reigning perspective.[44] The successful penetration of the world-view contained in Western advertising could (though there are those who differ) yield instability and a claim for change.[45] The most avid proponents of free-market television have, supporting this position, argued that the images of Western society, including its advertising, are entitled to some of the credit—to use an accepted formula—for the fall of the Berlin Wall and the collapse of the Soviet Union.[46]

The State as Participant

I have focused on the role of law and policy as a means for organizing and controlling the market for loyalties. But there is also the special, more identifiable role of the state as a participant in the market. Here the relationship between the state as censor and the state as generator of images is important. Some set of narratives, some sense of national identity, is an important aspect of the state's existence. Much of what the state accomplishes is a public good, and there is a danger that not all citizens or subjects will undergo their share of the costs of the state's undertakings. The benefits of security and peace are available to those who do not, as well as those who do, pay taxes. To engender sufficient loyalty to maintain cohesion, or to correct for perceived unfairness, the state can subsidize messages that it deems needed,[47] censor messages that are deemed antagonistic,[48] or itself become a vocal participant in the market.[49] Other things being equal, the pressure for censorship increases where cartelization has not been successful and the state, itself, has limited power to generate images of cohesion and loyalty. In the American context, for example, the public function of enhancing and enriching the civil narrative falls, fragilely, to public broadcasting. Cartelization or censorship efforts account for the fierce debate that continues over the structure and narrative of broadcasting. The felt need to address violence, indecency, obscenity, the misrepresentation of women or minorities—all of these are examples of this pressure.

There are, of course, profound difficulties with an approach that emphasizes officially instating the assortment of myths and narratives necessary for the achievement of a cohesive national identity. The approach assumes that there is a way of telling when the mix of messages that arises in the market-place, absent government intervention, threatens the cohesion of the society; that the government will have the judgement to know when this occurs; and that it will act with discretion to find the right balance. As to each of these points, the approach does not indicate how to define, in a democratic society, the proper limit on the state as a competitor or the proper limits on how the state articulates the grounds for cohesion. Even if one assumes that there is a role for the state in the competition for loyalties, as I have argued in Chapter 3, and that the state *should* participate in the narratives of legitimacy and cohesion, how, in a democratic society, is the limit of that role determined? Among all the images of cohesion, the narratives of identity, how does the state select the images it will subsidize and champion?

These are questions answered by the constitutional limits on the market for loyalties. In the United States, the First Amendment both limits the role of Congress as censor and precludes the legitimation of any particular religion as the carrier of national identity. Nothing explicit seems to limit the government as speaker or the President from using the bully pulpit of the White House, so long as the use is as one entrant in the market-place. A state monopoly in the competition for loyalties would be just another form of censorship, and such a monopoly is virtually the definition of a totalitarian society. On the other hand, a society in which the state has withdrawn completely from the field is not necessarily just and fair. The measure of the rule of law here is whether limits are articulated and observed; to some extent, it is tradition, the evolution of a process, that provides a sense that government functions properly within its limits.[50]

Locating the government in the market for loyalty flirts with the edges of propaganda theory. Propaganda is the name that we give to government use of symbols to influence or manipulate public opinion, at home or abroad.[51] There is much to be learnt about our conflicted attitudes towards this kind of speech, especially from those writers who recognize that propaganda is a word that does not necessarily imply a pejorative outcome and who see resort to propaganda as a mainstay of all modern governments, including democratic ones.[52] But most writings on propaganda do not use a market-place approach. Those who analyse propaganda are concerned with behavioural implications. They may use the metaphor of competition, but not its analytic implications.

Globalism and the Market

The problem of globalism re-emerges. The market for loyalties long functioned during a time in which technologies were more or less consistent with state sovereignty. The state had the capacity to serve as a forum for the cartelization of allegiances. As technology alters the power of the state to perform this role, the question is how the market for loyalties will be established, regulated, and policed in the future. After all, the capacity of states to use traditional forms of media law to establish barriers to entry and to parcel the market among various interests (including that of the government itself) is deteriorating. The media statutes that divide allegiances and control narratives already have the aura of being of another era, one in which the bounds of competition for national identity could be contained. True, the passion for using law to regulate loyalties and fence out competition proceeds unabated, but these efforts seem doomed.[53] Among the technologies that condemn traditional media regulatory practices are direct broadcast satellites, faxes, video-casettes, the rich potential of the electronic highway—all of which appear to preclude the kind of intervention by national governments that characterized the twentieth-century market for loyalties.

The market for loyalties will not disappear, however. What will occur is a massive shift in the profile of suppliers of loyalties and, in the definition of 'the audience', the relevant market of consumers. Each changing technology favours different political interests and causes changes in the locus and mode of regulation. National markets, constrained by borders, were long the key determiner of the market. For most of the century, as I argued in Chapter 1, the international order assumed that radio transmissions were primarily within the boundaries of one nation; the international function was to dispense frequencies so as to assure that these conditions of market division were met and enforced. International regulations and arrangements were built on the assumption of limiting broadcasting to 'national service of good quality within the frontiers of the country concerned'.[54] In the interlude between the First and Second World Wars there were, for example, bilateral and multilateral agreements to control propaganda subversive to the state system. For example, the League-of-Nations-sponsored Convention Concerning the Use of Broadcasting in the Cause of Peace provided that the

> high contracting parties mutually undertake to prohibit, and if occasion arises, to stop without delay the broadcasting within their respective territories of any transmission which to the determinant of good international understanding is of such a character as to incite the population of any territory to acts incompatible with the internal order of the security of a territory of a high contracting party.[55]

But the rise of new technologies, coupled with the fierce propaganda competition of the Second World War, rendered these arrangements a parody of actual behaviour. As the market for information became global, the capacity of governments to establish oligopolies, to assure market share, and to stabilize competition became much more difficult. In the post-war era, the rhetoric of human rights seriously competed with the rhetoric of the state system of sovereignty. The world has moved from a highly regulated, carefully divided market for loyalties to one that is less constrained, at least by national governments.[56]

Pioneer ways of dealing with the new technology suggest the kind of steps likely to persist in this transformative period. Regional multilateral arrangements, especially the Television Without Frontiers Directive, are harbingers. New technology serves as a prod for broader, supranational forms of regulation, for loci that provide more effective market division and policing given the geographical sweep of new media. Under the Directive, states are responsible to consult with other, receiving countries, where programming has destabilizing consequences.[57] The European Union is also a forum for eliminating internal national steps in which the government maintains close to a monopoly for itself. In the recent *Informationsverein* case, the European Court of Human Rights has raised, virtually to the point of prohibition, the cost to Austria of maintaining a state monopoly that protects a geographical area against competition. The last among its European compatriots, Austria did not license private radio and television stations, maintaining a monopoly for the public-service provider. The argument of Austria to sustain the monopoly was that it was necessary, in a small country, to further democratic values by maintaining tight control over the market, including the market for advertising revenues. A monopoly could assure 'well-balanced, objective and pluralistic programs', while a proliferation could yield 'one-sided programs . . . and the abuse of media power'.[58] The government made the argument of the benevolent monopolist: its legislation was 'aimed at preventing manipulation of the population and the concomitant serious disturbances of the public order'.[59] The European Court held that the public monopoly could not be maintained. The locus for making these decisions had shifted.

These are all new steps to re-divide the market or to establish rules for competition among suppliers. Those countries that oppose the content of messages coming from outside, for religious or political reasons, have, at present, little direct impact on the behaviour of the suppliers of programming. They must, often, control demand by increasing the price of viewing, or prohibiting it. In some settings, a partial or wholesale withdrawal from the mainstream of world-communications commerce will be attempted so as to prolong the hold of existing national identities. Banning satellite receiving dishes, moratoria on the award of broadcast frequencies, and the maintenance of an uncertain legal regime rendering investment in cable unlikely are all examples of their strategies. Such a withdrawal can be policed at high cost and is increasingly ineffective. In Singapore, a general ban on the purchase or use of satellite-receiving dishes without a hard-to-obtain licence is designed to keep out those programmes that are unapproved. Much more vigorous efforts to fence out foreign signals characterize Iran, where watching foreign programming may be a crime.[60] The steps these countries take are extensions of the barriers to entry employed during the early television era, limiting the number of television channels available for public viewing (by allocation or by treaty) and retaining control of the scarce resource.[61]

Similarly, while the introduction of advance technology and the multiplicity of channels have about them the air of the inevitable, the pace of their introduction and of the social organization for receiving information does not. States, concerned with extending their control over the competition for loyalties, will prefer the introduction of cable television to its alternative: the spread of satellite dishes at the home that can receive, silently, signals straight from abroad. With the cable system, there is at least a domestic intermediary, an entity that can be subjected to community influence. Acting in accord with the economic model, governments will prefer the cable system to be operated by a monopolist, and one with whom the government has some contact and potential for control.

It is often thought that censorship, the ancient and indispensable tool in shaping the market for loyalties, is rendered obsolete by the technologies of abundance and ease of access. But the architecture of electronic delivery of information permits innovation and efficiency in policing the sending and receiving of messages. The US government has been fighting, uphill, to insert special chips in the information infrastructure to facilitate eavesdropping when judicially or legislatively authorized. Other less gracious governments may introduce such monitoring technology in their systems without any public debate on their use.

Of course, powerful as it may be, television is not the exclusive factor in social change, nor is the availability of television sets and signals the only determinant of altered behaviour. States have, at their disposal, other socialization mechanisms, as do the varied traditional protectors of the culture (such as schools, churches, and the mass media themselves). It is popular to believe that television has a hypodermic effect, that 'repetitive exposure of media messages is sufficient to change the attitudes and behaviors of large numbers of people in important ways',[62] but a small scholarly industry has ridiculed the simple equivalence of viewing and impact.

Still, governments, themselves, act as if programming has consequences; and, because news-programming is so important a bearer of public narratives, the evolution of journalism in the era of new technology will bear special attention. If states have less control over accounts that come across borders, they will seek to exercise more control over journalists and the reports they export. In addition, formal or informal arrangements between states and large-scale international news organizations may become more frequent. CNN is an example of an institution with contractual ties to governments (to operate terrestrial transmitters, to broadcast via the national system, or otherwise merely to gather information). Implicit in the multilateral diplomacy of CNN is a set of images more likely to reinforce the narratives of prevailing governments, sending forth information that destabilizes only at the very margin, the margin from centres of power.

I have already suggested that enhanced acceptance of commercialization, and depoliticization of the media, is another possible response. If the competition has been among traditional national identities, and if product loyalties—consumerism—are a weak substitute, then governments would prefer an influx of MTV to a set of messages sponsored by a meaningful critic and proponent. A media filled with commercials is preferable to one crowded with opposing alternate identities, such as those of Islamic fundamentalists in Egypt, Basque separatists in France, or Kurds in Turkey. Commercialization may, in the words of its critics, undermine historic cultures; but it is far less subversive than destabilizing political messages. In this sense, at least in the short run, there is a benefit to governments in the gestation and entry of new and attractive commercial supply material, powerful influences through which it may be difficult for competing national identities to emerge.

Consistent with the idea of the market for loyalties, a likely response would be for the government to invest more in its own narrative of national identity, a point to which I return in Chapters 6 and 9. In some instances, this is what is occurring. In some corners of the former Soviet Union (Turkmenistan, for example), in the early period of transition, a strong central government has redoubled its efforts to maintain a monopoly over imagery. This has entailed censoring newspapers, precluding the distribution of dissenting papers, tightly policing the entry of foreign broadcast television signals, and monitoring those who are considered frequenters of foreign messages.[63] On the other hand, in Western democracies, the commitment to public broadcasting seems to be declining. There does not seem to be a convincing argument in the United States that the plethora of new channels require that the central identity be buttressed through the work of the Corporation for Public Broadcasting or the enforcement of public-interest standards on licensees of the public air waves.

The Market of the Future

Finally, other instruments for affecting the shape of the market for loyalties are emerging. Antitrust policy is a possible means of affecting tendencies towards evolving monopolies or oligopolies in the software industry, or in the film industry, or among the new vertically integrated giants, tendencies that may have a substantial impact on the competing narratives. This is not because Japanese-owned Hollywood firms will be more inclined to favour the country of their corporate owners. Rather, monopoly power anywhere in the chain of control can become a bottleneck, determining who has access to the technology and for what programming purpose. The European Union, in addition to its insistence on the power to discriminate in favour of locally produced film and television programmes, has developed a complex system of subsidies, politely called investments, and other inducements to create a common cultural space and to enhance the capacity of Europe to compete abroad in the area of programming.

But when all is said and done, the capacity of existing states to regulate the narrative of political discourse will be reduced by the new technologies and the mechanisms that are evolving for their exploitation. Even in an era of more limited broadcast entry, some argued that Radio Free Europe, Radio Liberty, and Voice of America helped destabilize the Soviet regime. If abundant channels become easily accessible, universally available, and used by powerfully charismatic unmediated voices, the potential for novel, widespread, populist alliances, spreading across wide areas, will certainly be realized.[64] There will be less control over which entities are destabilized. National identities are, of course, quizzical imaginings: a combination of the aesthetics of patriotism, romantic searches through the past, and the reinvention of old myths for sometimes benign, sometimes malevolent, manipulative purposes. These identities can change, and change rapidly.

The nature of the future market for loyalties remains a puzzle. Perhaps a world of hyperbolic home shopping, not just of consumer goods but political ideas, ideologies, and movements, will become divided into three great parts: the production empire, the consumer empire, and the Third World. The production empire creates a new kind of exploitation in which dollars are extracted from the empires of consumption. The Third World becomes even more marginalized, outside technology, outside the cash and trade nexus. Wiring the consumer empire (or interconnecting it by satellite) increases the technology that can expand the allegiances of consumerism, akin to establishing the infrastructure for resource extraction in the colonies of old.

There are other, more likely scenarios, linking changes in satellite technology to world demographic and economic tendencies. Religiously inspired reform movements, gaining global momentum, respond to deep inequities, the ravages of population growth, and the faith-based dissatisfaction with modernity. National identities spill out from their boundaries and become the foundation of potential clashes among civilizations.[65] Benedict Anderson, writing of contests for identity in colonial Asia, brilliantly captures the historical significance of reshaping boundaries: he writes of the old colonial maps, with each imperial state colouring their colonies in distinctive dyes (Britain pink-red, French purple-blue, Dutch yellow-brown). This logo-map, as Anderson calls it, 'penetrated deep into the popular imagination, forming a powerful emblem for the anticolonial nationalisms being born'.[66] The map of the future, unknown and unknowable, computer-generated and therefore infinitely changeable, will generate and render newly explosive allegiances and loyalties in ways still being determined.

The logo-map with its colonial dyes has not wholly disappeared. There are maps, now, of the skies, of orbital slots and transponders. It is those maps that increasingly concern leaders, speaking to audiences they never see, whose views they seek, none the less, to shape. Longitudes and latitudes are replaced by geostationary reckoning. It becomes the spatial reach of AsiaSat and Astra, and the political content they spread across borders and boundaries, which requires bargaining and decision. The now-reigning oligopolies will be weakened, replaced by new allegiances, reinforced by new media structure. That will be the case because the old market for loyalties survives no more.

Part Two

Raising the Curtain: Freeing Speech in the Transition Societies

5 Inventing Independence

In the austere lobby of a hotel in Kiev, time stops; the receptionists move from behind their counter, leaving telephones unanswered. A group of soldiers, garbed in the dark flannel grey of their Soviet past, file through the simple hotel doors to join them. Four heavy women, wearing white culinary caps, descend from the kitchen and quietly take their seats. All form a tight semicircle around the television set. No hero appears, no celebration of freedom. It is the hour of the soap opera, made in Mexico, dubbed into Russian, shipped by satellite, transmitted from Moscow, watched in Ukraine. Here is a brief period of the 'normal'; a moment of respite as the amalgam of life and representations of the public good turbulently change. After decades of Soviet domination, after centuries of Tsarist control, Ukraine has so long been a story about a country, not a country itself, that the task of finding the attributes of nationhood—flag, language, foreign relations, broadcasting policy—becomes a matter of complex and sophisticated articulation.

This moment in Kiev, among the curved naugahyde chairs and the faintly erotic flickers on the television screen, is part of a contest for control of imagery, a contest in which the competing parties have not yet been clearly identified. The glimmering reflections from a Mexican soap opera watched by the anxious viewers of Ukraine may provide more of a guide to the future than do the language of statutes, parliamentary debates, or claims to represent the national identity. In the short run, there is an intensive, internal contest for destiny, but, in the longer term, technology, global politics, and the reshaping of public taste will have their own imperatives. Kiev, becoming part of the larger market-place of images, determines its relationship to the strong cultural influence of Moscow, represented now as the 'other'. There is an effort, though hardly forceful enough, to create a clearly Ukrainian cultural presence, with a strong connection to the populace, serving as a domestic force competing with cosmopolitan imagery. These are issues which are and will be repeated not only in Kiev, but in Tbilisi and Almaty, Vladivostok and St Petersburg. All these places in the former Soviet Union constitute a zone of past pervasive impact from which the component parts are now seeking to withdraw. The capacity and strategy to accomplish that cultural, as opposed to political, withdrawal are the subject of scrutiny and agony.

By the spring of 1994, not only Ukraine, but Estonia, Lithuania, and other states of the former Soviet Union were threatening to limit or terminate the transmission of Moscow's Ostankino within their borders. At times, these threats were justified on the basis of the costs of transmission; at times, on the basis that Moscow was using the instrument of transnational television to spin the news in ways that undermined the new governments and that reinforced Russia's stance on controversial issues. For the twenty-five million Russians among the 'near abroad', the curtailing of Russian television could be seen as a discriminatory, over-nationalistic act. The aura of television was such, however, that government decisions concerning whether to continue to foster Russian television touched memories of empire and concerns over spheres of influence.

The situation facing the former Communist bloc countries of Central and Eastern Europe and the former Soviet Union renders these places useful crucibles for testing the opportunities and limitations facing government in a period of broadcasting globalization. They must fashion their own identities and, in doing so, decide how pluralistic those identities should be.[1] They must often determine whether programming from Russia should be encouraged, especially in the light of the large numbers of Russia's 'near abroad', and they must decide how much authority to muster so as to regulate the extent of programming from other countries (from the West or, in Central Asia, from Turkey and China). These are states which have a conscious need to fabricate themselves, to build loyalties, and to define citizenship. If the 'market-for-loyalties' hypothesis is useful in describing changes in law and regulation of the media, then the transition societies—Central and Eastern Europe and the New Independent States of the former Soviet Union—should provide an excellent test bed. At a time when liberal democracies are being manufactured from the detritus of command economies, the purposive transformation of their historic and monopolistic broadcasting systems has been a matter of the highest priority.

All states are constantly involved in the process of inventing and nourishing traditions, or they are doomed. In the transition states, the nation-building is transparent, the problems and approaches are far more visible, the motives more clearly stated, the conflicts more certainly evident. These states require, at the instant, new mythologies, new leaders, new histories, new narratives. Whether spontaneously or by instruction, a virtual transformation in public attitudes—towards economic life, towards political life, towards citizenship and individuality—is in the process of taking place. Decisions concerning the shape and content of the media are inevitably involved in this process. The processes of transformation have included harnessing media in the project of change in a manner harmonious with liberal democratic norms. In a society where the media have so pervasively been used in the task of indoctrination and education, their employment for a new narrative might seem ironic. Government use of the media in the process of state-building is too much a reminder of the old totalitarian regime, a tool inconsistent with present seemingly democratic aspirations. To further coherence, these new states combine the rhetoric of freedom with a celebration of national cultures, hoping to place a stamp of national character on their enterprise. Transition societies are a small warring ground for competing external views about what foreign model a transformed post-totalitarian system should resemble. They have been under pressure to conform to the practices of the West, but the lethargic impulse to retain their former ways remains.

Defining Independence

In this context, one of the most difficult issues has been the expansion of 'independent' media. While, throughout the region, there has been a blossoming of non-government newspapers, the evolution of independent broadcasting has been far slower. The preoccupation with Russian television in Kiev and the general search for new mythologies make tolerance of effective, truly separate and competing media hardly an unmixed blessing for struggling leaders. 'Independence' of the media is a key mantra, a defining hope in the period of transition. But what constitutes independence is far from obvious; certainly not the mere incantation of the phrase, or a stumbling understanding of its complexity.

In Chapters 6 and 7, independence is examined in terms of the drafting of laws, formal efforts to establish a legal structure that purports to increase independence by protecting the broadcaster from the state, the small broadcaster from powerful programmers, or weak programmers from powerful media giants. Some laws protect the editor from the publisher or even the journalist from the editor. Looking in detail at the Russian context, the relationship between law and violence is explored. In addition, while Chapter 6 focuses on the Russian Federation, Chapter 7 reviews transitions elsewhere and seeks to determine what yardsticks should be used to evaluate media-law reforms both in the former Soviet Union and in the remainder of Central and Eastern Europe.

In this chapter, the problem of defining independence is approached from different vantage-points. The formal language of statutes and judicial decisions cannot be understood without some insight into the historic origin of words and concepts. These transition states have a specific legacy in which a complex terminology and elaborate doctrine have had extraordinary sway; some familiarity with that legacy is necessary to understand the transfer of mind to a new set of jurisprudential expectations. In addition, the turbulent aspect of inventing independence is a human function as well as a legal one: some insight into the aspirations, motivations, and capacities of those who have been pioneers of independence is essential. All media transitions build not only on the innovators, but on those who were previously in control, the existing pool of journalists and the existing journalistic tradition. An important aspect of these processes of law reform is the effort by Western entities—governments, foundations, private entrepreneurs—to expend passion, treasure, and talent to further the concept of independence. It will be useful, in understanding the evolution of media law in the transition states, to have a greater grasp of the objectives and efforts of these doctors of free speech.

In the Republics of the former Soviet Union, declarations of media independence proliferate at the same moment as the states themselves grope for a definition of their own power in a radically different world. Just before the break-up of the Soviet Union, Moscow's Second Channel, representing the fierce identity of Russia, announced independence from its parent, Gosteleradio, but became immediately dependent on the Russian Federation. In the summer of 1992 a group of Russian business men, led by Eduard Sagalaev, announced a joint venture with Turner Broadcasting System (TBS) (of CNN fame) to create the first private sector, independent television station in Russia. That same year, Boris Yeltsin, President of Russia, appeared on television with a group of editors to reaffirm his commitment to the freedom of the press, and, in particular, the 'independence' of *Izvestiia* from the state; but the paper remained dependent on the state for newsprint and access to printing facilities. *Pravda* declared independence from the Communist Party, but a year later was suspended by the government for advocating the violent overthrow of the constitutional order. Debates between President Yeltsin and Parliament, before its 1993 dissolution, were most vituperative over which institution most supported press independence. A strong commercial entrant, NTV, backed by a banking group which sought widespread media influence, declared itself, in 1993, the first truly independent entity with extensive news programming. In January 1994, newspapers, as a group, threatened a strike to maintain their independence; but, in their demands for continued subsidies and other protections, the need for old relationships was clear. Despite abundant declarations, the sense persisted that the elixir that produced autonomy had not yet been discovered.

These varying formulations of independence are indicators that absolute independence—coupled with financial security—is usually chimerical. Most journalists, though independent of the state, are dependent on a publisher or an editor. Most publishers and editors are dependent on advertisers or their banks or other funding sources. Perhaps only the wilfully poor or boisterously successful are persistently independent. Robert Karl Manoff has addressed these definitional aspects of independence, challenging common formulations. The media in the former Soviet Union, he has written, can achieve a certain measure of political independence but at the cost of increased dependence on non-state institutions. 'To put the matter simply, one needs to weigh carefully the consequences of trading dependence on government, party, administration, and the state for dependency on captains of industry and individual commercial enterprises.' For Manoff, the 'independence' of the media even in long-standing Western democracies is not absolute. Everywhere, including in established, functioning democracies, the relationship between the media, politicians, and government is an ambiguous one. Governments control and allocate the broadcast spectrum, they grant and rescind preferred postal rates for printed matter, they pass and enforce official secrets acts, alien and sedition acts, national security legislation.[2]

At its simplest, the essence of independence is independence from something or someone. In the American vocabulary, independence means immunity from government, particularly from government-sponsored inculcation of national identity. A report of the Commission on Radio and Television Policy, an unusual consortium headed by former President Jimmy Carter and concerned with the development of broadcasting policy in the former Soviet Union, sought to establish goals and define conditions for broadcasting autonomy.[3] These goals included ferreting out truth 'without fear or favor'; empowering ordinary members of the public in the democratic process; gaining credibility so as to minimize citizen alienation and encourage participation in democratic processes; controlling abuses of power by government through exposing misdeeds and establishing a countervailing centre of power; providing a forum for ordinary people effectively to press their interests upon and command resources from powerful institutions including government; and providing access to means of self-expression.

Definitions like those of the Carter Commission centre on freedom from accountability to government, freedom to maximize economic profits, freedom for broadcasters to pursue 'any goals they choose', disciplined only 'by the pressures and incentives of a competitive free economic market'. While this approach is laudable, like so much that vaunts independence and autonomy, it has a built-in weakness: there is too little evident relationship between the goals articulated for society and the specific immunity demanded from societal regulation. The prophets of independence and supporters of free television assume that the societal goals of discourse and individual empowerment will be realized through the growth of independent broadcasters. It is hardly clear, yet, whether these assumptions are realizable.

Partiinost to *Glasnost*

One place to begin the process of understanding 'independence' is the historical context in which it arises. Even in the most enlightened of the newly freed societies, the transition to independence is transfused with obstacles; the range of difficulties cannot be fathomed without a sense of the long-standing relationship between media and state. Television and radio have been so basic an extension of the state and Party in the former USSR that it is necessary to understand how their respective roles were articulated to fathom the post-Soviet legal structures. From the outset of the Soviet era, Lenin and then Stalin harnessed the arts—and imagery in general—in the service of the state, and an aesthetic of social realism was founded to further the ideals of the revolution.[4] Among the first decrees was an order for the establishment of public sculptures celebrating a specific set of heroes of the revolution. The art of the 1920s and 1930s was used to bring the message of central authority to distant villages, small rural settings, everywhere embracing the periphery in the mission of the Party.

Lenin, early on, and in no uncertain terms, established the principles that should guide artists, writers, and other media workers in the plying of their crafts. Journalists can be understood as having had functions similar to those in other professions for the makers of images. Scenes of hard-working peasants, a brooding omnipresent Lenin, or, later, a cheerful fatherly Stalin were to fulfil a set of detailed criteria that distinguished superior from inferior, acceptable from unsupportive art. Similarly, there were genres of writing and formulae for stories for journalists to follow. *Partiinost/ideonost*; *obyektivnost/pravdivost*; *narodnost/massovost*; and *glasnost/otkrytost*: these were the principles established by Lenin after 1917 and reinforced in books for cultural training as part of the education of artists and generators of imagery.[5] The idealized early understanding of these principles must be discerned to interpret developments in the current transition. They establish the vocabulary of the past, a use of words that must be kept in mind when dealing with the present. Without such a grounding, the contemporary usage of words like 'independence' or 'objectivity' can be a snare.

Partiinost

In the Leninist armament of language, *partiinost* was the doctrine that all communication is the conscious repetition of a class-view and ought to be a direct and open defence of working-class interests. The Party is the vanguard and the spirit of the Party should infuse all decisions, all manifestations of the government's activity. The Decree on the Press, passed by the Soviet of People's Commissars on 27 October 1917, the government's first day in office, provided a clear insight into the relationship between central knowledge and attitudes towards unfettered independence:

> The bourgeois press is one of the most powerful weapons of the bourgeoisie. Especially at this critical moment, when the new government, that of the workers and the peasants, is only just consolidating its position, it would be unthinkable to leave this weapon intact in the hands of the enemy when it is no less dangerous than the bullet or the machine-gun.[6]

Interesting, in terms of exceptions for censorship included in the 1991 Mass Media Law,[7] were the grounds, in the Decree, for the closure of the press: 'inciting open opposition to, or disobedience of, the workers' and peasants' government'; 'sowing discord by means of a clearly slanderous distortion of the facts'; and 'inciting clearly criminal acts'.

In modern liberal democracies, the principle of 'impartiality' is heralded, but a Western idea of impartiality was inconsistent with the Leninist perspective that 'neutral information' is an illusion.[8] After the Decree on the Press, and certainly by 1919, the leaders had made *partiinost* easier to accomplish by outlawing private ownership of press, printing, and broadcasting, and placing social ownership of instruments of mass information solely in the hands of Party organizations, government bodies, and such public organizations as trade unions. Under the aegis of these 'founders', it was the task of the instruments of mass information to function, as Brian McNair put it, as 'tribunes' or platforms for the organizations with which they were affiliated.

In the first years after the dissolution of the Soviet Union, the relationship between 'founder', the mass media, and notions of independence remained ambiguous, with the tradition of *partiinost* largely responsible. The concept of 'founder' captured the essence of *partiinost* —namely, that wisdom existed within government organs and not in diverse private hands. As is discussed in Chapter 6, newspapers had to wean themselves from their official and Party founders, and problems of ownership and control were rampant. The 1991 Russian Federation Law on Mass Media (the Russian Media Law), for example, strictly regulates who can be a 'founder' of an instrument of mass communication. Problems with founders plagued the transition from a more controlled to a free press. Without a sense of the Leninist past, without the concept of *partiinost*, the important status and function of a publication's 'founder' in the time of transition were difficult to translate into Western terms.

Obyektivnost

The second concept, *obyektivnost/pravdivost*, also underlines the contrast between Marxist–Leninist definitions of socialist–realist objectivity and Western ideas of impartiality and neutrality. These different perceptions of objectivity are an important factor in understanding the transition. The essence of the doctrine lay in the scientific confidence of those who professed the Leninist perspective. Confidence in Leninist theory meant that, the greater the amount of information and the more thorough the reportage, the greater would be the fidelity to the political truths. A Soviet textbook for journalists states that 'objectivity is the fundamental demand of Leninist methodology',[9] where objectivity 'is premised on the assumption that historical materialism is . . . a *scientific* worldview'. In the transition, requirements that journalists be objective and truthful remain; requirements that a journalist be objective are contained in the 1991 Russian Media Law. For those schooled in the Soviet period, for those with a memory, the new objectivity could mean simply that a new theory—the theory of capitalism—would be the scientific world-view, and objectivity would consist of demonstrating its wisdom. Objectivity might become that picture of the world that corroborates the then-government's scientific approach to a particular problem.

Narodnost

Another principle, *narodnost* or *massovost*, seems very much at risk during the transition to a market economy. *Narodnost*, or spirit of the people, imposed a responsibility on instruments of mass information to be linked to the masses, not to increase circulation for purposes of raising revenue, but for reasons of ideology. 'Our press . . . can have no tasks or interests distinct from the tasks and interests of the people.'[10] Brian McNair puts it this way: *narodnost* means that 'the media must be open to the views and opinions of the masses'.[11] But *narodnost* also means maintaining a link with the mass of workers, avoiding trivialities and providing strong reinforcement, re-education, and re-organization of the people. *Narodnost* and *massovost* underscored the desirability of near universal availability of newspapers and television and a consciousness that the media should be prepared to assist the government in educating the public to the goals articulated by the state.

Among the transition debates that contain a tinge of *narodnost* in the post-Soviet period are those that concern the pricing of newspapers, the extent of subsidies, the availability of newsprint, and access to printing facilities. Of course, fundamental fear of a free press, critical of government and somewhat indifferent to its agenda, is one of the strongest speech-related remnants of Marxist–Leninist principles. But so is concern over a tendency for newspaper prices to rise sharply and circulation, thereby, to fall. A free-market solution to demand and supply of information is inconsistent with principles of *narodnost* if it means that large sections of the community would be without access to information. Continuing subsidies for newspapers, regardless of disputes over the difficult question of determining who should receive such funds, bespeaks a societal determination that information ought to be linked with the largest possible audience. Proposals that newsprint and printing facilities be made available to all who need them at reduced prices are connected, as well, to these old traditions. How these issues have surfaced in recent years is a matter for discussion in Chapter 6.

Glasnost

Understanding the fourth Leninist principle, *glasnost*, is vital because it was so important an underpinning of the Gorbachev reforms. *Glasnost*, in Lenin's meaning of the term, included making widely known the positive aspects in the march of Soviet progress. But it also had a meaning which could be, somewhat deceptively, likened to Western notions of freedom of the press. Newspapers must, Lenin wrote, reveal 'shortcomings in the economic life of each labour commune, ruthlessly branding these shortcomings, frankly laying bare all the ulcers of our economic life, and thus appealing to the public opinion of the working people for the curing of these ulcers'.[12] 'Critical *glasnost*' assumed that the power of propaganda would be enhanced if the élites and the operation of the economy were subjected to press analysis. But critical *glasnost* was, in that sense, instrumental: criticism in the right amount was useful because it lent legitimacy to the press and, consequently, lent the government that controlled the press credibility. By the same token, the doctrine was self-limiting; too much criticism or criticism of the higher levels of Party and government could undermine both *partiinost* and *narodnost*. The concept of *glasnost* includes one other aspect which helps in the understanding of post-Soviet legislation and debate: access by the public to sources of information. The notion of access to information was reflected in provisions of the 1991 media legislation that required officials to hold press conferences, mimicking 'open polemics between comrades', in Lenin's phrase.[13]

Anxieties of Transformation

Not only governments, not only newspapers and broadcasting outlets as institutions, not only laws, not only government agencies, but men and women, as individuals, were affected by the complex transition from old patterns of thinking to the new. Departments of journalism would have to undergo the agonizingly slow task of altering curricula, changing books, 're-educating' themselves and their students. Judges, steeped in the precedents of a prior law, would have to alter patterns of thinking.

Among those who felt most trapped in the habits of the past were the veteran journalists who had made their peace and found their security in a prior order. These journalists—like journalists everywhere— have their favourite places for drink and conversation and for talk of decline and fall. The bar of the Foreign Press Association in Moscow in the period just after the break-up of the Soviet Union was a reminder of better days. It was then the place, among others, for saddened writers of the last decades, former reporters for institutions torn to shreds by a combination of ideological shift, death of empire, and firings caused by the shrinking of state budgets. The talk was of the price of liquor when Brezhnev was in power. The mood was like that in Eugene O'Neill's *The Iceman Cometh*, men yearning for former times, former dreams, old securities. True, journalism was in the service of the state, in the bondage of the Party. But those who had accepted the bonds, who had proclaimed what they had been asked to proclaim, were conditioned to think of themselves as not less independent than their Western counterparts. They saw themselves subject only to different and, perhaps, more noble pressures: governmental rather than private, ideological not commercial.

Now unemployed, they weighed the pains of transition, the opprobrium resulting from their prior office, the economic hardship of a new order. They were often scornful of the new independence, seeing in their more successful brethren journalists who, learning new tricks, could dance to a more flashy, more prosperous drummer. The talk, at the bar, was of the transformation of newspapers, all earlier controlled by state and Party, now finding other forms of ownership structure. For them, comparative independence—American versus Soviet—turned on that oddity of Soviet journalism, the fact that most publications were instruments of government or Party organs. Censorship could be said merely to be the decision of the founder—a state-related entity—as to what should be in a journal, a decision taken by publishers world-wide. Most journalists of the old order concluded conversations about the myth of independence with the assertion that all writers were subject to the whim of the boss. Thus it had been, and thus it would be again.

Typical of the regulars was a man who had lived in Prague for five years, working for a Soviet-financed international organization of journalists; his task, during that period, had been to demonstrate just how free journalists behind the Iron Curtain really felt themselves to be. Now, he sat at the Foreign Press Association and wondered why the price of whisky was so high, what had happened to the old certainties, and whether the new order would survive. Around him, filling the room, were the human forms of transition. They and the institutions for which they worked—newspapers, press agencies, broadcasting entities—would endure an agonizing wrenching over the next several years, losing ties to former sponsors, losing the security of state support, losing the predictability of an established context in which to write and edit.

These journalists and editors would face a market system in which foreign publishers would seek to invest and where strange entities, American and European foundations, would lecture on freedom, and old government agencies would retain power through newly defined financial incentives. It would be a market in which new government would provide support for some participants and harass and sometimes close others. Many of these men and women would adapt, even seeing skills developed in the old regime as useful in the new. But for many around the bar, the habits of the past would make change hard, no matter how much training or re-education they received.

Pioneers of Independence

A different frame on 'independence', a different source of energy for transformation, would come from scruffy pioneers, many new to the media, often combining goals of free enterprise and profit with hopes of making a positive change in society. Almost any event in the former Soviet Union involving the invocation of independence refracted the spirit of the shift from old to new. In the autumn of 1991, two hundred of the new journalists, producers, news directors, and television entrepreneurs from what was still the Soviet Union met their American counterparts, trying to find their way in a brave new world, reaching for new vocabulary, seeking to establish new institutions such as the launching of an organization for independent broadcasters. The meeting was in Novgorod, carefully selected because it was not Moscow, nor St Petersburg, not the locus of post-Soviet dominion.

For many of the new journalists attending, part of the idea of 'independence' was liberation from Moscow as the dominant cultural force as well as independence from the Party or independence from the state. A large red banner stretched across the main boulevard, the kind of gold-lettered billowing sheet that used to announce Party Congresses; but this one proudly announced a new kind of Congress, a forum on free expression, with the auspicious title: 'Independent Television in a Post-Totalitarian Society'.

For three days the city became home to an odd collection of foundation executives, investment bankers, financial planners, and public-interest lawyers: American idealists meeting the new Russians, television magnates, ragtag hopefuls, organizers of business ventures, hip producers, nineteenth-century dreamers working with twentieth-century technologies. In a sense, the title said it well. This was a group of people trying to search for what independent television might mean in the new Republics, in the world after Gorbachev's *glasnost*. The delegates trooped to meetings in the recently liberated Political Education House of the Communist Party, so recently freed from its prior purposes that the seals placed on the doors by the local government were still evident. One of the meetings was in a board room panelled in light wood, with an inlay of Lenin in contrasting hues. The Great Hall had the hierarchical architecture of the old order—the curved arc of the power structure on the stage hovering over the audience below.

As at any conference, most of the intense talk was in breaks and in the corridors. A technician from a private commercial station in Kharkov, a city of nearly two million people in Ukraine, told the following story: he worked for a young Ukrainian who had seen the opportunity to create his own television station and who had made his own miracle in Kharkov, rehabilitating an old transmitter, borrowing money, and cadging a few video cameras. Showing American films obtained in questionable fashion, he had founded a commercial station that in a short time had become one of the most watched in Ukraine. To raise more money, the talented young entrepreneur appeared on the screen to tell viewers that they would have to purchase descramblers because the signal would be encrypted. Almost 200,000 viewers sent in 200 roubles each (then a considerable sum), part for a descrambler and part as a contribution to a programming fund. Here was a programming equivalent of political change, support for some kind of independent programming, independent of the entertainment decisions of the state enterprise. The signal was never scrambled, the funds had not been needed, and possible skulduggery was not a matter for public sorrow. As in politics, there were plans, always plans, just around the corner, plans to use the money wisely. In a time of hope and transition, that was enough.

In a session on commercial financing, the journalists heard from Leonid Kolnakov, who had a licence for a private commercial station in St Petersburg. He was one of the new breed: an already successful business man with a profit interest, not a political motive, for favouring independence for the media. He sounded confident and had the trappings of success. He had a precise plan: to go on the air for four hours a day, gradually increasing to eight hours in six months or so and then more. His programming would be pitched in part to the foreign population living in St Petersburg. This was the independence of the entrepreneur, the freedom not to cater to some imposed ideal of what constitutes appropriate programming, but rather to respond to the market. The entrepreneur could afford to wait and he did not plan to turn a profit during the next two years. An example of the altered tendencies, he had, as a partner, a wealthy Californian who was an investor with his own combination of idealistic and financially related plans. To demonstrate his acumen, Kolnakov flashed a licence, a paper suitably signed and sealed and held in a velvet pouch. Licences are needed for everything, but they are hardly ever completely the right licence. This one was from an All-Union minister, just prior to the break-up of the Soviet Union, and already the intimation was in the air that some additional paper, a visit to another set of bureaucrats, would be needed.

The Americans at these conferences were as important to the story as Russians or Ukrainians. Some were purveyors of their own personal views of American democracy, populist and strongly capitalist as well, reminiscent of the democratic vision captured by the cable television industry as it peddled cable from city to city across the United States. These were idealists who wanted to demonstrate that, somehow, a free press could emerge from scruffy self-invented journalists without the intervention of substantial economic interests or the protective intervention of the state. Under the influence of the Americans, there was a palpable reaching-out for 'little-d' democracy that seemed so reminiscent of a now-fading California optimism and a nostalgic faith in community efforts and voluntarism. It was a charming hope, though it was unclear how durable independence might be. One of the most popular of the Americans was a San Francisco investment banker who, fairly selflessly, had flown to St Petersburg to help the conferees understand the alchemy of balance sheets. He was besieged by those with a naïve fascination with money and with the relationship, yet to be plumbed, between the rapidly increasing 'joint ventures' and the aspirations for unencumbered speech.

Another example of the crude early steps towards independence lay in the transformation of the nearby Novgorod television station. Housed in an old villa, with the look, inside, of US cable television in its earliest days (one tattered studio, a spotted, upholstered chair and couch, slightly sagging bookcases, and plastic flowers for the inevitable talking heads), Novgorod television was seeking to reconstitute itself for the new world. The offerings were limited: at the time, it produced a forty-five-minute feed about twenty times a month that was carried on the Russian Second Channel from Moscow as a regional window of identity. In addition, as a sign of the new entrepreneurship, it had seized a local UHF channel. There it experimented with the new pleasure of selling advertising, broadcasting four hours a night of films obtained at the video rental store without the payment of foreign licence fees.

Novgorod television was said to be private, to have been privatized; yet the composition of its ownership told much about the complexity of independence. The new station appeared to be owned by a stock company in which 10 per cent of the stock, in late 1991, was held by the municipality, about 10 per cent by a local union or organization (one which might well have had prior links with the Party), and roughly 80 per cent by private individuals (including former high officials during the state-owned era). This early case of privatization provided a clue to later problems: those with power, sitting around a table, deciding that they (often the journalists and editors), themselves, were the best potential owners for a valuable medium. How the charter owners were chosen, whether the privatization was at all competitive or fair, whether the public received adequate compensation—these were questions that were rarely asked.

Given the overwhelming prior role of the state, one thing was clear at this early time of dissolution: the machinery of independence unravelled from officialdom itself as much as it sprang from the new class of 'independents'. At Novgorod, a high-ranking government technologist dealing with broadcasting and satellite in the Russian communications ministry described the role of the government in shaping more elaborate instruments of future competition. Like many ambitious Russian officials, the official was half-way between his government role and a lofty new enterprise that would promise a bright future. Within the government, he had been part of a high-level group preparing a new programming service, satellite delivered, that would use a Sputnik transponder. Like many projects of the early post-Soviet period, this one was scheduled to begin 'in the very near future'.

The project was large scale, a monumental dream. And, clearly, if it occurred, the technocrat would leave the Ministry to be part of it. There would be a privatization, with convenient opportunities, all in the name of independence. The footprint of the satellite would extend from Eastern France deep into Russia and from the north all the way to Northern Africa. The current 'owners' of the project were two Ministries, All-Russian State Radio and Television, and others. The programming service would be completely commercial; it would be received in the future by cable television systems, and by television services such as Novgorod Television—i.e. independent television with transmitters and no programmes. This was a period of bold ideas, in which the future promised the prosperity of the West, filled with new media, each one finding its own niche and financing.

The complications of fighting for independence were marked by two spirited bureaucrats of the old Soviet information agency (TASS), Vladimir Zaretsky and Victor Litanko. The pair realized that, like most other bureaucracies in Moscow, their agency would be scrambling for its life, scrambling to find the means to employ its people, scrambling to find new sources of income. Zaretsky and Litanko were involved in the application for a new radio licence, but, given the nebulous process for obtaining frequency rights, they continued to be frustrated. Three weeks before the Novgorod conference took place, they were told that the Russian Federation government had given to the existing near-monopoly, All-Russian State Television and Radio, the power to grant interim authority for new radio licences. True or not, the young entrepreneurs found this delegation disturbing, because the state broadcaster would not be in a rush to give a licence to a competitor. Like their counterparts in the West, Zaretsky and Litanko sought to use the power of contacts rather than the process of reason, currying favour with the Parliament and hoping that the President himself would intervene on their behalf. Independence, if it came, would come, as in times of old, from connections, relationships, and political ties.

How competition would evolve was also underscored by Sergei Duvanov, a sallow, thirtyish figure visiting Novgorod from Alma Ata (now Almaty), the capital of the Republic of Kazakhstan in Central

Asia. Like so many new 'producers', Duvanov was trying to determine how to get or make or sell television products for alternative transmission. Poll-taker as well as producer, Duvanov had documented how the viewership in Kazakhstan for its central television had fallen off since pirate independent television transmissions had begun to show American films. Reading from a hand-written sheet with polling figures for every station viewable in that capital, for spring and autumn, he claimed that the infant commercial stations were making heavy inroads into the traditional government television market. A very high percentage of viewers—more than 50 per cent—said that they watched the new stations (which were often dependent on pirated American movies) regularly.

Within his account of triumph lurked potential dangers. Language and other problems loomed on the horizon if independent television too markedly threatened its official competition. Viewership for the official station, with its reliance on the Kazakh language, was declining in Alma Ata for two reasons: the high Russian population and the fact that many Kazakhs themselves had weak Kazakh language skills and prefer watching in Russian. Independence, here, could be read as inconsistent with the aspirations of a Republic struggling for identity. Because the 'independents' used the government transmitter and government-supplied housing for offices, too much success, or the wrong kind, might be their undoing.

A serious byplay in the Novgorod forum came from an odd tension between the French and the Americans. There were about a dozen people from France or connected with French radio and television, and, as a portent of a mild competition of the future, the conference had become a skirmish ground in some unconscious struggle, among Western interests, for the mind and soul of the Russian people. The French representatives did not want the conference to appear to be too American, or to have Americans in control of all the principal organizing forums, and the Americans, almost unconsciously, were suspicious of the European influence. When most of the conference wanted to hear the American investment banker give a standard business-plan talk, the French more or less walked out. While the Americans had planned an ambitious set of seminars for training independent journalists in the skills of reporting, the French were planning a Franco-Soviet Institute in Broadcast Management for the training of high-level administrators. None of the Westerners represented their governments. But all carried the baton of unstated domestic strategies in their knapsacks.

The intensity of Franco-American rivalry was combined with other rivalries in a debate over the formation of an independent broadcast association. The organizers of the Novgorod forum hoped that such an association would emerge from the forum, but, in advance of the conference, Sergei Korzun, the dashing director of Radio Echo of Moscow, had set up such an association on his own, with the word 'Russian' in the title. At the conference, the Russians from St Petersburg expressed their resentment that Moscow had stolen the march; and the representatives from the other Republics expressed *their* resentment that the organization was, like so much in their past, Russian- and Moscow-centred.

Korzun, whose tiny station had famously carried the news (partly through a balloon-supported transmitter) during the August 1991 *coup* attempt, sat in a wooden chair, with a crowd of excited young producers, discussing plans for the nascent broadcasters' association. The setting was much like that of old 1930s paintings of revolutionary times: the intense leader and the inflamed discussants posturing in the background. This time, the hero was wearing blue jeans, and mimeographed copies of his proposed purposes and by-laws were at his side.

Independence and the West

The Novgorod conference was just a foretaste of the involvement of the governments, foundations, and entrepreneurs of the West. By the mid-1990s the field of Western warriors for press independence had become crowded. The International Media Fund, established with a grant from Congress, exulted at the prospect of launching American-style media in the bleak desert of a government press; its cadre of alumni of American newspapers and broadcasting travelled through Central and Eastern Europe and the former Soviet Union, establishing outposts of training and technical assistance. The Freedom Forum Foundation, the well-financed heir of the Gannett publishing fortune (publishers of *USA Today*), sent ambassadors of independence to the former Soviet Union and brought deans of journalism schools, journalists, and media specialists to the United States. George Soros, the billionaire money manager with a passion for Karl Popper, established a dozen active foundations throughout the region, their minions scrambling to encourage civil society. The United States Agency for International Development (USAID) announced, in the summer of

1994, a US–Russian media Partnership Program, to use approximately $10 million to help selected stations, newspapers, and news organizations become financially stronger, and, free of public-sector constraints, produce high-quality programming, in a professional and ethical manner. The Carter Commission for Radio and Television Policy issued reports on election coverage, reportage of ethnic conflict, and the economics of running an independent media.

One of the most aggressive exporters of American ideas of independence was Internews, by far the largest recipient of USAID funds for encouraging democracy in the former Soviet Union. In Kiev, with $7.7 million from the US government, Internews had established an International Media Center, and by doing so had had an immediate and pervasive influence in the fragile world of independent television journalism in Ukraine. In terms of funding and activity, the Kiev project was the equivalent of the establishment of a major military outpost, though here the battle was to change the nature of the press. Another indication of the ambition of Internews—not only in Ukraine but throughout the region—was its announcement of the 'Open Skies Satellite Exchange' which was to link independent stations and media centres across the former Soviet Union and Eastern and Central Europe for the exchange of news programmes. The programme, the result of a $2.2 million grant to help develop independent television in the former Soviet Union, was designed to establish an independent news distribution system and an improvised and infant network. The dream was to produce a competitor to the state-delivered television news system; but in the beginning there were merely acorns, not even seedling oaks.

Similarly, in contrast to the dark and sullen mood at the old journalistic hangouts, the Russian–American Press and Information Center, a recently painted and modernized eighteenth-century mansion near the hubbub of Moscow's Arbat, became a symbol and embodiment of the new and of the influence of the West. Financed by American foundations and USAID, the Press Center was dedicated to strengthen Russian journalism, especially journalistic independence. The Center became an advocate of facts: computers, arrayed in the Center's cubicles, would be gateways to the huge data banks available to most Western reporters, but by no means common to the Russian experience. The Center would become the regular stopping-off place for American journalists and publishers certain that, if American-style 'independence' could be brought to Russia, then political democracy would be more likely to endure.

The tasks of such an institution are complex. To provide a sense of joint direction, and so as to underscore independence from The United States, governance is nominally bilateral, Russian and American, an attempt to avoid the appearance of an arrogant US operation. The agenda or curriculum of the Center, over time, is to include ideas of independence related to achieving a more perfect public sphere: critical perspectives on government that are influential in enhancing democratically based change. The building is inhabited by enthusiastic Americans, some in their post-college wanderings, some scholars with experience in Russian studies. Cramped space is allotted to the Committee for the Protection of Journalists, a group monitoring continued examples of imprisonment and torture in the post-Soviet era. Upstairs, there are press conferences, given by visiting American dignitaries, respected journalists and publishers, Russian officials, or, more unruly and emotional, protesters against police roughing of reporters and censorship in general.

Characteristic of the pot-pourri of activities was a seminar there of twenty young men and women from around what was then still an active Commonwealth of Independent States, aspiring to be independent television reporters. They were being trained by a Berkeley journalism professor and had been brought—from Kazakhstan, Ukraine, and other Republics—for several days of intensive seminars. This was Western instruction in independence. The students discussed a story the young reporters had been told to cover in Tashkent. Afghan veterans had taken over apartments in a newly built housing complex and the government was trying to oust them. The story was strong visually and emotionally compelling: veterans who thought they had not received adequate benefits were asserting themselves against the government. These were stand-up television stories about the failure of the government to act; they would have a certain rhythm, a familiar narrative, the aura of critical independence. But as a result of the journalists' attention, there was a further development: the Afghan veterans, feeling sorry for homeless people in Tashkent, decided to liberate additional housing for them. Now, the story was more complex: the facile script of criticizing government gave way to such issues as how new housing stock should be allocated, and what role should force play in the allocation scheme. The capacity to engage in sustained criticism, knowing when to criticize, when to abandon, a skill difficult to develop in any context, proved hard to teach here as well.

At the Press and Information Center's training session, one of

Moscow's most important radio personalities related a tale to exemplify the evolution of the new journalist. What was the journalist's salute to an official during the Communist reign? A stiffly outstretched arm, reminiscent of the Sieg Heil. What was the journalist's salute in the first years of the post-Communist era, when the yoke of the past still existed and the new traits had not been learnt? A wan and weak waving of the hand. And what would be the journalist's greeting in a time of mature independence? The derisory, irreverent upward jerk of the forearm with the disrespectful strike of the opposite hand in the cupped elbow. It was a witty story and self-satisfying, a reminder for the young journalists of the bravery of their profession. For someone watching the evening news, it was clear that this heralded third stage of independence had not arrived, and was hardly on the horizon. And when it would come, as during the 1993 election campaign discussed in Chapter 6, the response by the government was not altogether welcoming.

Centre and Periphery

Independence, as has already been suggested, meant more, in the period of transition, than independence from government, or independence from ancient theologies of reportage, or independence, even, from the influences of the West. In the emerging battle for identities, independence for Ukraine or Kazakhstan, Estonia or Azerbaijan, was primarily freedom from the images of Russia, not from the images fostered by their own governments. In a shakily independent Ukraine, in Kiev in late 1992, a major question was autonomy from the imperial centre, from the cultural forces that had held sway for seventy, if not for hundreds of years. The television transmitter in Moscow was, itself, a monument, a steel pylon with a huge concrete base, massive in proportion like the Egyptian pyramids, that represented the power to send a signal throughout the vast domain not only of Russia, but, metaphorically by satellite, through the entire territories of the former Soviet Union. It epitomized the power of the Party and of the state, a physical manifestation of the desire to assert the monopoly of public thought. Now, the transmitter became a saddling remembrance of the past and, as well, an indication, through the signals it transmitted, of the complexities of defining the independence of the future.

In Kiev, for example, Russian, not Ukrainian, had predominated as the language of the state, and the basic language of the media as well.

Surprised at its independence, Ukraine now had to determine what attention should be given to the cultural element of identity. This was not only a question of changing street names, that everywhere were being recast, nor of finding new purposes for the palatial Lenin Museum, that now stood empty. The very imagery of nationhood was to be forged, a challenging task.

Nevertheless, for an average household in the Ukraine, on an average evening, the television set was turned to Moscow, to the glitz and professionalism of Ostankino, the First Channel, as opposed to the more amateurish, more unpractised presenters at home. Moscow was now the home of a post-Soviet teenage music culture, producing short videos with quick cuts, computer graphics, and the look of the West. Lights flashed on and off, electronic effects cast their technological spell. Ukrainian folk-songs and country dances could not compete. And the tendency of the young Parliament to demand time for its deliberations compounded the problem of fashioning a Ukrainian alternative for the Moscow diet.

In the remembered days of the USSR, *Gosteleradio* had been the supreme voice of the state and the Party. There had been no competition, and the stolid presentation had been a tribute to the theory of monopoly behaviour. Television in the Republics had been organized with some minor modicum of separateness, but the organization in Kiev had been subordinate to the administration in Moscow. The executives and the news presenters had all understood what it meant to be in a command society and what risks not to take. They had been charged, as well, with using the medium not to underscore the differences that could divide, but to reinforce solidarity and, indeed, the cultural and political superiority of the centre.

It was not only in the living rooms of Ukraine that one could see the consequences of these practices of cultural domination. In the offices of Ukrteleradio—the Ukrainian state radio and television monopoly—there was a virtual acknowledgement of the continued drawing power of Moscow television. The officials there, like their compatriots at home, had seen how television from Moscow had become miraculously younger and Westernized in the Gorbachev period. Programmes had more razzle dazzle; rock video appeared together with culture and news. Anchors had brand recognition. There were glamorous hosts and hostesses, fashionable and daring clothes, beguiling, softly erotic shots of 15-year-old rock stars. Moscow had chosen to deal with the problem of which culture to carry, in its new regional look, by going global.

Moscow's transformations were important, with repercussions all over the empire. At the beginning of 1992, with the decline of the Soviet Union, the First Channel, formerly the flagship for Gorbachev and for each leader before him, was in danger of abandonment. A centrepiece of the Soviet Union, the enterprise now needed a client. Russia itself was the major candidate, but there was an intriguing alternative: an all-commonwealth channel, one dedicated to maintaining an informal sense of region, finding a voice that acknowledged the new sovereignties but remembered the old ties. Such a role might have been all the more important if the budget of the First Channel were to be dependent on specific allocations from each of the republics. And, indeed, it was initially considered by a Council of Presidents of all the republics that such an arrangement might be appropriate.

But this view placed the new sovereigns, like Ukraine, in an unusual position. In the first year of their independence, Ukrainian officials were sensitive to every slight. Tested on all fronts as to their distinctiveness (from military to language policy), trying to appear separate and distinct, they believed that Moscow television was particularly biased on Ukraine–Russia relations, inflammatory and insulting. The daily news and the interview shows were scanned for a Russian, anti-Ukrainian perspective. Furthermore, for the media czars in Kiev, it was a matter of concern, if not embarrassment, that, although they had obtained political severance from Russia, Russian television dominance still continued. Indeed, the ministers of the new Ukraine considered alternatives: pressing for the closure of the Moscow First Channel and the dividing of its assets, jamming its signal, or imposing a governing structure—through the Council of Presidents—that would make the channel less biased, at least from the Ukrainian or non-Russian perspective. Instead, there was a temporary compromise, not easily comprehensible. Ukraine and the other republics would no longer finance programme production on the First Channel. Russia would have to be guarantor of that substantial amount. On the other hand, Ukraine would not charge for the transmission of the signal to its country's inhabitants. The consequence was a curious, impermanent, intermediate cultural imperialism—one that recognized historic links and the substantial continuing Russian population, the 'near abroad'. The force of this now-external source of programming was so ingrained that no government, particularly at a time of economic deprivation, could risk the consequences of its elimination.

The struggle, then, for 'independence' assumed may forms, human, historical, geographical, financial. The citadel of the old, Moscow-controlled state television sought a new future and a charter to find and promulgate a national identity—one that would support the new status quo. In Kiev, in the last decade of the Soviet empire, a large modern complex—a broadcasting city—had been planned and built for a Ukraine still under the thumb of Moscow. Now, rather than consider the new edifice as an inappropriate symbol of the role of the press in a post-totalitarian state, the old bureaucracy was destined to dedicate this monument to a brave new world of a statist broadcasting in which a new officialdom and a new national identity needed buttressing. Maybe architecture would be as good a guide to the future as the images that scurried across the reformed television screen.

Three years later, the question of imagery and geographical independence from the centre was sharpened as the relations between Ukraine and Russia became more severe (as would be true between Russia and many of the former Republics). In spring 1994 the tense relations between Ukraine and the Russian Federation found a spark in the rights of Russian correspondents, now called 'foreign', to accreditation in Kiev and Kharkov. Leonid Kravchuk, then President of Ukraine, had stated that coverage on Ostankino and in other Russian media was biased on questions concerning Ukraine, and that the consequence was a weakening of support for his state. Ostankino journalists working in Kharkov and Odessa were denied accreditation. The question was whether this action was in retaliation for an ill-received slight, was the start of a 'media war', or had some other basis. An adviser to the Ukrainian Embassy in Moscow, Vadim Doganov, contended that the action was specific to these journalists and was because of 'nonobjective reporting' by them. He claimed that the government acted in accordance with the new Ukrainian media law.

'Independent' broadcasting was emerging, but it was not necessarily serving the goals which had inspired its advocates. The central broadcasting empire of the state had been weakened. That was certain. But it was far from evident that the gap had been filled with indigenous broadcasters independent of the state, using that independence (to use the Carter Commission formulation) to ferret out truth, empowering ordinary citizens in the democratic process, and providing access to means of self-expression. True, a generation of publishers, editors, and journalists was training itself and being courted from abroad. True, the process of adaptation was proceeding full tilt. But a vacuum, created by a declining state sector, was increasingly filled with networks coming from abroad. The commitment to a great deal more television news and public-service broadcasting was little in evidence in a society where an appetite for advertising and a new mood of deregulation were the call of the day.

It is in this context that efforts to establish law and legal structures must be evaluated. Almost from the beginning of the transitions, at the beginning of the 1990s, projects to reformulate media laws existed throughout the former Soviet empire. These statutes sought to encapsulate how the old state broadcasters and the many incipient attempts at independence could, if at all, contribute to ideas of national identity, the public sphere and the reconfiguration of the market for loyalties. These statutory approaches, their evolution, their construction, and their impact are matters for the next two chapters.

6 Law, Force, and the Russian Media

LOOKING at the development of mass-media law in post-Soviet Russia is like examining the wrists of a recently freed prisoner where the marks of the chains are still present.[1] The very claims for freedom and the guarantees of change bespeak past injustices and old allocations of power. In the short moments that have transpired, issues of law in the defining of communication have already had a dramatic cycle: the rule of law has been followed by the assertion of military force and bloodshed, and force, in its turn, has been followed again by a clumsy reaffirmation of law. In 1995, Vladislav Listyev, the first head of a newly-organized Russian Public Television, was assassinated. Television has been an arena for bitter struggle, political and armed. In this context, the evolution of rules for the organization and governance of the press has reflected changes in political and economic powers in a society seeking definition and stability. The forms of a media law—its words, its constructions, its hermeneutics—cannot be understood without its embedded context. Like other laws, those concerning broadcasting can be studied like shards from an archaeological site, as clues to the nature of their social and political origins.

The Russian Mass Media Law of 1991

The Mass Media Law, signed by President Yeltsin just two days after the formal dissolution of the Soviet Union in December 1991, was practically the first effort throughout all of the transition societies to enact a modern framework for communications policy.[2] Drafted by journalists and academics in a time of dramatic change, the law is an awkward version of an ideal, a sometimes apolitical formulation of the proper relationship between the media and the state. The Mass Media Law is not a statute that begins with language glorifying the state, or in which the state is even the central actor. The idea of the statute is to involve the state as little as possible, to move towards autonomous information providers that have rights against the state, rather than the other way around. As an embodiment of Western traditions of independence, the statute might be an emblem of democratization—an ingredient, like a new flag, of a new national identity—rather than the means to implement or require aspects of loyalty.

Censorship provisions have such significance and scope that their treatment deserves closer attention as an example of how law is deployed as an engine of reform and, simultaneously, as a badge of power. The opening chapter of the 1991 Mass Media Law is a basic guarantee of freedom from censorship for 'instruments of mass information'. There, and in the media laws of each transition state, an explicit prohibition of censorship has been important to proclaim.[3] But the obligatory post-Soviet declaration is accompanied by another form of law—namely, what is specifically excluded from the sweep of anti-censorial zeal. Article 4 of the Mass Media Law lists the permissible content prohibitions, and by doing so defines the proper zone of national concern with the shaping of public consciousness. Instruments of mass information, for example, are prohibited from calling for a change in the existing constitutional order by force; from arousing religious animosities; from fomenting social, class, or national intolerance; or from proliferating war propaganda. These exceptions, these nodes of sensitivity, recall areas of exclusion in article 10(2) of the European Convention for the Protection of Human Rights and Fundamental Freedoms and articles 19(3) and 20 of the International Covenant on Civil and Political Rights.[4]

In the turbulent post-Soviet environment, however, the excessive dependence on the words of law are expressive, also, of the overriding concerns of an insecure officialdom. The law's prohibition against a call for revolution in the existing constitutional structure tells of remembered wounds and an institutional aspiration for stability, the preservation of basic elements of the status quo, for a political debate that has important bounds. The state has a duty to defend against the promulgation of messages that could be destructive to the process of openness. A prohibition against arousing religious animosities revealed the sensitivities that, in 1991, were already evident and affirmed a new role for the state as fostering, not suppressing, religious organizations. Sanctions against speech fomenting social, class, or national intolerance denoted an important role for the state in ameliorating the harsh schisms and ancient hatreds between ethnic groups. Finally, a statutory prohibition against 'war propaganda' could be understood as a footnote to past dogma that a private, capitalist press, the press of the future, could stir the people into unwarranted aggression.

The Mass Media Law demonstrates, in article 3, an effort to exorcise the demon of pre-publication registration and discretionary approval of instruments of mass information. The drafters knew too well how power could influence the question of who should be registered and who should not. Such measures historically invited substantive intervention from the state. Here, too, there is faith in words. The Mass Media Law contains requirements to register, but seeks to make the scheme less intimidating by limiting the discretion of the registration authority. It also provides the skeletal framework—anticipating a supplement that has long been in gestation—for the issuance, regulation, and annulment of television and radio broadcast licences.

Limitations that seem automatic, not requiring the exercise of dangerous discretion, are built into the design of the law. Because article 7 places limits on who can be the founder of an instrument of mass information, authorities can refuse registration under article 13 if the ownership or structure is improper. Article 7 denies foreign citizens and persons without citizenship who do not live continuously within the boundaries of the Russian Federation from establishing a mass-media outlet. Registration is a tool for enforcing this rule. Much more troublesome is the power under article 13(3) to deny an applicant's registration when the registering authority claims to know in advance that the content of a new publication would violate the law (for example, that it would foment class or national intolerance). Even factors that once seemed clear can become fuzzy, so that the power to register can easily be abused. As media ownership becomes more complicated, as relationships with foreign broadcasting entities and press investors become more common, the simple structure that looked adequate in 1991 begins to founder.

National power to register—to legitimate—implies a power to deregister, to close, to delegitimate. The relationship between a publication and the state, and the capacity of the state to influence content (often not so subtly), are functions of this harshest of sanctions: the power of the government, already, as we shall see, exercised in the post-Soviet era, actually to close a newspaper down. Law, in this sense, limits, but it also empowers and legitimates state activity. One could conceive of a statutory scheme that had no power to close an instrument of mass information, relying, if necessary, on the ordinary authority of the state to punish individuals for criminal acts, or to collect taxes, or to impose damages for injury inflicted.[5] In this respect, the Mass Media Law has the beguiling appearance of liberalization, but also the more than implicit threat that the government can step in when something is deemed dreadfully wrong. Under article 16, a section too-often invoked in the years since 1991, the Ministry of Press and Information, later succeeded by the Committee on the Press, could and did force closure of a publication, if, in the view of officialdom, it persisted in violating statutory prohibitions such as promoting conflict. The requirement that there be a prior court order was only sometimes respected.

Restrictions concerning ownership of the media provide another set of insights into how law incorporates or limits dreams and establishes visions of identity. In the 1991 Media Law, ownership restrictions, especially in a context where the institutions of official power had an earlier monopoly, are an index to the dedication to pluralism, to assumptions about the future role of the state in shaping national identity, and to the pace of change. The Mass Media Law, as in all transitions, was to determine whether the government, directly or indirectly, would be able to establish and operate a substantial subset of instruments of mass information. The statutory approach was, therefore, an important determinant of the nature of the state and its potential for shaping public opinion and fostering loyalties.[6]

The 1991 law permitted, in article 7, any 'state organ' to found a mass-media outlet.[7] This provision signifies continuity with the environment of the past, a situation in which great powers in the society—the Communist Party, ministries, trade unions, even Parliament—could be founders of newspapers or broadcasting entities, a legacy of the principles discussed in Chapter 5. The shift from public to private, one of the most difficult aspects of any transition, was shaped by this provision. State broadcasters and print media form a crucial element in Russia's mixed system of state and private mass-media outlets,[8] and state-owned mass media became hotly contested focal points of conflict between the executive and legislative branches—a conflict that erupted in October 1993. In the autumn of 1994 the State Duma had approved a draft law 'On Amendments and Additions to the Existing Law on Mass Media' that would prevent federal and regional 'bodies of power' from being founders of mass media except for those which published only official documents. The question of severely curtailing the power of state organs to participate actively in the direction of the media as founders or publishers remained a matter of much debate.

The Mass Media Law, like many of the first generation of media laws throughout the region, is a time-bounded monument to the experience of new freedoms and the traumas of transformation. Transition laws, as a group, are idealistic in construct and artefacts of a new order still being born. But in their idealism, many of these early laws, including the 1991 Russian law, did not adequately address what should occur to the previously all-powerful state broadcasting authorities or the encouragement of private competition at the margin. The law did not address whether the media should, substantively, incorporate and offer a voice for the many voices rising in Russian society, including those with agendas very different from those of the ruling authorities. Financial necessities quickly put much of the newly private press at risk and made them increasingly dependent on government subsidies.[9] As to these issues, the 1991 Mass Media Law, like many other mass-media statutes, was tantalizing and complex in its enshrinement of aspects of independence but not sufficiently detailed to ensure that independence would actually ensue.

Organic to the vision of this transitional statute was the preservation (and modification) of the idea of the founder from its important historical setting, discussed in Chapter 5, in which the Party, Party organs, and the state were the traditional and exclusive sponsors of mass media. The transition to another form of collective ownership had to take place, in the view of the drafters, through the creation of a new kind of sponsoring organization, not the full equivalent, yet, of private publishers. Consequently, the device of 'founder' was reinvented, as an intermediary between government and Party, on the one hand, and journalists, on the other. Part of the complex notion of 'founder' and a law-driven definition of independence is contained in articles 16–24. These sections provide a detailed programme for the internal organization of mass-media activities. The explicit direction is not censorship, to be sure, but, in its meticulous concern with the way editorial (primarily newspaper) ventures are organized, the hand of the state is present.

The statute illustrates its preoccupation with any authority, even the authority of a newspaper's internal hierarchy, by requiring an agreement between the founder and the editor-in-chief, and, beyond that, setting forth arrangements, both editorial and functional, between the editor-in-chief and the journalists. Independence, or the capacity to act freely, becomes the function of a code of law.[10] Article 26, for example, allocates power from the publisher or founder to the editor by mandating that a publication can be distributed only after its editor-in-chief has given permission. The Russian statute, like many of its transitional comtemporaries, differs in this respect from US law, which does not, normally, order that there be a particular design for the internal structure of a newspaper organization or a television network. In the United States, as in many national systems, there is no guarantee that an editor will be 'independent' of the publisher, however desirable the goal. To the extent that an editor is independent, it is a result of tradition, and, in rare instances, contract, but not a constitutional or statutory right.

In the same vein, the Mass Media Law uses the forms of law to accord greater rights than are typical in the West to those who work for the mass media. Under article 20, the journalists' collective has the right to approve the editorial charter—the mass-media outlet's by-laws or regulations—by a majority vote, provided that no less than two-thirds of its membership is present and that the regulations are also approved by the founder. These regulations would cover the manner of appointing the editor-in-chief, the manner for ceasing operation, and the manner by which founders or publishers could be changed. In the United States it is unusual, unless reflected in the ownership structure, for journalists, as a body, to have rights independent of collective bargaining agreements.

Emblematic of past frustrations, the 1991 Mass Media Law in articles 38–40 guarantees access to government reports and provides for audiences or press conferences with officials themselves. Because the Mass Media Law confers special privileges on journalists, the category of those so blessed must be legally differentiated. Article 49 provides a code of behaviour: journalists are obliged to verify the reliability of information reported to them, protect confidential sources, honour requests for citation by those who provide information, obtain prior permission when it appears that a news report will be an invasion of privacy, notify those persons whose pictures have been taken, keep superiors informed of possible lawsuits, and refuse assignments that might entail violation of the law. If a journalist does all this, article 49 states, the government then 'guarantees the journalist protection of his honour, dignity, health, life and property' as a person who performs a public duty.

As meritorious as these ethical goals for reporters might be, the imposition of such government standards suggests a relationship between journalist and government that is reminiscent of the sometimes velvet, sometimes steel prison of the past. Journalists are, in article 4, provided special rights of access, including a kind of post-Chernobyl right to visit calamities, catastrophes, and places of 'mass unrest and mass gatherings of citizens, as well as areas in which a state of emergency has been declared'. Somewhat chillingly, they are burdened with responsibilities as well. If journalists fail (e.g. if they distribute false information which defames the honour and dignity of a state organ), article 48 provides that they can be stripped of accreditation by that agency. Because article 47 provides journalists with a right of access, there must, as a result, be a defined category of 'journalist' who has more of a right than others to enter prisons, rummage through government files, or see what is going on in defence installations.

Article 51 provides that the journalist is forbidden to use his or her privileged position to cover up falsification of information, to transmit rumours under the guise of truth, to collect information for unauthorized persons or organizations, or to distribute information 'for the purpose of defaming a citizen or individual categories of citizens exclusively on the basis of sex, age, racial or national affiliation, language, attitude toward religion, profession, place of residence and work, or in connection with their political convictions'. Articles 59 and 60 provide a list of potential sanctions for journalists who are not true to these responsibilities.[11]

The Russian Mass Media Law of 1991 remained an experiment in the use of the statutory form—laws arrayed on a page—as a way of fashioning a transition from control to greater pluralism. But the form of law without a commitment to the rule of law is not sufficient. Dedication to complex terminology could not alter reality in the absence of institutions in which law could be interpreted and enforced by government officials and judges with a common commitment to pluralistic goals. Clumsy formulations, lengthy recitations, awkward adjustments of old ways to new political realities could not suffice to ensure the evolution of a free press. The Russian Mass Media Law of 1991 was a breakthrough—a shining example of the move towards law as a means of assuring an altered public sphere and a more pluralistic national identity. The victory of passage, however, was followed by the recognition of the hardships of adjustment.

From Law to Force

In the brutal year after the dissolution of the Soviet Union, during adjustment to new realities, perspectives on the nature and function of law substantially altered. Deepening conflict over the distribution of power in the society meant that the immediate achievement of the dreamed-of paradigm, a non-manipulated press, the hope of the media law, was impossible. Like similar laws being considered elsewhere in transition societies, the 1991 law was largely about press immunity from government intervention, focusing on the rights of journalists against their publishers and editors, and the rights of citizens and journalists against the state.[12] But the earthquakes within the ruling order —the disputes for control among interest groups and institutions— meant that the goal of immunity was unrealizable. In the first years after passage, it was hardly independence, hardly the structuring of a public sphere, that took centre stage. Instead, reallocation of control of the media, especially television, became the harsh focus of struggle and political division.

Nothing in the 1991 law dealt explicitly with the allocation of power between branches of government, between the President and Parliament. But, as the intense division among competing forces for public loyalty took place, the media were a flashpoint. Controversy over the media's role in society contributed to President Boris Yeltsin's calling for new elections and the closing-down of the Parliament. Disputes over the division of media power, unresolved by law, would disintegrate into the storming of the great production facility that housed Ostankino, the massive factory of state central television. The text of law and the institutions for its interpretation could not hold the hostile energy within competing camps. Law and force alternated in defining the control of the media. As had proved to be true elsewhere in the transition societies, the appointment and dismissal of the chief officers of the state broadcasting service became levers for violent disagreement and the reimposition of state influence.

Private newspapers, freer than broadcasting, were also an arena for battles for control. As paper and printing costs skyrocketed in the post-Soviet period, government subsidies became necessary for survival for most publications. The 1991 Mass Media Law did not address the tensions that would arise in determining which journals would be favoured by government largess. Here, too, a dispute arose between the President and Parliament as to the criteria for distribution. An assertive Parliament sought to impose a legislative standard with the appearance of political neutrality, and suspicion mounted between that institution and the Ministry of Press and Information.

A dramatic example of the struggle for control was the status of the great newspaper *Izvestiia*. Established as the organ of the state at the dawn of Revolution, *Izvestiia* was always under the direction and control of the Supreme Soviet of the Soviet Union. With the dissolution of the Soviet Union, the question of succession arose. Journalists voted to claim the paper for themselves, invoking the spirit, if not the letter, of the 1991 Media Law. Here was a test of the rights of journalists against the historic 'founders' of instruments of mass information. For *Izvestiia*, as with much of the Russian press of the post-Soviet period, daily life consisted of the transformation of institutions which were the projections of political entities, to institutions which would be independent of such organs and subject to owners, investors, and subscribers. The Russian Parliament claimed that, as inheritor of the mantle of the Supreme Soviet, it controlled the editorial direction of the paper. The issue became especially important because, at a critical moment in the constitutional life of the nation, the influential paper, though once the child of the legislative branch, favoured the President over the views articulated by the Parliament and its Speaker, Ruslan Khasbulatov. 'Freedom of the Press' became a rallying cry for those supporting the journalists and opposing greater parliamentary power. But a vote for freedom, here, as elsewhere, was also decidedly a vote for one side in a power struggle. The journalists succeeded and the victory was marked as a tribute to greater press autonomy. In fact, the outcome was also a measure of shifting political power.

The battles over control of the media escalated in 1992 and early 1993, reflecting the deadly enmity between President and Parliament, an enmity that produced governmental crisis after crisis. The crises served as a major justification for a national referendum on 25 April 1993 throughout the Russian Federation and the narrow adoption of a new constitution in December 1993. But the run-up to the referendum itself produced an aggravation of government–media relations, and the conclusion of the electoral contest did not improve matters. The April referendum tested the commitment of President and Parliament to a truly free press, and the commitment was found wanting, though the flag of independence was waved by all sides. Both the forces behind Boris Yeltsin and the forces of the opposition manœuvred for control of television, radio, and print media.

The first decree of President Yeltsin, announced during the spring campaign, established a new effort to 'protect' the mass media, under the President, as 'the supreme official personage of the state' and as 'guarantor of the rights and liberties of the individual'.[13] His opponents saw the decree as a law designed to compel press loyalty. Citing its authority under the 1991 Law on Mass Media, President Yeltsin's Ministry of Press and Information, a few days prior to the 25 April referendum, initiated court action to close down two opposition newspapers, *Sovetskaia Rossiia* (*Soviet Russia*), and *Den'* (*The Day*), on the grounds that they were abusing that law by fomenting inter-ethnic conflict and violence against the state.[14] In St Petersburg, local authorities, supporters of the President, temporarily removed television commentator Aleksandr Nevzorov from the air in late March, claiming that his calls for volunteers to defend the Motherland against Yeltsin's 'unconstitutional coup' were a violation of the mass-media law's prohibition against appeals for armed insurrection.[15]

Just a month before the April vote, in the mid-sized city of Saratov on the Volga, local deputies, opponents of the President, marched into the local television station and seized the microphone from a surprised reporter. A Moscow news account of the Saratov incursion quoted a weary and angry journalist as follows: 'In the old regime, we were told not to show empty wheat fields, or to show workers on their knees so that the wheat looked taller. Maybe that will happen again.'

Yeltsin's decree ordering that the press be guarded from hostile abusers of media rights was mild compared with the activities of the legislative branch and the President's opponents. The Congress of People's Deputies (the super-Parliament), angered by perceived imbalances in news coverage of the crisis that favoured Yeltsin, passed its own Resolution, before the referendum, requiring the formation of their own supervisory councils (the membership to be chosen by federal and local legislative bodies) in order to 'insure objective coverage' and 'prevent political monopolization' of broadcasting.[16] In addition, the Congress ordered government agencies to transfer to the Supreme Soviet their powers to start and partially to supervise media activity. Aleksei Simonov, the head of the Glasnost Defense Foundation, said, at the time, that Russian television was only fragilely an example of 'fantastic pluralism'. He cautioned against reading too much into the clash of opinions and the presentation of different sides of the great constitutional questions. 'It's the uncertainty about the future that leads to pluralism. This is still government television. The only problem is defining who is the government. As soon as there is clear evidence as to who will win, the content of television will change.' 'You have to remember,' Simonov presciently observed, 'the relationship between television and the state is governed by people and loyalties, not by law and constitution.' Change is still too recent, he claimed.

'Government thinks it owns television, that it is not just another source of information, but far more.'

Typical of the Russian media war, and similar contests in other transition societies, was the invocation, on all sides, of the duty to protect the freedom of the press. Parliament strengthened and extended the power of supervisory councils it had established in the name of guaranteeing freedom. Oleg Poptsov, Chairman of the All-Russian TV and Radio Company, condemned, however, the 'extraordinary hostility of the [Supreme Soviet] committee on mass media toward the mass media'.[17] The President's Minister of Press and Information, Mikhail Fedotov, resigned on 21 August, calumnizing the Parliamentary observation councils which, he claimed, had already been set up and started to operate throughout the regions. 'They are already dividing up air time. They are deciding who is to be shown and who isn't. Lists of desirable and undesirable speakers are being compiled. . . . The whole purpose of the game is to call freedom censorship and censorship freedom.'

The continuing duel among institutions brandishing competing media laws was one of the principal zones of bitterness between the President and the Supreme Soviet during the summer and fall of 1993. Finally, President Yeltsin's 21 September dramatic suspension and later disbanding of the Parliament led to the immediate institution of censorship. At least ten newspapers in Moscow were closed down following the violent events of early October,[18] and, at the outset, all newspapers were subject to censorship, having to submit material for government review before publication. On 23 September, citing the Mass Media Law, the Council of Ministers ordered the suspension of additional media, namely the newspapers, magazines, and radio and broadcast programmes of the Supreme Soviet. The Council's resolution declared that, with the Parliament suspended, a new 'founder' for its publications was needed, and the successor would be the government itself.[19] Shortly after the 23 September Council of Ministers' action, the government installed a new editor-in-chief at the newspaper *Rossiiskaia Gazeta*, Natalia Ivanovna Polezhaeva, who initiated radical changes in personnel and editorial directions. These actions brought her into conflict with the journalists of the paper, who, in a 27 September meeting, voiced their unanimous objection to the take-over and claimed that the substitution of founders had been illegal.

When, in early October, the government suspended 'extreme' newspapers, including *Pravda*, *Sovetskaia Rossiia*, and *Den'*, it was pursuant to 'emergency powers', the basis, as well, for asserting prior censorship for two days over other publications including *Nezavisimaia Gazeta* and *Sevodnia*. A St Petersburg daily, *Chas Pik*, reported that one censored item, a short report on the suspension of a number of newspapers, angered the censors, not for the story itself, but for 'the lack of exaltation' about the decision. St Petersburg's *Vedomosti* (*The Record*) published details on the suspension of Aleksandr Nevzorov's virulently anti-Yeltsin television programme, '600 Seconds'. The order received by Bella Kurkova, chair of the television company, on 5 October was signed by Deputy Minister of Press and Information O. Yusitkov and Director of the State Inspectorate to Protect Freedom of Press and Information, Yu. Luchhinksii. The full text of the order (implemented by Kurkova) was as follows:

In accordance with the introduction of the emergency rule in the city of Moscow by the Decree of the President of the Russian Federation No. 1578 of October 4, the Ministry of Press and Information of RF has been instructed to provide, starting from October 4, 1993, the execution of Article 23 (*b*) of the Law on Emergency Rule. Since the program '600 Seconds' on St Petersburg's Channel 5, retransmitted in Moscow, stirs up ethnic, class, social, religious intolerance and enmity, we require you to stop its transmission to Moscow pending the lifting of emergency rule. If you cannot do it technically, you must suspend airing of TV program '600 Seconds' until further special instruction.[20]

The shift from law to force was epitomized by the bloody battle at Ostankino, one of the last acts in the conflict between President and Parliament. Except for the White House, home of the Parliament, and the Comecon building, housing the Moscow Mayor's offices, Ostankino was the only major site for massive struggle. An October night of violence left at least sixty-two people dead and scores wounded, members of the television staff and foreign journalists included. Cameras panning through the corridors and studios showed scenes of rubble and destruction. In doing so, the cameras revealed something else: that the control that comes from law is just a thin overlay beneath which the armed march, the terrorist act, the seizure of transmission towers, and the arbitrariness of censorship are ready to emerge.

Strengthening the Rule of Law

After the battle of Ostankino, a condition resembling the rule of law was reasserted. With increasing speed, new institutions were put in place and decrees issued re-employing the language of independence and free speech. Even the earlier acts of censorship were justified on the basis of law. The October close-down of several newspapers had, as indicated, been based not only on the President's 'emergency powers', but also on article 4 of the Mass Media Law (authorizing closure if a publication engages in appeals for seizure of power, for violent change in the constitutional order or integrity of the state, or incitements to national, class, social, or religious prejudice or intolerance), as well as international human-rights law.

In an obeisance to the reinstitution of law, President Yeltsin, who had, just months earlier, suspended the Constitutional Court, also established a new 'arbitration tribunal' that would ultimately be transformed into a unique instrument for deciding and mediating information disputes.[21] With the disbanding of the Russian Parliament and the announcement of elections to a new Federal Assembly, to be held on 12 December 1993, the already contentious question of media access became an issue of great concern among potential candidates. In response to critics who argued that the press was predominantly pro-Yeltsin and that the government continued to treat state-owned television as its own propaganda tool, Yeltsin included a provision in the Statute on Elections aimed at providing equal access to the media. According to article 28 of this statute, all mass media 'whose founding agencies include a state body, organization or institution, or a body of local self-government, or mass media whose financing comes partially or entirely from state funds or the funds of bodies of local self-government [were] obliged to afford equal opportunities of pre-election campaign presentations to all candidates for deputy to the state Duma'. Article 28 was soon expanded in the Statute on Information Guarantees, adopted on 29 October. In addition to dealing with questions of equal access and other matters, the new tribunal created by the Statute could issue warnings to candidates who in their campaigning made false statements 'demeaning the honor, dignity [or] business reputation of candidates [or] their agents'. Both the Arbitration Tribunal and the Russian Electoral Commission in early December rejected the demand by First Deputy Prime Minister Vladimir Shumeiko that the Communist and Democratic parties be removed from the election lists because they declared themselves against the proposed constitution.[22]

In December 1993, and January 1994, President Yeltsin and other officials issued a series of additional decrees relating to mass media, largely designed to establish a legal framework for a free press. These included a renewed commitment of financial benefits for the state broadcasting apparatus, including, temporarily, substantial outlays for signal distribution. A decree of 10 January, 'Issues Ensuring Publication and Dissemination of Mass Media Information and Printed Matter', called for preferential taxation of the print mass media, a system of state subsidies, and improved access to printing facilities. A decree guaranteeing Citizens' Rights to Information, issued on 31 December 1993, ordered news programmes of state radio and television to 'inform citizens without fail of the principal provisions of legal acts and decisions of state bodies on fundamental domestic and foreign policy questions on the day they are issued'.[23] Of course, the order to promulgate government decrees, while increasing citizen access to information, raised the possibility of greater intervention in day-to-day editorial decisions made by state entities.[24]

In the wake of the December elections, Vyacheslav Bragin, who had been the head of Ostankino, was ousted, a reminder of the relationship between the forms of law and the exercise of power. Bragin's downfall was partly attributable to the results of the election in which nationalists had done surprisingly well and the results had not been so favourable to the government as had been hoped. Television was supposed to have the aura of fairness, but, when it counted, those in power wanted the unifying quality of television, its persuasive capacity, to be used in a way that would redound to the benefit of the Yeltsin reformers. In a move of considerable importance for the development of a pluralistic broadcasting system in Russia, linked perhaps to the failure of state television during the elections, President Yelstin ordered the granting of a television broadcasting licence to a private entity, NTV. The cause of pluralism and access was advanced, but the rule of law was nicked: the just recently established mode of awarding valuable channel rights seemed to be circumvented so that a favoured (and talented) broadcaster would prevail.

Intense societal conflict, threatening the existence of legal institutions, was felt throughout early 1994, with the legitimacy of many of the new bodies (including the Duma and Federal Council) very much at issue. In the spring of 1994, President Yeltsin, to achieve a moratorium among contending forces, put forward a Treaty of Civic Accord, a novel instrument that was more a public-relations device than a binding agreement among its signatories. The Treaty sought to place a frame around a debate that had, a few months earlier, erupted into battle. The Treaty could also be seen as an effort by those in a broad status quo position to establish standards of discourse that might discredit their most radical challengers. The Treaty provided that 'the parties . . . consider that the grandeur of Russian history, with its heroic and tragic pages, obliges one to avoid simplified or insulting appraisals of the past and to prevent the distortion of historical fact'. In addition, under the Treaty:

> the parties . . . stress that love for the fatherland, freedom and moral duty to society, creative labor, all the values common to the whole of mankind, spiritual and moral traditions of the multiethnic people of the Russian Federation should become the basis for its revival. The parties to the treaty pledge to uphold, in word and deed, the norms of moral behavior in politics, the economy and public life.

To render clearer the relationship of the press to this process of establishing a consensual social order, the Treaty provided that 'a special role in all of this belongs to the mass media . . . the efforts of which should be supported by the state and society'.[25]

By the summer of 1994 the Duma was also able to develop a draft statute on radio and television broadcasting to supplement and build on the 1991 Mass Media Law. Passed on a first reading by the Duma on 26 October, the draft statute maintained its rhetorical commitment to prohibiting censorship, but it also imposed on the state the obligation to employ the media for 'the defense of public morals and morality, the strengthening of the family, and the confirmation of a healthy lifestyle'. Under the bill, government ought to ensure that broadcasters 'satisfy the wide and variegated informational needs of viewers and listeners' and encourage the 'wide distribution of education and culture'. The language of the bill also foresaw as an underlying principle of broadcasting 'creating the conditions for the maintenance and development of a national culture' and co-operating 'in the formation of a law-based state'.

More unusual was a proposed law prepared in the summer of 1994 to take in hand, rearrange, normalize, and shift control of elements of state underpinning for financing the media. The draft, 'On State Support of the Mass Media',[26] was the creation of Mikhail Poltorianin, the powerful chair of the relevant Duma committee and former Minister of Press and Information, and it sought to address a number of demands and concerns of the emerging independent press. The proposal sought to reduce publishers' dependence on state printing monopolies and substitute indirect subsidies (such as tax relief) for existing, more onerous programmes. The bill, as reported from its committee, like the government's earlier decree, was designed to provide favourable tax treatment for profits earned by editorial offices of mass media, publishing houses, news agencies, television and radio broadast companies, and similar enterprises. Video equipment and printing presses could be brought into Russia free of duty. Media institutions would be able to keep foreign currency and use it to acquire equipment and materials. Favourable postal rates and special rents for the use of public buildings would be established. Equally important, the bill provided a scheme for the systematic transformation of all state-owned printing facilities used in newspaper, book, and journal output. Such enterprises would be privatized: up to 30 per cent of the stock would remain in federal hands for three years, with the rest distributed to workers in the enterprise, newspapers, magazines, and book publishers that historically used the printing facilities. A certain amount would be reserved for the general public as investors.

The most creative innovation of Poltorianin's proposal was the establishment of a National Fund for Media Development which would hold, for a limited time, the government's own stock in printing enterprises. This Fund would accumulate and invest funds to strengthen the printing and distribution structure for mass media and book publishing. It would be a vehicle which would manage funds and control stock in privatized mass-media assets, such as printing-press and book-publishing operations. The Fund would work with the state as it determined its own 'needs . . . for the solution of nationwide tasks in the spheres of education, culture, science and technology as well as the development of new printing technologies'.

In this respect, the Poltorianin approach sought to redefine a state role in ways that mediated between an American hands-off tradition and the practices of the Soviet past. The state would redefine its requirements in terms of purchases of books for libraries and educational establishments, in terms of encouragement of manufacturing, and in the redeployment of existing subsidies. The Fund was attacked by Sergei Gryzunov, the head of the government's Committee on the Press, who criticized the Fund as 'a fresh approach to monopolization', to 'accumulating all money in single hands and a new handing out to "ours" as opposed to "theirs", to those who are liked as opposed to those who are not'.

Seizing the language of free enterprise, in the autumn of 1994, President

Yeltsin approved the privatization of Ostankino, in a manner that seemed to equip it to compete more effectively with private entrants while, at the same time, maintaining control in government hands. Under the decree, signed on 30 November 1994, approximately 50 per cent of the company would be owned by the State Committee for the Management of State Property, with the remaining stock distributed among a dozen hand-picked major companies. The 'privatization' took place against the threat of the merger of the once-proud first channel into what had once been its mere appendage. The alternative to privatization and the injection of new financing was, for Ostankino, a slow and depressing decline and death. The increasingly combative Poltorianin attacked the plan on grounds clearly linked to national-identity concerns as 'breaking up the common information space' and 'edging closer to the dismemberment of Russia'.

While the resolution of control over the great instruments of state television seemed to become settled, elements of strength among new independent competitors became more prominent. The joint venture in which Turner Broadcasting System was linked to Russian partners dissolved as those in Moscow found more favourable financing at home. Under the direction of Igor Malashenko, a young hero of television in the Gorbachev period, NTV, financed by Moscow bankers, posed a threat to central television's domination of the news, so much so that the government threatened to withdraw its licence because of unfavourable coverage of Yeltsin's military campaign in Chechnya.

Notwithstanding the rhetoric of independence, there seemed to be a systematic discouragement of the growth of non-governmental television even five years after the dissolution of the Soviet Union. Local and regional governments proliferated efforts actually to use television to produce and distribute information themselves, thereby increasing their control over the messages available to the public. A 1994 draft statute on the coverage of the Duma provided that the legislative body would have its own production capability and command time, at least on the state channels. Many municipalities and other local or regional bodies were gaining their own channels or participating in private channels as joint ventures. Enforcement of copyright law lessened the power of independents, depriving them of their ill-gotten lifeblood: pirated American films and cartoons. Discriminatory pricing of government-controlled transmission facilities and discrimatory taxes on equipment purchases inflated costs. In addition, the government, in the spring of 1994, ordered that the state channels should restrict the time independent entities were given as 'windows' to broadcast their material. The market for advertising was being manipulated to injure small independents as the large state channels expanded the number of minutes they would sell. Independents saw the boundless appetite for advertising at Ostankino or Russian Television as a purposeful threat.

In this environment, official, philanthropic, and business entities from the West sought to buttress whatever they deemed to be moves to 'independence', sometimes with little concern about the relationship between different forms of privatization, control, and political divisions. By the autumn of 1994 USAID was moving to implement its Russian American Media Partnerships to foster independent television, radio, and the press in theory because of the role they could play in enhancing and reinforcing democracy. These partnerships would help 'high-quality non-governmental Russian media organizations become sustainable and independent institutions'. In terms of objectives, the Agency provided three justifications for US aid to the internal press of a third country. First, a financially viable and politically independent non-government media sector 'is a central mechanism for keeping a democratic government accountable for its actions'; second, such a sector is useful in ensuring that the existing state media remain honest; and, third, such a sector safeguards freedom of the press. USAID wished to diminish the leverage that the state continued to exert over the non-governmental press because of its economic control of printing presses, distribution, and information networks.

Free Press and Democratic Values

Frances Foster has written that the initial Russian justifications for freedom of the press were strikingly similar to those of their US counterparts.[27] Proponents argued that an independent Fourth Estate would expose and check potential abuses and 'mistakes' by executive, legislative, and judicial branches. They would provide the citizenry with the 'full and objective' information essential for democratic self-governance. A free press would assist in the spiritual liberation of the populace from the shackles of socialism and offer a forum for the introduction, comparison, and debate of reform proposals. A free press would 'consolidate' Russian citizens in support of their embattled government during 'a time of most difficult sociopolitical changes and economic trials'.

Reality, Foster concluded, 'has diverged markedly from these high-sounding phrases'. Leadership attempts to influence and subordinate the Russian mass media by direct and indirect political and economic means characterized the first years of transition. Escalating to the media wars of 1993, there was a rapid implementation of prior restraints on publication and restrictions on press access to information. In addition, numerous criminal and civil actions were taken against media organs and personnel and draft legislation was introduced to expand liability for disclosure of state secrets and to punish publications that insulted top officials, attacked constitutional organs of power, or violated the 'integrity' of the Russian Federation.

Observers committed to the freedom of the press, Foster writes, attribute this backlash to the Russian leadership's unfamiliarity with, insensitivity to, and, ultimately, intolerance of Fourth Estate criticism and opposition.

> A closer look, however, suggests an additional, less obvious explanation. The recent moves against the media may reflect not only the early success of the Russian press as an embryonic Fourth Estate, but also its fundamental failure as a force for societal consolidation and moderation during a period of profound national crisis.

Foster draws an important contrast between the American justifications for a free press and the Russian reality:

> One of the most compelling but least cited United States defenses for freedom of expression relates precisely to the issue of crisis management that confronts Russia today. In the words of Thomas Emerson, 'freedom of expression . . . is an essential mechanism for maintaining the balance between stability and change'. In the United States context, the press has traditionally promoted this equilibrium in two main ways. It has acted as a 'safety valve' for the release and 'domestication' of popular discontent and frustration. Equally importantly, it has communicated to and persuaded the United States citizenry that established political and legal institutions and processes are both predictable and flexible enough to accommodate change.[28]

Enhanced press independence in post-Soviet Russia might, in this analysis, have contributed to a destabilizing, not moderating, role. In a period of turmoil, the Russian press, with its 'unrelenting criticism and exposure of personal and systematic failings . . . eroded rather than fostered public confidence in the post-socialist Russian leadership and evolving norms, rules, institutions, and procedures. Thus, the press has demystified and delegitimized the present as well as the past.'[29]

Defending his aggressive position in fashioning new media laws, Mikhail Poltorianin argued, in the autumn of 1994, that the strategic objective of Russia's information policy should be to 'deepen democracy'. With the destruction of the totalitarian regime, 'the importance of its mouthpieces—the central newspapers—fell off as well'. He blamed a decline of support for central television on its 'propaganda for spiritual emptiness'. Society, he argued, 'has grown tired of boundless freedom for impudence and slander, of freedom for instigation and political foppishness'. The state, Poltorianin argued, could no longer 'continue a policy of peaceful nonresistance to evil'. He recalled how Ostankino and Tass 'assailed' Yeltsin and his associates from every point in 1990, leading to the creation of the All-Russian State Television and Radio Company (Russian Television) and the Novosti Russian News Agency to 'break the information blockade'. Now it was time for a new set of alternate forces to break a new information blockade.

A central tenet of the US rationale for broad expressive rights, in Thomas Emerson's formulation, is that 'an open society will be the stronger and more cohesive one'. But Thomas Emerson identified two limitations that may help explain what Foster identifies as an apparent contradiction between general theory and Russian practice: (1) 'society must be committed to democratic procedures or rather in the process of committing itself', and (2) 'men [must] have learned to function within the law'. For Foster, the post-Soviet mass-media experience provides ample evidence that Russia has failed to satisfy either of these requirements. Everywhere there is serious doubt about the level of current commitment to democratic procedure and enforcement and observance of law. 'This prompts a perplexing question that has far-reaching implications for the reform process in Russia and other former socialist states. Is conventional wisdom correct that press freedom is a precondition for the democratic, law-based state? Or is the democratic, law-based state a precondition for press freedom?'[30]

7 Text and Context

As societies move from one political paradigm to another, the transitions in their media law reveal much about them. In the midst of reconstruction, the scaffolding of reform is evident as press and broadcasting organizations are transformed (or fight to remain the same), and as state functions are reorganized, destroyed, or reformulated. Justifications for control that once had the quality of faith are suddenly publicly useless, but new justifications take their place. Not only in Russia, the subject of the last chapter, but throughout Central and Eastern Europe and the severed Republics of the former Soviet Union, the process of transition has led to local media wars. Everywhere, beneath the frequent and fervid search for a free and independent press, lies an active and changing market for loyalties.

In these moments, formal changes in the law are abundant. New laws and regulations have been painfully produced. But, especially at times of transition, formal statements captured in the words of laws cannot be taken at face value. The rhetorical zeal for a 'free press' obscures, not always so completely, a recartelization of interests. When powers shift within states that are, themselves, newly independent, law shifts as well, disestablishing the state's monopoly over imagery and reducing its power to reflect and sustain new alignments. A 'free and independent press' is many things; but, in this context, at a minimum, its advocacy is a useful and respectable tool for previously suppressed competitors to assure that the market for loyalties allows for new entrants. Anecdotes alone do not provide a sense of what is meant, in these transition societies, by a free or freer, an independent or autonomous press; and the subtleties of the relationship of market to text often escape reformers dispatched to improve the broadcasting laws of Belarus or Kazakhstan, Albania or Ukraine, Hungary or Poland.

The language of media statutes may have a purpose of camouflage or may be designed to placate an international community rather than to serve as the operative guide to conduct within the state. Preoccupied with the escape from the past, these statutes and draft laws rarely come to grips with the new order, the consequences of globalism, or the weakening of a national voice. Formal texts, intentionally, often crudely, reflect the working-out of important differences among interest groups. At times, those features that seem the most obvious flaws, from a free-speech perspective, are consensual arrangements that represent a division of loyalties, a settled framework within which debate and discussion can take place. In this chapter, several central issues in the formulation of media law and policy in transition societies are examined. In some cases, the focus is on laws that were actually enacted. But, by definition, transition societies are fluid and their laws still unformed. For the purposes of understanding the relationship between law-making and society, draft approaches and political responses to them can be as important as the final statute and set of regulations themselves and are, therefore, considered as well.

Governance and Power

One example of controversy over text relates to the method of selecting, supervising, and discharging those in command of the state broadcasting services: who appoints the director-general (or the local equivalent) and who organizes the structure of the supervisory or regulatory council. Eric Barendt has written that 'broadcasting freedom is certainly endangered if there are no legal limits on the ability of government to pack television authorities with its supporters'.[1] Since broadcast freedom, in the liberal democratic spirit, is measured by the absence of governmental power, surely the state must be limited in its capacity to determine and constrain the personnel who run state television. But the very issue at the time of transition remained the relationship of the state to the imagery of its existence. Tenacity in holding the reins of loyalty could be expressed in terms of the governance of public broadcasting.

An early transition debate in Hungary took place against the backdrop of a parliament in which the majority, but not a super-majority, represented the Magyar Democratic Forum (MDF), a coalition of somewhat rightist factions, more or less nationalistic organizations, and religious groups. The second party, the Free Democrats, represented a liberal, cosmopolitan, European tradition. Under an agreement dating from the formation of the government, a consensus of the two groups was required for passage of a new media law. In the interim, while the majority party inserted the right to have the Prime Minister nominate the presidents and vice-presidents of the Hungarian radio and television companies, the authority to remove those officers was unclear. Governance of the media was of utmost importance because it had the potential to define not only a vision of the future (and the past), but also an ideology that might influence forthcoming elections.

As the drama of competition unfolded, each of the two major sides in the Parliament drafted an alternative form of governance, though neither, without consensus, could prevail because a two-thirds rule applied to passage of the new law. The Free Democrats proposed that the presidents of radio and television be, in the future, elected and discharged by the Parliament (after a hearing by its Cultural and Press Committee), with a two-thirds vote required. The MDF proposed that the heads of radio and television be appointed by the President upon the initiative of the Prime Minister, thereby more firmly lodging power in the government.

The crisis, almost predictably, arose over discharge of the the head of the television system, a sociologist, Elemer Hankiss, whose supervision of the news programming did not yield coverage to the liking of the MDF. The Prime Minister instructed the President of Hungary, Arpad Goncz, to dismiss both the heads of radio and television, reflecting the view of his majority, and, most likely, to have a more pliant director prior to the next national elections. The President refused to be bound by the Prime Minister's request, and the issue was pursued in Hungary's Constitutional Court, which decided in favour of the President.[2] The situation was eased by the President's announcement that he would eventually follow the procedure set forth under the new legislation, including a commitment to recognize the Prime Minister's power to hire and fire, and ultimately by the decision of the heads of television and radio to resign.

What was significant in both the drafting process and the arguing of the constitutional case was the shift between the language of law and the language of politics. At the grand level, this was a debate about institutions: how ceremonial was the role of the President of Hungary to be; what was the nature of the power in a parliamentary government when the Prime Minister has majority support? Also at the grand level, it was a debate in which 'freedom of the press' was invoked. Those who sought to maintain the heads of television and radio in power represented their position not as a struggle between two parties, or even between the President and the Prime Minister, but as a matter of resisting the government's power to intervene in the management of the media. In that respect, the debate represented a test of the pace of transformation, of the rate of adoption of Western (perhaps American) ideas. Providing to the directors-general of the state television system immunity from arbitrary discharge would assist in buffeting broadcasters from government pressure and would be a token of a shift towards the West.

Disputes over the appointment and discharge of directors-general of state broadcasting entities have been rather common. We have seen, in Chapter 6, how the political waves that afflicted Moscow were reflected in the rotation of heads of Ostankino. Convulsion was also a characteristic of the direction of Polish television, as is traced below. Throughout the former Soviet empire, transition hardly meant comfort and independence for those who managed so powerful a set of tools as the nation's broadcasting facilities. The nature of the appointment process was telling in terms of the extent of politicization, competition for control, and existence of a rule of law.[3]

The controversies over appointment of directors-general were complemented by debates over the composition of governing or supervising councils. These bodies, or buffer organizations, have rich precedents in European pluralism, and especially the German practice. They have had varying powers, usually over policy, with some having the authority to allocate frequencies. Because of their power, they were similarly seen as an important field of contestation. The stated objective, in many transition settings, was to depoliticize such councils by removing them from the direct control of government. With European precedents, many of these bodies were composed mostly of government officials or parliamentarians, and the politicization of these bodies remained high.

In most of the transition societies, the German system of a *Rundfunkrat*, which provides for broad representation by officials, parliamentarians, and citizens, was taken as a model, though revised substantially to reflect local political exigencies. The Estonian Broadcasting Act provides for the nine-member Council of Radio and Television Broadcasting, elected for six-year terms by the State Assembly and nominated by the Committee of State Culture.[4] A 1994 draft law on broadcasting in Russia provided a more typical fifteen-person Federal Radio and Television Broadcasting Commission with one-third of its members appointed by the President, one-third by the Federal Council, and one-third by the Duma of the Russian Federation.[5]

In Budapest, draft legislation would have established a Supervisory Committee of Hungarian Radio and Television that, at least in form, would have functioned only at a policy level and be precluded from intervening in the daily activities of the state companies. About half of the committee would have been composed of appointees from government and Parliament; a parliamentary member would represent not the body as a whole, but rather the political parties represented in the Parliament. In addition to sitting members, each political faction would appoint a public member. From a prepared list, selected organizations would delegate a member. These organizations would have included national and ethnic minorities in Hungary, nationalities outside Hungary, religious organizations, and organizations of journalists, environmentalists, and employees. A substitute version would have provided rotating membership for the historic churches of Hungary; the nationalities of Hungary; trade unions; youth organizations; pensioners' organizations; environmentalists and conservationists; and women's organizations.[6]

Poland provides another example of the dispute over governance. After Solidarity came to power in September 1989, Prime Minister Tadeusz Mazowiecki, in his maiden speech to Parliament, announced that the government would maintain control over state television and radio, in part to promote beneficial change during a period of severe economic constraints and austerity measures.[7] In Poland, as in Hungary, there had been a struggle between government and the President for control of broadcasting, though in a context in which the position of the President was far more powerful and the prime ministers were dependent on the President for patronage. Accordingly, the prime ministers followed the President's wishes regarding appointments to the top positions in Polish state broadcasting. As Karol Jakubowicz, one of the great cataloguers of the statutes of the region and a veteran of ancient Polish media wars, has put it, there was 'little real belief in the ideal of autonomous, impartial and politically neutral public service broadcasting', and it was quietly assumed that every government would seek to bring pressure to bear on the state media in any way it could:

> In political terms . . . Polish Radio and Television [was] poised between the government and the president. There [was] direct political intervention in the running of television, especially as regards news and current affairs. This [took] the form both of securing the appointment of ranking executives (like the

head of the news department) known to support either the president or the prime minister, and of residual day-to-day 'manual steering', with government officials influencing coverage of particular stories or making their displeasure known if news or current affairs departments dealt with issues in a way they [did] not accept.[8]

The mechanisms for structuring the broadcasting councils—bodies that supervise the public-service or state broadcasting companies and sometimes allocate frequencies for private broadcasters—also reflect the struggle for power. The Polish law provides for a Broadcasting Council that is, in aspiration, relatively autonomous, outside the government, subordinate neither to the Council of Ministers nor to the Parliament, and immune from political pressures. The President nominates the head of the Council, which would consist of nine members: three nominated by each of two chambers of the Parliament, the Sejm and the Senate, and three nominated by the President. But, despite the aspirations for autonomy, intervention and efforts to control occurred with regularity. In the spring of 1994, for example, the Polish Constitutional Tribunal ruled that Lech Walesa's recall of Marek Markiewicz from the post of chair of the National Broadcasting Council (partly over the award of channel licences) was unlawful, and disputes continued over political interference into both the work of the Council and the administration of the state's television service.[9]

Slovenia has adopted a Mass Media Law and a Law on Slovenian Radio and Television,[10] influenced substantially by a 1991 Slovenian draft. In the draft, councils advisory to the founder were mandated as a means of placing a public perspective in the editorial process. As outlined in article 9 of the draft, one function of these councils would have been to enhance 'the influence the public has on the realization of the content and editorial policies of a public medium'. Also indicative of these efforts is the detail in which the draft statute described a citizen's right to access for the purpose of replying to damaging published information. While the rights of access survived into the final law, the function of the advisory councils was reduced. Both the draft and the final law require that the editor responsible for the whole of a publication (or for parts, where there is more than one) be clearly identified so that citizens' rights can be more easily implemented. The Slovenian law places great emphasis, and provides enormous detail, on a right to reply. Emerging from a context in which accusations could go unanswered, the revisionists seized on the right of reply as providing the model of a better society.

The early Slovenian draft created, at least as one alternative form of supervision of the editorial process, a collegial entity called the Chamber of Journalists. This Chamber, a separate and presumably independent entity, would examine and license journalists 'who fulfill the conditions defined by the Chamber . . . and successfully pass its professional examination'. The Slovenian draft, while describing and imposing journalists' responsibilities, did not establish a set of rights and duties as comprehensive as those in the Russian Mass Media Law discussed in Chapter 6. Still, the process of ascribing a definition to journalists can be understood as the professionalization of the public sphere: taking what is a desire for a consultative process and locating it in a specialized social entity charged with important general obligations (such as providing for the free flow of information and the openness of public media to a variety of opinions).[11]

Emblems of National Identity

The evolution of law in Slovenia also provides insight into the relationship between government structures and issues of national identity. Article 3 of the 1994 mass-media law requires the Republic of Slovenia to promote and develop public media 'important for the fulfillment of the rights of Slovenian citizens to be informed and for the preservation of Slovenian national identity'. The original draft obliged the government to design and furnish news and information especially relevant to the Italian and Hungarian nationalities in Slovenia and to reach out to the Slovenian nationalities in Italy, Austria, and Hungary. This focus on the relationship between the government and national minorities recurred throughout the draft legislation. For example, article 8 required that, if a newspaper or television station is founded to provide information for the Italian or Hungarian nationalities, the relevant community must be consulted regarding not only content, but also the appointment and dismissal of the editor, unless the newspaper or television station was founded by the national community itself. Further, as a kind of substantive fairness, Slovene-language national radio and television programmes would have been required to exhibit the life and work of the Italian and Hungarian nationalities.[12]

The Hungarian draft law included, in article 14, exhortations that public broadcasters pay 'special attention . . . to the cultural heritage of the Hungarian people, [and] of the national and ethnic minorities living in Hungary, as well as to the European cultural heritage'. These broadcasters must provide 'extensive, comprehensive, objective and unbiased information about Hungarian . . . events . . . which are of interest to the general public'. Further, the draft statute required substantial ownership by Hungarians, or Hungarian-based entities, of the private television distribution systems.[13] Consistent with other transition media statutes, the 1994 Estonian Broadcasting Law establishes it as the duty of the public-service radio and television entities to further the 'development and promotion of Estonian national culture', to encourage use of the Estonian language, and to promote the international reputation of Estonia and to reinforce the Estonian political system.[14] A 1992 Ukrainian statute provides that 'information may not be used to call for an overthrow of the constitutional order, a violation of the territorial integrity of Ukraine, or as propaganda for war, violence, cruelty, fanning of racial, national, or religious enmity or as an instrument to violate human rights and liberties'.[15]

Hate Speech

A further window on loyalty and imagery in the transition societies can be gained from an examination of the family of issues now categorized, in the United States, as involving 'hate speech'. Andras Sajo has written about the judicial tolerance of extreme statements in Hungary.

> Unrestrained speech . . . given the social and political conflicts racking Hungarian society during the transition, may endanger social stability. Restricted speech, on the other hand, may immobilize nascent civil society, limit fundamental freedoms, and stifle the lively criticism of government so essential to democracy.[16]

The 1989 Hungarian Constitution protects the basic freedom of thought and the right to express an opinion and disseminate information and assures the freedom of the press. The Press Act, however, in article 3(1) prohibits the use of press freedom that constitutes a crime, incites people to commit crimes, violates public morality, or breaches another individual's personality rights—human dignity or the right to be free of defamation. The Hungarian Criminal Code makes it a criminal offence to incite hatred through publication in the press against 'the Hungarian nation or any nationality' or 'against any people, faith or race or single groups of the population'.[17]

In a case concerning anti-Semitic, anti-gypsy, and anti-Slovak periodicals, *Szent Korona* (*Holy Crown*) and *Hunnia*, the President of the

Hungarian Constitutional Court wrote that such statutes governing the arena of speech were constitutional as a means of protecting the public order. According to Professor Sajo, the Court recognized that

> ideas of racial superiority endanger civilization, and that incitement to hatred against groups may disturb the public peace and engender social conflicts. . . . Incitement to racial and other forms of group hatred contradicts the constitutionally protected democratic and peaceful order of society, denies human dignity, and deprives people of their right to be different.

While the Court refused to provide constitutional protection for offensive speech, it did recognize the need to protect the press from criminal liability, even for words of hate. 'Criminal sanctions are not intended to shape public opinion and political styles.'[18]

In each instance, laws concerning incitements to hatred and offensive speech are an integral part of a formal reshaping of a market for loyalties. The general outline of the working of the market for loyalties is set forth in Chapter 4, especially the function of law in establishing rules: what speech will be permitted, how forcefully that speech can be proclaimed, how important wealth or other attributes of power will be in putting forward one idea as opposed to another. The market for loyalties is a vital aspect of life and democracy in the transition societies; the very transition involved is a reorganization of the marketplace of ideas with the opening-up to new entrants and the limitation or exclusion of some of the old ones. The process of determining the shape of broadcasting and the press (including the role of foreign owners, the tolerance or suppression of hate speech, rules for the conduct and financing of elections, and protective quotas for internal programming) is a jostling for the levers of power over the minds and votes of the citizenry.

Defamation laws, laws licencing the press, laws providing for injunctions or criminal libel are all used by interest groups as a means of reflecting and allocating power. Take the question of the power the press itself should have, as compared to other institutions or individuals, to help shape public opinion and to reinforce and accentuate the position of particular interest groups. A statutory framework, hardly uncommon in the transition states, that makes broadcasters and newspapers liable for defaming public officials (whether or not the defamation is true), necessarily weakens the press.

In the United States, the Supreme Court, in 1952, upheld the conviction of the president of Chicago's White Circle League for organizing the distribution of a leaflet to the City Council 'to halt the further encroachment, harassment, and invasion of white people, their property, neighborhoods and persons, by the Negro'.[19] Illinois had enacted a statute declaring it unlawful to distribute any publication that 'portrays depravity, criminality, unchastity or lack of virtue of a class of citizens, of any race, color, creed or religion' or that subjects them 'to contempt, derision, or obloquy'. It is quite unfashionable to cite the case *Beauharnais* v. *Illinois* approvingly, and most influential scholars consider it to have been, at the least, *de facto* overruled.[20] Yet it stands as an example of the use of law and judicial enforcement to police the market-place of ideas and limit both the manner and the substance of arguments designed to change loyalties.

The process—in Central and Eastern Europe—of achieving a pluralistic society, a society in which there is an effective public sphere, may require limits, like the ones upheld in *Beauharnais* or at issue in the cases before the Hungarian Constitutional Court. In Russia, Boris Yeltsin sought to gain signatories to his Treaty of Civic Accord, discussed in Chapter 6, to limit voluntarily the parameters of speech so as to provide an interim period of stability. Throughout the region, there is a revived interest in those aspects of international law and practice, like the United Nations International Covenant on Civil and Political Rights which requires that 'any advocacy of national, racial, or religious hatred that constitutes incitement to discrimination, hostility, or violence shall be prohibited'.[21] Where untoward claims can lead to war and the dissolution of public order, those who hold the fragile status quo together have a stake in setting boundaries to the marketplace of ideas.[22]

Foreign Investment and Domestic Content

Just as concerns over hate speech reflect the remaking of national identities, so too do media-law restrictions on foreign ownership and requirements of domestic programming content. In an essay for the Council of Europe,[23] Karol Jakubowicz summarized, for example, the policies of various countries towards capping foreign capital investment in domestic media enterprises. Poland had a 33 per cent ceiling, Bulgaria 25 per cent, Latvia 49 per cent, with Slovakia, at the time, having an absolute bar. The 1994 Estonian Broadcasting Law limits ownership in radio or television transmission facilities to citizens of Estonia who have a permanent place of residence in Estonia or a business registered in Estonia where more than 50 per cent of the ownership and control rests with Estonian citizens.[24]

Domestic-content minimum requirements have also been imposed. Those countries which wished to become part of the Council of Europe moved from general restrictions to ones in which the quota was not only national but European. Poland first demanded at least 30 per cent domestic production, and then, by decree of the National Broadcasting Council, set higher quotas: 60 per cent for the national public television channel, and 45 per cent for the national commercial television channels. The Czech Republic, in granting its first licence, required from its licensee a high percentage of Czech-produced material. Under temporary licences in Estonia, granted to private broadcasters in 1993, foreign programming could not exceed 30 per cent of air time.

These were states in which the institutions that had been the producers of culture—film and ballet companies, orchestras, publishers—were all in shock with the precipitate decline in subsidies. Television had been a consumer of their output, and they wished and needed the relationship to continue. The mass of workers involved in the technical side of television and the making of local programmes (and in each case the inherited payrolls included thousands) feared a shift to the purchase of a much greater proportion of programming from outside. For these reasons, statutes, even if they did not include specific domestic-content requirements, often included general goals. The 1994 Estonian Broadcasting Law, listing the tasks of public-service radio and television, included 'development and promotion of the Estonian national culture', 'recording and preserving Estonian national culture', and 'reinforcing the Estonian political system'.[25]

The existence of these rules does not necessarily disclose what actual changes have taken place in the programmes made available and actually watched. Law, alone, was no guide to the permeability of the borders, either in terms of investment or in terms of content. In Poland, in 1994, the National Radio and Television Council awarded the country's first private terrestrial nation-wide system to a small local company, Polsat, rejecting bids by Time Warner, Bertelsmann, Reuters, and others, largely for reasons of proclaimed national ownership. No sooner was the award made, than it was revealed that Rupert Murdoch and his News Corporation had a large-scale holding in the licensee, which would become part of Murdoch's global strategy. In the Czech Republic, a heated competition for its major private network resulted in an award to Central European Development Corporation, a company controlled by Ronald Lauder, the former US Ambassador to Austria, and headed by Mark Palmer, the former US Ambassador to Hungary. The conditions placed on the licence, more than thirty in number, were designed to render the channel as Czech as possible, but it was American films which gave the channel its initial character and power to draw audience. Time Warner, through its HBO International subsidiary, invested heavily in cable systems in Hungary. In Romania, while the new audio-visual law imposed no requirements for domestic production, it did require that licensees include 'illustrations of the national culture'. Still, it was noticeable that 'the protection of the national programmes was not even taken into consideration as licenses were granted mainly to TV companies that offered rebroadcasting of TV5 Europe, CNN and Eurosport'.[26] In many parts of the region, hundreds of small operators and entrepreneurs began the process of becoming television or radio stations. Too rarely, however, did these entities—sometimes broadcasting just an hour or two on the state transmitter—create or even rebroadcast indigenous programming. These fledglings, encouraged as symbols of free speech, cited in the speeches of diplomats and ambassadors of the Western press, were, rather, place-holders for programming emanating from London or Paris, Hollywood or Hamburg.

Yardsticks for Evaluation

In the first years of the post-Cold War era, the traffic from the West to the transition societies was substantial in experts and advisers on freeing the press. There was a kind of odd intercourse, reminiscent of the time of European exploration of exotic lands: Western journalists and scholars spent time in Central Europe or the former Soviet Union conducting interviews and lecturing; Czechs, Poles, Russians, and Slovenians were flown to London, Washington, and Paris, like native exemplars of a distant past. They performed, were studied, and sent back again, local guides helping Westerners to determine the lay of the land. Meetings took place in castles and conference centres or by fax and phone. But what was communicated, even face to face? The problems are probably similar to those that plagued eighteenth- and nineteenth-century scholars and civil servants moving among sharply differentiated societies. Formal language difficulties aside, a fundamental hurdle was uncertainty about the transferability of concepts.

For those who made these travels, a persistent problem was determining how rooted in a particular history and experiences a set of practices might be. Even sophisticated experts, schooled in the relativism of anthropology and sociology, find it easier to conclude that laws and institutions come in ready-made, almost modular packages (as sometimes they must), such as model statutes or constitutions. Not only the translation of words, or even of concepts, but the translation of deeply engaged settings and the machinery of administration must be taken into account. The words of the First Amendment, for example, are embedded in the music of their context. For Americans and Europeans, plying these intellectual waters, a serious problem involved the portability of these magic constitutional words or their continental equivalents. It is sometimes difficult for those from Washington or Boston who market the First Amendment in Kiev, Prague, Zagreb, and Budapest to understand or translate the complexities of their adaptation. One cannot talk of 'judges', of 'neutral principles', or of 'accountability of government officials to a rule of law' without sensitivity to the differences that might unravel the hidden meanings of these terms. The post-modern, post-critical, post-legal realist is more than a naturalist working with cabinets stuffed with statutes, pinned like butterflies under glass. To examine change formally, there is the project of chronicling specific statutory drafts and laws, country by country, organizing them by category, and engaging in a textual analysis comparing proposed and achieved transformations in one state to those in another. Various units for archiving and evaluative analysis automatically come to mind. These include the persistence of a monopoly in state television, the existence of prior censorship of the press, arbitrariness and corruption in frequency allocation, and recognition of the rights of journalists. Examination of the formal framework can also focus on the depoliticization of the appointment of chief executive officers of public-service broadcasters, broadening the composition and appointment of supervisory or regulatory bodies, and the application of the rule of law to the decisions of government agencies.

In the early 1990s an absence of state interference was hardly the norm in the republics of the former Soviet Union and the states of Central and Eastern Europe. War or the threat of war, irredentism, fierce debates on population movement and 'ethnic cleansing', and the general instability of economic transformations meant that the competition for loyalties was at an extraordinary pitch. The very definition of the state was often at issue. These transition societies could see themselves swept into the global information network, but they still had the isolation of the periphery. Television structures showed as much continuity as change: channels remained highly scarce and state controlled. Except for struggling independents with largely bootlegged material, television featured surprisingly little programming that originated from the West. Virtually everywhere, the hand of the government was felt as a mocking reminder of the ambivalences and ambiguities wrapped up in the emerging freedom of the press. Yet in each of these states, the pressure for media-law reform was intense. There was pressure not only for privatization, but for greater openness for sexually explicit programming, for a shift to commercial support for programming, for greater editorial freedom, and for news that had the formal hallmarks of programming from a free society.

The resulting laws and legislative drafts in these beleaguered states reflected far more than the ideals of social reform. Intrigue, xenophobia, corruption, a search for modernity and compliance with international pressures—all were part of the mix that produced the initial legislative efforts. The blanket of the past was everywhere, with its purposive, penetrating, stifling controls, a complex backdrop for the evaluation of any proposed approach. As a result, these laws and legal drafts, as we have seen in this chapter and in Chapter 6 in the examination of the Russian Mass Media Law, are clues as to the nature of the transformations. The laws help tell us whether what we witness represents a revolution of rights or an attempt to restore—as Andras Sajo, the Hungarian constitutional scholar, has argued—some hard-to-locate pre-Socialist order of an imagined national past. They exhibit a reordering of interest groups, but largely among those within, not without, the borders of the state.

Broadcasting legislation might be the actual working-out of conflicts, or it may be evidence of the inexorable anxieties that plague the society. The new laws of broadcasting reveal the idealized hopes of outside models, a mirror pointed outside towards the face of the West. These emblems of transition expose the scars of a remembered history; they can be read as articulated triumphs over some torturous practice, seemingly rejected, but retained in the very act of forceful repression. Broadcasting statutes can be useful indicators of the definition of power in the new societies; they can show the competition between legislative, executive, and judicial, and the assertions of personal authority.

How should these statutory drafts be evaluated? Given the basic context—transformations *from* authoritarianism *to* greater political involvement—it is insufficient that statutes adopt Western formalities, turns of phrase, the statutory equivalent of clichés and slogans. Too often, especially for American observers, the test of whether press freedom is actually transformed seems to be privatization and as much removal as possible from connection to the state. More broadly, the point is whether a restructuring of the broadcasting system contributes to a pluralistic, democratic society, a strengthening of the public sphere. Is there greater information flowing to the citizenry than before? Is there more of a zone for public discourse than previously existed? And is there the capacity for a broad diversity of views to be expressed in a way that has the unfettered opportunity to be critical of government?

The relationship between this cluster of standards and new broadcasting and press structures is difficult. In most, but not all the regions, a relative absence of censorship means that more information and a greater diversity of views is available. As economies pinch and majority tastes are indulged, the actual results are ambiguous for the publication and reading of newspapers. Common assumptions about how much of the news, whether biased or not, was available under the former Communist regimes may be far wide of the mark.[27] Despite the absence of competition, news programmes were watched more consistently by a greater range of the population, despite doubts about their veracity. Economic differentiation may mean greater access to information by the newly rich or middle class, and less access by others; a pronounced tendency in this direction has developed as government subsidies for the printed press decline, subscription prices rise, and circulation figures alter drastically.[28]

It is also important to know whether a new media statute contributes the incentive and machinery for a more secure and enduring national identity. Here the meaning of national identity is neither the romantic nor the cynical version described in Chapter 3. Rather, it is a pluralistic national identity, one that gives ethnic and religious and political minorities a sense that the system provides them with voice and recognition. We have seen that some draft statutes quite explicitly make reinforcement of the new national identity a duty of the broadcasting enterprise and do so in recognition that pluralism is an essential part of that identity.[29] It remains a risk that regimes which are shaky look to the state-controlled media to help strengthen their power; these are often states in the process of being invented, to use Hobsbawm's term,[30] or imagined, to use Benedict Anderson's.[31]

Another yardstick for evaluating the new media statutes is whether a broadcasting transformation contributes to the strengthening of a market economy, both by enhancing the market for information and ideas and by enlarging the market for other goods and services. Privatization of the broadcast media is not necessary for either objective, though it is often assumed that is the case (the European Court of Human Rights, in fact, has held that a monopoly of broadcasting in state hands is a violation of the right to receive and impart information[32]). The market economy makes headway through the introduction of advertising, which has become an acceptable, if not mandatory, source of revenue for almost all broadcasters, public as well as private.[33]

Translated through the lens of observers from the United States and Western Europe, these statutes and their purposes take on a slightly different hue, related to their transnational significance. The outside perspectives are summarized succinctly in a report of the National Telecommunications and Information Administration of the United States Department of Commerce:

> An open international marketplace not only serves US trade goals . . . but is fundamental to the continued vitality and diversity of the domestic US mass media industry, a major goal of US communications policy. An open international marketplace, in which the electronic mass media industry ties the nations of the world together, also can foster the growth of freedom and democracy worldwide.[34]

To parse these goals, think of the United States as a participant in the market for loyalties in each of the transition societies. Consider that those on the outside have several possible interests in the structure of broadcasting in these states. Somewhat playfully, I have labelled these interests as missionary, trade oriented, and grounded in defence or national security. The 'missionary' basis stems from a profound moral belief in human dignity and a concurrent duty to ensure that others see the light. Legions of advocates for freedom of information spend their valuable time writing and advising on transformation of broadcasting structures because of a commitment to immunity from state intervention and a wish to extend the bounty of the First Amendment. As far as trade is concerned, it is, as the excerpt from the Department of Commerce makes clear, an opportunity for American businesses to acquire television licences and to sell programming. Therefore, enhanced networks of communication are the infrastructure for substantial developments in trade.

Finally, and more problematic, there is the basis for advocacy in a frequently stated equation: free speech yields a democratic state and democratic neighbours are less likely to engage in war. In its more elegant, but sadly unproved, formulation, the argument is made that reason prevails where discourse is open and unencumbered. This is the formulation favoured by diplomats and assistance providers, such as the United States Agency for International Development. Statutes that encourage independent television and an end to censorship provide, indirectly, the pleasures of an open society, the television taste of material possibilities. On the receiving end of the narratives of freedom, people begin to think that individual efforts, not the actions of the state nor of great forces beyond their control, are accountable for despair and depression. The narratives of freedom yield the belief that, whatever the economic strivings, they can be attained.

The commitment to open speech has its inherent international limitations. Transborder speech can subvert governments as well as promote democratic forms, and sometimes the governments that are subverted may be democratic ones or somewhat more democratic and far more friendly than their predecessors. For American foreign policy, piping truth behind the Iron Curtain was considered therapeutically destabilizing. Among the shaky neophyte republics, now partners, the destabilizing aspects of truth may not continue to be such a high priority. Subversion is thus double edged. The time has already come when Western passions for freedom cool and censorship is tolerated if acceptable transition states require it.

In evaluating the formal statutes regulating television and radio, there is also an overwhelming tendency to think of broadcasting automatically as part of 'the press', bringing to mind outlets of communication that contain news and information about the place in which the signal is viewed. But much of the broadcasting that emerges in the transition societies is not about news but about entertainment *simple*. These channels may deserve protection, but not necessarily because they contribute to the public sphere. And in terms of the generation of images of national identity, the institutions of broadcasting have to be seen among other media that perform similar purposes. A reconstruction of the education system, the strengthening of language: like the broadcasting system, but more so, these hold the elements of cohesion and the power of encouraging orderly change.

Transition and the Market for Loyalties

In the transition societies, globalization, the move away from the state, and the growth of autonomous media, can be reinterpreted in terms of the transnational market for loyalties. Easily, with some frequency, language becomes a mechanism for encouraging or discouraging loyalties across old borders. I have already recited the many examples, after the first years of dissolution, of ending or limiting drastically Russian-language programming. Russians in Central Asia and the Baltics, as well as Russians in Ukraine, found that the proud networks that marked their dominance were now consigned to minor hours, or inadequate frequencies, or not broadcast at all. The new freedom for channels to spring up and reflect the programme needs of their audiences meant, also, that divided populations, within a single boundary, could have their prejudices honed and sharpened. In the West of Ukraine, German, Polish, and Ukrainian broadcasting gained popularity. In the East and the Crimea, the standard programmes of Ostankino and the Russian Television Company barely withstood the onslaught of independence. Crimea's most credible threat of secession occurred in the wake of a policy in Kiev to end transmissions from Moscow.

In Romania, where differences between the Hungarian and Romanian populations had led to tragic confrontations in the past, the challenge to a national television system came through the technology of cable. In a city of sizeable Hungarian population, where primitive cable systems linked the massive apartment buildings, the private operators, with only a handful of channels to fill, often totally excluded Bucharest's productions. Channels from Hungary, as well as satellite channels from the West, were preferred. There are many who claim that the intense, repetitive, unabashed separateness of regional television in the former Yugoslavia has contributed to its years of violence and war.

In Tajikistan, in the winter of 1994, a decree was signed which forbade the activity of any non-state electronic media, closing down the several dozen independent TV stations in the Republic until the acceptance of a new television law which the Council of Ministers was instructed to devise. The decree, unlike any elsewhere in the former Soviet Union, seemed to be a response to the growing strength of the country's two main independent TV stations, Somonen in Dushanbe and Temurmalik in Khojent, which caused a certain amount of fear in the country's leadership. Another, less important reason was the perceived invasion of Western morality through films on the independent

TV stations. A key leader, fearful of Islamic fundamentalism and its potential to usurp the ruling élite's privileges, did not wish to alienate the predominantly Muslim population.

Arguments for free speech, whatever else they accomplish, serve to justify a change in the mix of imagery: making room for the narratives of the West. Formal law does not automatically disclose this aspect of change. Statutes and regulations do not, on their face, show how the global television drama transcends the internal or regional rearrangement of political forces. The old competitors, such as the Voice of America, Radio Liberty, and their European counterparts, are now joined by Rupert Murdoch, Bertelsmann, the American networks and Time Warner, and a newly aggressive BBC. They are engaged in contests for new licences, arguments against quotas, and the weakening of central broadcasting entities. The failures and successes in these pursuits fill the pages of financial papers and are followed, by *aficionados*, as if great sports pursuits were under way.

Far from being neutral, each form of introducing competition brings its own transformation in content. Openness alone, without subsidy for existing media or preference for citizenry, results in a preference, understandable to be sure, for those with global wealth and experience. A statute which restricts foreign ownership of broadcast licensees has a different narrative import from one that does not. How open television is to competition is now a function, too, of technology, the availability of satellite signals, and the proliferation of cable channels. But form still makes, and is thought to make, an important difference. For example, texts that open the field of newspapers and television to all competition have a predictable, almost determinative outcome in the market for loyalties. Technology aside, there are strenuous efforts, often supported and encouraged by the governments of Western Europe and the United States, to ensure that entry is very open, and that conditions for competition are evident in regulations, licensing schemes, subsidies, and the composition of state broadcasting organizations. Such formal motors of change as statutory law and regulatory policies inscribe the ways public-sphere and national-identity concerns are conceived. Of course, formal statutes are not wholly revealing: many were the statutory paeans to freedom in the Soviet era.

In Chapter 3 I noted the observations of Ryszard Kapuściński about the resistance, in Iran, to messages of secularism and from the West. There, a 'walling-in' used every technique possible to screen out the permeating, compelling, seductive voices from abroad. What Kapuściński wrote about Iran hardly applies in its wilfulness to most of the restored democracies, to Hungary, the Czech Republic, Poland, and much of the former Soviet Union. Freed from a stifling Soviet Iron Curtain, a new walling-in was the last objective: sovereignty, for many of the newly independent states, was a relentless openness to influences from the West. Yet no society is fully immune from qualities that characterize those few which establish a wholesale campaign to control imagery. Already, there is the experience of bitter ethnic struggles in the Caucasus and the unrelenting rhetoric of Vladimir Zhirinovsky in Russia, examples of the sinister ideologies that can compete with the narratives of progress.

It is sometimes thought, perhaps in vain, that the stories of Hollywood and London and Paris, and the soap operas from Mexico, can trump and overwhelm the bitter stories of local differences. The commercial services are willing to undertake the task, almost without prodding, because of the relatively low marginal cost of spreading the availability of their product and the potential that a market will be developed. And where these services falter, justification is found for the external voices of Western governments, the BBC World Service, the American 'Radios' and the Voice of America. Besides, filling the space with Western imagery is justified, if not celebrated, by Western principles of freedom of speech.

The United States and the West, thus, reinforce their political ascendance by taking advantage of the role of the media in the market for loyalties. A controversy over Radio Liberty and Radio Free Europe in the United States provides a somewhat too obvious example. As a result of the new world order, a presidential commission had recommended eliminating these entities, which formerly had the responsibility for providing 'surrogate' news services within Central and Eastern Europe and the former Soviet Union.[35] The perceived propaganda and national-security needs of the United States had changed, and the surrogate 'Radios', as they were called, would be outdated. Now, it was argued, the Voice of America, with its very different role of projecting democracy and the American way of life, should be strengthened: there was less need for focusing on the question of local 'objectivity'; more reliance could be placed on domestic journalism for that purpose. But, as competition for power and for national identity has intensified, as the issue of journalistic control has deepened, the arguments for retention of the Radios has become stronger and stronger. The new defence was that these surrogates were playing a kind of preventive role in the global struggle; a back-up, as it were, if the domestic press faltered in the pursuit of objectivity. Whether this would be evidenced by increased government control or a backsliding into an anti-American pose was never clear.

The direct propaganda of one government to the people of another has long been deemed a questionable intervention in domestic affairs; but the yearnings encouraged through the extension of commercial broadcasting are a matter of the free movement of ideas and goods. The programming called 'American', but really global, carries the burden of advancing a particular style of life, the narrative of modernity. It may be the cheapest, most effective way of carrying out the implicit motivations of what might be called the Kapuściński theorem. In terms of promulgating and advancing attitudes towards modernity, Western governments believe themselves better off proposing advanced technology and a free market for ideas than establishing elaborate propaganda machines. Private advocacy, cheaper from the taxpayer's standpoint, produces an odd message. Michael Schudson, the scholar of advertising, has, with irony, compared what he has called 'capitalist realism' to its socialist counterpart. The argument is that 'advertising [particularly] is part of the establishment and reflection of a common symbolic culture'.[36] Advertising 'tends to promote attitudes and lifestyles which extol acquisition and consumption at the expense of other values'. Schudson abstracts five principles that animated socialist realist art as a basis for comparing the organizing principles of American advertising:

1. Art should picture reality in simplified and typified ways so that it communicates effectively to the masses.
2. Art should picture life, but not as it is so much as life as it should become, life worth emulating.
3. Art should picture reality not in its individuality but only as it reveals larger social significance.
4. Art should picture reality as progress toward the future and so represent social struggles positively. It should carry an air of optimism.
5. Art should focus on contemporary life, creating pleasing images of new social phenomena, revealing and endorsing new features of society and thus aiding the masses in assimilating them.[37]

Advertising incorporates a set of aesthetic conventions linked to the political economy whose values they celebrate and promote.[38]

Of course, while there is a superficial resemblance between the strategies of the socialist realism of the past and 'capitalist realism', the differences are vital, and they should be mentioned even before the similarities. Stalin's socialist realism was not only government controlled, but it was a monopoly with a vengeance. Deviation from the line was punishable, not with demotion to an inferior ad agency, but with Siberia or worse. Though there is little about 'capitalist realism' that is official and state sponsored, the very structural choices about broadcasting have a subtext of public sanction. It is not the news alone that carries the messages that affect the market for loyalties. It is MTV, advertisements for beer, and the soap operas that influence the political imagination of the millions.[39]

Part Three

American Identities: Imagery and the State

8 The Search for the Public Interest

I have focused on the transitions in Central and Eastern Europe and the former Soviet Union because there has been, in them, a visible, often painful, coping with the problems of harmonizing national-identity concerns with democratic values. In addition, in these states, the process of building patterns of citizen participation has allowed examination of the role of law in constituting a public sphere. Though it is difficult to recognize, the United States, like these states, is a transition society. Revolutions in communications technologies, sea changes in the role of government, upheavals in the structure of the broadcast industry—all these are characteristic of the American setting. True, the context is extraordinarily different from that of Central and Eastern Europe, but in the United States, as well, these changes produce their own crises in the operation of the democratic process.

As a consequence, it is fruitful to examine, in connection with the regulation of television, the development of national-identity and public-sphere questions in the United States. The task is difficult because the ideas themselves have not been explicitly cited and discussed in judicial opinions in the United States. More important, the Bill of Rights mandates that 'Congress shall make no law abridging freedom of speech, or of the press'. What the Bill of Rights means by 'no law', whether there are speech limitations that do not constitute 'abridgments', and whether the prohibition affects 'speech' and the 'press' equally are all questions that have been so meticulously and thoroughly canvassed that I shall only obliquely try to explicate them.[1]

The core of First Amendment doctrine has been a clamp (if not a prohibition) on government involvement in areas of identity and discourse. The United States has argued the most limited view of government power over speech, in any form, in international forums and pressed these views upon newly democratic or post-totalitarian societies. An expansive first amendment view is on the ascendancy in US courts, fuelled by the cable television and telephone industries, manufacturers of tobacco, and purveyors of home-shopping programmes.[2] The First Amendment is a banner which rises over a great and important trade in films, television programmes, musical performances, and other aspects of intellectual property. The First Amendment has not, however, prevented Congress from launching efforts, proudly and openly, to use radio and television to mould loyalties elsewhere in the world.

And the First Amendment has tolerated a statute, the Communications Act of 1934, which has required licensed broadcasters to serve 'the public interest, convenience and necessity'.[3] Summarized as the 'public-interest' standard, interpretation and administration of this statute have indirectly and clumsily encapsulated the concerns at the heart of this book. The public-interest test is not, nor was it designed to be, a perfect surrogate for continental doctrines. It has, however, been used to shape America's market for loyalties and improve the operation of the public sphere. The content of the public-interest test and its justification reverberate interestingly against transitional travails. Its relationship to the First Amendment, its justification in scarcity, the use of a common resource of the air waves, and the impact of broadcasting on society are also important for comparative debates.[4] In examining the history and use of the public-interest doctrine—and its disappearance—commonalities between the US and world experience will be evident.

The Impact of Broadcasting

In the waning days of 1992, John J. O'Connor, the long-time television critic for the *New York Times*, uttered the periodic wail of those who, for a living, must watch too much US television. Unlike the situation elsewhere in the world, O'Connor lamented, there is an assumption 'ingrained in the history of American broadcasting, that television is merely another business. . . . Shortsightedness is rampant, along with an inability even to consider that concepts like culture and the national heritage might be too important to hinge almost entirely on corporate interests.' In Japan, O'Connor could report, NHK, the national broadcaster, was wholly committed to a strong public-service broadcasting system. In the United Kingdom, the BBC had just issued a report that recognized that 'Broadcasting is at the heart of British society. The structure and composition of the broadcasting industry, the purpose and motivation of broadcasters, and the programmes and services that they offer are vital factors in reflecting and shaping that society.' The BBC would continue a 'commitment to reflect and nurture the UK's rich cultural heritage . . . fostering and nurturing the national talents, originating and commissioning new works and developing excellence in the arts'. O'Connor called for 'an apparatus to evaluate and oversee the functions and responsibilities of television as the 21st century looms . . . Pollution of the physical environment has become, despite formidable naysaying, a serious public concern. So, by all means, should pollution of the mind and the spirit.'[5]

O'Connor was far from alone in his plea. On both the left and the right, massive complaints have long been voiced at the impact of broadcasting on society. Church groups, parents organizations, representatives of ethnic minorities, Republicans, Democrats—all have expressed serious concern. Around the same time as O'Connor's lament, David Bollier, a public-interest media critic, wrote a despondent essay on the wasteland of the previous decade: the United States had become home to amazing new technologies—networks proliferating, the promise of renewed competition from telephone companies, startling developments in interactive video. A unified vision was not to be found. Social architects who had tried, in past decades, to influence the Federal Communications Commission and the Congress were in almost full retreat. 'The market-place' was increasingly the answer to every question; and shapers of the new market-place would be cable-system operators, programmers, broadcasters, telephone carriers, newspaper groups, and on-line information services. Though these market-place changes 'will have profound consequences for American democracy and culture for decades to come', Bollier suggested, 'disturbingly, there is virtually no concerted effort to articulate a set of public interest priorities for this new medium'.

These evocations of a golden age and restoration of a greater role for organized society in its self-definition are poignant in a time of increased globalization. They may be based on an incomplete and faulty diagnosis, an inadequate sense of the radical changes presented by the situation. Not doctrine alone, but also the changes in technology itself, seem to render it far more difficult than ever for government to play a strong role in influencing output—all the more reason why the relationship of broadcasting to society must be rethought. The impacts of broadcasting on identity and democracy continue to be important, though the ancient ways of thinking about these impacts are less availing.

Government as impetus for excellence has been a persistent but frustrated theme over the almost half-century of broadcast television. Now, however, the call for action—like O'Connor's—comes at a time when a new generation of distributors functions freer of intervention and when viewers have their hands on the remote control. Technology seems to be making a mockery of the very idea of a central agency harnessing television for the public good. Old state as well as private monopolies face new competition; state licences no longer owe their value to their status as the exclusive way to broadcast. Public control of gatekeepers is diminishing, as technology promises unhindered, almost unfiltered personal access to information. This freedom, so abundant in the United States, is the essence of future patterns, and with it comes the reduction or elimination of the impact of the state on the content of television.

In the transitional societies of the post-Cold War era involved in defining a post-Soviet identity, it is hardly surprising that debates over the future of television reflect a preoccupation with national identity. But we have seen how difficult it is, in a globalizing world, for any nation to maintain control over imagery, even if doing so were consistent with democratic values; the new technologies have the capacity radically to alter the way in which speech, information, and political discourse occur in the society. When these technologies are combined with a deep and rigorous free-speech tradition limiting the role of government, then the nature of potential visions is quite limited. The excitement about new technologies, of course, has been exuberant. But, given the reluctance formally to engage the government directly in aspects of content—in matters of national identity and democratic discourse—there has been a reserved, almost stilted quality to official discussion. What is little understood is how these changes may work and how they affect or ought to affect the power of society to respond to the operation of the new speech market-place.

The persistence of ties between broadcasting policies and community coherence, throughout the world, renders suspect the separation attributed to formal US doctrine. Too much is at stake, as the architecture of the new electronic age is established, to leave old premisses unquestioned. Even in the United States, governmental intervention has had its play, and the rhetoric of non-involvement, the formal doctrine, has a quality of denial. Important principles underlying free speech become manipulated and distorted as they are reoriented in a world far from their eighteenth-century origins. Nostalgia for cohesion arises as society evaluates such disparate public concerns as the impact of a monopoly structure of cable television, the survival of over-the-air broadcasting, the future of news and sports, the nature of political campaigning, the pressure on education in an electronic age, and the long-term justification for public broadcasting. If the infrastructure of citizenship is being rebuilt, not only in broadcasting but throughout the domain of communications policy, important questions concerning the design and function of that infrastructure must be discussed. Invoking the First Amendment as a barrier to the examination of these aspects of cohesion and community is popular, but not necessarily true to its history.

There are basic distinctions in the US experience that differentiate it from the European agenda of encouraging cohesion. These distinctions are deep in a unique and triumphant American free-speech tradition. Born in mild rebellion, at a time of rising rationalism and individuality, the function of the central government was, from the beginning, different from that of its European counterparts. The idea of limitations, not powers, was at the heart of the founding vision, so that the articulation of denial, an injunction against the *abridgement* of freedom of speech, shaped the constitutional definition of the role of Congress in relation to free speech. A nineteenth-century frontier mentality, still flaunted and generative of the American character, has always, at its heart, been anti-government, and, often, healthily so. Gritty independence, in action as well as speech, had been one of the key elements of national identity. In the twentieth century, the continental United States has not suffered the debilitating wounds of bombardment, actual invasion, and occupation, either physically or culturally. Great spaces, protected by the insular nature of the continent, and a long period of seeming single-language unity contribute to a history in which this comfortable dominant narrative of national identity, rarely challenged, persists. Unlike those of its European counterparts, the borders of the United States were buffered, and its lands stood contiguous to seemingly non-aggressive cultural influences. Furthermore, and distinctly so, the American experience, cunning, hegemonic, or fortunate, was of a long-term, now-ending isomorphic relationship between prevailing language and space. There was less of a perceived need, during the development of broadcasting, for the state to intervene and mediate among contending cultures.

Interpreting Free Speech

Beneath the calm of a set of accepted stories, the national identity has always been subject to dispute, from contested colonial settlement, to sharp sectional disparities, through the Civil War, through the rise and decline of cities to the current contests over race and gender and language. Broadcasting, in the twentieth century, long provided an envelope of seeming homogeneity, helping to produce and reinforce a national identity of domestic security and economic growth. But now, as history is told and retold, a more explicit struggle to redefine American national identity, to determine how plural it should be, seems keenly obvious. Any formulation of national identity carries within it the consequences of competition for power; it is no accident, then, that the contest for the regulation of images in American society arouses great passion.[6]

The major difference for the United States may be its place in the graph of maturation of a speech and broadcasting commonwealth, not necessarily the shape of the curve. The United States has been a broadcasting pioneer, with an intensive and pervasive television service which grew in soil so remarkably nourishing that the vector of changes that we now see elsewhere took place in the United States earlier and much faster. The process of 'regionalization' that is the hope of the Broadcasting Directive in Europe, trying, there, to establish a 'cultural space', was realized, or so it has been thought, in the United States, with the emergence of the nation constituting the triumph of the integrating whole over the identity of its parts. The United States could be viewed as the first flowering, internally, of a globalizing tendency, a test run for some of the technological consequences now felt throughout the world. An institutional history of broadcasting in the United States, one that traced its national and international dimensions, would emphasize the development of the radio chains or networks that crossed local American cultures, that exploited the trappings of localism but established a relevant market that eventually encompassed the vast and disparate regions of the land. The United States constitutes the first place with a mass population subject to the thing called American television. The oft-told story may be too simple: the story in which 'American television' is the aggressor, becoming global, engulfing the rest of the world with the United States as the subject, not the object of cultural change. Broadcasting for the United States, itself, can be reinterpreted as a dress rehearsal for globalization, altering identities here first. As the comedian Jay Leno joked in the inauguration of NBC's Superchannel, 'We're going to ruin your culture just like we ruined our own.'

To understand US practices afresh, not so bound by existing premisses, is to see that many of the difficulties that plague the relationship between state and imagery abroad confront American culture as well. Much of the history of broadcast regulation can be read as an effort to broker the impact of radio and television, though often in ways so subdued as to disguise the task. What is at stake is a mild counter-history of the American free-speech tradition. The tendency is to neglect the larger practice of government in its relationship to speech and public debate. It is often said that the very existence of the First Amendment sharply distinguishes the United States from other Western democracies as well as totalitarian societies.[7] In the United States, the written constitution precludes Congress—and by extension all government officials—from abridging freedom of speech and the press. The text of the First Amendment, however, has been mediated and interpreted in ways of varying strictness through successive eras of the nation's history.

At almost the original moment of its creation, the First Amendment did not prevent the US Congress from enacting the Sedition Act of 1798, which prohibited 'False, scandalous, and malicious writing against the government of the United States, or either house of the Congress of the United States, or the President of the United States', a rule that would now be thought unsupportable, more characteristic of a maladroit transition society than a Western power.[8] Since the meaning of the Amendment turns on interpretation and patterns of enforcement, a similar vigilance against government interference could exist in a parliamentary system, like that of the United Kingdom, where the clear words of a written constitution are not present. With the establishment of the European Convention on Human Rights, enforced by the Court of Human Rights in Strasburg, another distinction between Europe and the United States dissolves, for both have a tradition of judicial review against inscribed words from a written constitution, of executive and legislative acts.[9]

If it is not *the constitution* that is the difference, then it is the constitutional tradition. The extended free-press tradition separates the US case from many others. But the tradition contains strong protectionist elements, strong indications of a government concerned with affirming positive attitudes towards the state and suppressing those adverse to a particular perception of national identity. It is also true that the relationship of media to government in the United States is unique because broadcasting enterprises, like newspapers, are virtually all—even those devoted to non-commercial purposes—held privately. Undoubtedly, this ownership factor has been important, not least because it has meant a continuing and well-established lobbying force against a government role.

Given the predictable concern with the impact of imagery on the course of society, expressions of national officials—including Supreme Court Justices, Commissioners of the Federal Communications Commission, and Members of Congress—are a source for insight into the government role. It is within these statements that the concept of 'the public interest' was articulated. Decisions concerning frequency allocation, limitations on foreign ownership, moral qualifications for licences have furnished ample opportunity for discussion of the larger questions of identity, democracy, and communications policy. These have been augmented by endless debates on violence, indecency, and other aspects of the public-interest standard. In comparative hearings where the Federal Communications Commission (FCC) had power to select among competing claimants for a broadcasting frequency, standards had to be employed that would reflect underlying values.

For the most part, the rhetoric of US broadcasting decisions leaves very little space for explicit sanction of the tools for shaping national identity, such as the affirmative use of language, or the imposition of standards relating to national culture, cohesion, aspiration. Fragments of legislative history, such as the discussion surrounding the introduction of radio licensing and regulation, provide insight into some early idea of future function. For some visionaries, radio was conceived not as a mere medium of entertainment, not even as a linear extension of the newspaper, but as something wholly new, a major mechanism for improving the nature of American democracy. The language of the public sphere entered into the notion of public air waves and public trust.

In 1924 Herbert Hoover urged Congress that no single person or group should 'ever have the right to determine what communication may be made to the American people', and that radio is 'a public concern impressed with the public trust and to be considered primarily from the standpoint of public interest to the same extent and upon the basis of the same general principles as our other public utilities'.[10] The idea of the public utility is one of universal service, non-discriminatory rates, evenness of access. A utility assures fair distribution of a scarce commodity as an element of a democratic society. Here, the scarce commodity is not spectrum, but rather information and culture; its supply should not be controlled in ways that might be abusive, and access to it should be rendered in ways that are just. To say that radio is 'a public concern impressed with the public trust' is to have, as it were, the shell of the public sphere with some premonition of its content. And the idea that radio is not to be considered as 'merely a business carried on for private gain' provides some negative suggestion as to what the content should be. Much of the early rhetoric—by Herbert Hoover and through the enactment of the 1927 Radio Act—reflected a patrician sense of national purpose and national propriety. Hoover's idea of duty was a legacy of the great nineteenth-century idea of the gospel of wealth, the responsibility of the fortunate for those who were less so. In Hoover's mind's eye, occupying a licence for a radio station might be thought to be not much different from being on the board of the Metropolitan Museum of Art.

A member of Congress stated what were, even then, in the early days of radio regulation, general fears:

> There is no agency so fraught with possibilities for service of good or evil to the American people as the radio . . . The power of the press will not be comparable to that of broadcasting stations when the industry is fully developed. . . . it will only be a few years before these broadcasting stations, if operated by chain stations, will simultaneously . . . bring messages to the fireside of nearly every home in America. They can mold and crystallize sentiment as no agency in the past has been able to do. If the strong arm of the law does not prevent monopoly ownership and make discrimination by such stations illegal, American thought and politics will be largely at the mercy of those who operate these stations.[11]

Here, too, are intimations of the threats to the public sphere, not only in the anti-monopoly sentiment, but in the way in which radio is differentiated from the 'press' in terms of its impact on the political system. These were astute politicians; they could recognize, even at this moment of beginnings, that the nature of political debate could be altered without conscious impact on the social organization and management of radio. In the 1926 debates concerning the 1927 Radio Act, Congressman White stated:

> the right of all our people to enjoy this means of communication can be preserved only by . . . the doctrine that the right of the public to service is

superior to the right of any individual to use the ether. . . . The recent radio conference . . . recognized that . . . licenses should be issued only to those stations whose operation would render a benefit to the public. . . . If enacted into law, the broadcasting privilege will not be a right of selfishness. It will rest upon an assurance of public interest to be served.[12]

For him and his colleagues, it was the power of radio, not just the scarcity of spectrum,[13] that motivated concern for the new technology's relationship to American democracy. The right of an individual to use the ether was a privileged access to a kind of public magic, conferred upon condition. The ether was a resource in which selfishness alone would not be sufficient.[14]

The Regulatory Tradition

These quotations are samples that could be endlessly duplicated.[15] They reflect early recognition of a place of public discourse. The vagueness and generality cover a persistent problem, an inability to find and implement a useful expression of an operative public interest. Maintaining radio in public hands or placing it in the vessel of a public corporation, as in the United Kingdom, would have provided an approach less laden with ambiguity and doubt. The determination that radio (and then television) licences should be privately held has meant the imposition of unclear conditions, unclearly stated in pursuit of difficult objectives, and therefore harder to achieve. To say that a licence is granted in the public interest is hardly enough to guide a licensee who is inclined to employ the licence for the greatest personal benefit. So a machinery of definition and enforcement is necessary, and it is there (and in the courts interpreting legislation and administrative action) that the lack of clarity and confusion in the notion of public interest is manifest.

The judicial tone was set in one of the first modern cases—*NBC* v. *FCC*—a 1943 case involving possible restrictions on the power of the great radio chains to control programming on local outlets. While Frankfurter J., writing for the Court, upheld the rules of the FCC restricting the behaviour of these emerging networks, he was not expansive in describing the government's power. Frankfurter recognized that, given the scarcity of the air waves, government could not constitutionally be confined merely to the function of traffic officer and could exercise judgement in allocating their use. The duty to provide 'the best practicable service to the communities', to 'realize the vast potentialities', 'to provide maximum benefits' is a cautious opening for the government role in shaping the media, or affecting the media's shaping of the society. Furthermore, in that early case, Murphy J., another New Deal Justice who ordinarily supported government power, used words that more clearly predicted the future attitude of the Court. He issued a chilling warning.

Because of its vast potentialities as a medium of communication, discussion and propaganda, the character and extent of control that should be exercised over it by the government is a matter of deep and vital concern. Events in Europe show that radio may readily be a weapon of authority and misrepresentation, instead of a means of entertainment and enlightenment. It may even be an instrument of oppression.[16]

Over the next quarter century, the FCC developed a fitful social meaning of the 'public-interest' standard. This laborious, inconsistent work was a product of interactions between the Commission, the industry it regulated, Congress, the courts, and the White House. In 1946 the Commission published a book entitled *Public Service Responsibilities of Broadcast Licensees*, which established a series of performance goals for licensees (then radio). How well licensees performed would be considered at the time their licences were up for renewal. The Blue Book, as the document was called, urged (too soft a word given the power to deny a licensee's extension) broadcasters to serve as a vehicle for creative expression in their local communities by carrying live programmes. Some obligation existed to mount discussion of public issues and 'sustaining' programming, the predecessor of educational or non-commercial efforts. Amending the Blue Book, and using the public-interest standard, the FCC fashioned the fairness doctrine which I discuss in Chapter 10,[17] and in doing so used language hauntingly similar to the notion of the public sphere.[18] In its 1949 Report on Editorializing, the Commission said:

One of the most vital questions of mass communication in a democracy is the development of an informed public opinion through the dissemination of news and ideas concerning the vital public issues of the day. . . . we have recognized . . . the paramount right of the public in a free society to be informed and to have presented to it for acceptance or rejection the different attitudes and viewpoints concerning these vital and often controversial issues . . . It is the right of the public to be informed, rather than any right on the part of Government, any broadcast licensee or any individual member of the public to broadcast his own particular views on any matter, which is the foundation stone of the American system of broadcasting.[19]

The standard does not provide an assurance of equal access to the zone of opinion-making, or guarantee the quality of public debate, but the emphasis suggests the right of the public *qua* public. It is also a reference to a public in a general sense of the term: the 1949 statement deliberately excludes the notion that the 'foundation-stone' right is the opportunity of any particular individual to have views expressed. The conception is of a public, separated from the government, separated from specific persons, that has the right of expression. As early as 1941 the FCC argued that radio would serve as an 'instrument of democracy' only if the air waves were not used to support candidacies in a discriminatory way, only if radio was a locus for the fair and objective exchange of ideas. A licensee could not devote the space to 'principles he happens to regard most favorably'. The broadcaster was not to be an advocate.[20]

In 1960 the Commission issued a Report which emphasized that licensees must engage in 'a diligent, positive and continuing effort . . . to discover and fulfill the tastes and desires' of viewers in their communities. The Commission listed fourteen programming elements that constituted the public interest.[21] And, in rulings that provided a specific role for the public to influence the very content of information programming, the Commission obliged licensees to 'ascertain' the needs of their community. Broadcasters had to identify the leaders in the community, interview them, and keep a record of their articulated preferences. The rules did not force broadcasters to abide by these ascertained conclusions; the process of being involved with the community was as far as a government agency could go in bringing the public into the tent of decision-making.[22] Under FCC obligations, broadcasters did have a duty affirmatively to cover local news and provide opportunities for independent producers by setting aside time, during the prime time for audiences, that could not be used by networks.

Of course, words may serve as a disguise. Perhaps these speeches at the creation and through the construction of the Fairness Doctrine build a model of discourse based upon illusion: a false image of the United States as a congregation of local communities, of those communities searching for outlets for a local voice, of a continued need to bind the communities through local news. It was an imaginary world in which one could define the controversial issues of public importance and treat them fairly by showing all (usually both) sides. Local station, local management, a duty to serve the public interest and to ascertain local needs—together, these were the focal point, a modern cracker barrel. The illusion may have been adopted from a variety of motives, conscious and unconscious: to enable officials to distribute new radio channels as rewards for local political contributors; to maintain local sources of political support for Congressional candidates; to hamper new radio entrepreneurs in their competition with existing enterprises (the established printed press), or to crystallize a nostalgic and invented set of eighteenth-century democratic practices seen as quickly passing. At a time of growing newspaper chains and powerful publishers with the capacity to affect the views of urban masses, the radio could be a restorative, a recreator of the golden past.

For the first several decades, administration of the Communications Act followed a traditional US model of assuming that competitors in the commercial market-place would bring to the public forum a panoply of the questions that needed to be decided. It was disappointed applicants for radio, and then television, licences that raised issues about the appropriate standards for public service. In theory, competition among applicants would lead to the best proposals offering public service and the FCC would be the keeper of the public conscience, the representative of the citizen. This theory was sharply challenged; despite some heroic efforts, the FCC was deemed, like most regulatory agencies, to be 'captured' by the industry it supervised.[23] Only later—during the 1960s and 1970s—was there a public interest movement, a touch of reform, a citizen effort to enforce the public-interest standard.

This movement, which still flutteringly persists, had, as its primary goal, gaining a place for the ordinary citizen at the table where decisions were made, whether in the courts, the FCC, Congress, or the corporate headquarters. Through that access, citizens could employ whatever leverage they could legitimately find to try to make the stations operate more closely to the hope or promise of the public interest. The concept of who could protest, who would have the right to oppose or affect government action—a legal doctrine called 'standing'—was the hinge for change and another indicator of a quiet public sphere. As a result of the work of the public-interest movement, ordinary individuals or groups were allowed to go before the FCC and articulate some independent public view and seek to impose it on the agency and to take an appeal to court.[24]

One of the most important victories of the public-interest movement came in a case—*United Church of Christ*[25]—premised on improving the capacity of the citizenry to be informed and act upon that information. A television station in Jackson, Mississippi, in violation of the Fairness Doctrine, determined, at the height of the civil-rights movement, that it would favour programmes advocating the preservation of racial segregation. When national news reports showed civil-rights leaders in a favourable light, the station would put a card on the screen saying that weather, or circumstances beyond its control, interfered with the delivery of the national signal. The Citizens Communications Center argued that the station, a supposed instrument of discourse on the key issues facing the public, was in fact blocking discourse. The court found that representatives of the listening public did have standing to challenge the renewal of the licence.

The public-interest agenda was aimed, case by case, at improving the operation of broadcasting by having greater coverage of controversial issues, increased fairness, greater and better reflection of minority communities, and greater competition among networks through more channels of information. Pragmatic in an American sense, any radical rethinking of communications in society was only implicit, with faint intimations of a public sphere or notions of national identity. The model of the great broadcasters, a top-down model, feeding news, information, and political discourse to a mass audience, remained at the heart of the enterprise, to be improved but not displaced until the prospect of cable and other new technologies emerged.

The new technologies were embraced with the hope that they would alter the mix, particularly through the abundance of channels and the new possibilities of interactivity.[26] Early debates over cable contained the promise that the public could create a zone for discourse, using a different technological universe for a redefinition of the role of the citizen and the nature of the forum.[27] Cable proclaimed the opportunity to undercut old forms of regulation: suddenly, there could be room for all points of view, for labour and management, for many political parties, for the dissenter as well as those in the main stream. A new term was invented—narrowcasting—to describe the prospect of intensive, special-interest-group, constituency-building channels.

A critical moment for any reinterpretation of the public-interest standard, and its intersection with the free-speech tradition, was the so-called 'seven dirty words' or *Pacifica* case,[28] in which John Paul Stevens J. justified FCC regulation of indecency (pursuant to Congressional authorization), not on the ground of scarcity, but because of the unusual and pervasive impact of radio in the lives of America's children. 'Patently offensive, indecent material presented over the airwaves confronts the citizen, not only in public, but also in the privacy of the home, where the individual's right to be left alone plainly outweighs the First Amendment rights of an intruder.'[29]

The *Pacifica* case was roundly denounced and considered an exception from the ordinary course of First Amendment jurisprudence. Critics argued that speech should not be subject to regulation merely because it is more effective. *Pacifica*, however, became the possible narrow point of origin for justifying and acting on the actual effect of broadcasting. Stevens J. transformed consideration of radio from a free-speech issue alone to a public-health question as well. It echoed, strangely, an early decision in which the Commission had denied a licence renewal to a church minister who had continuously defamed government institutions and viciously attacked labour and various religions. Dr Shuler (the minister involved) could, the affirming court said, freely criticize religious practices, and privately engage in malice or slander, 'but he may not, as we think, demand, of right, the continued use of an instrumentality of commerce for such purposes'.[30]

A political, technological, and rhetorical shift in the late 1970s totally undermined the public-interest movement. Steadily, starting with the Carter Administration and continuing through the Reagan period and beyond, the FCC saw deregulation—the very abandonment of previous rules—as the substance of the public trust. The Supreme Court seemed constantly on the verge of retreating from its high point of support, expressed in a decision holding that the Fairness Doctrine was constitutional. The legal and constitutional shift matched the technological: because of the rapid expansion of cable television and the prospect of channels of abundance, the end of scarcity as a justification for government intervention was disappearing. The economic metaphor of the market-place gained immense power, such power that the former construct (ascertainment, content requirements, and fairness) virtually became an object of ridicule.

The rules struck down or diminished had hardly been a model of the public sphere. The Commission had established principles that were often meaningless and harassing, and enforcement was haphazard. The new Commission saw in the Fairness Doctrine an annoying federal intervention in the life of the newsroom, unconstitutional at best and without redeeming social purpose. The new goal was to take action to eliminate scarcity once and for all, increasing the number of broadcast outlets, populating the market-place with more 'speakers'. If scarcity of spectrum was the only justification for government intervention, government could eliminate its role by encouraging a flood of new modes and opportunities for expression.[31]

By the 1970s a rapidly changing technology was affecting the strategies of those who sought to obtain a greater mix of voices, more of a public sphere. Access in terms of cable television became the source of a complex set of new and superficially radical ideas. These included compelling cable operators to carry specific channels for government and educational entities and to carry the services of local broadcasters. But, most remarkably, there was federal sanction for a brand new idea: a 'public-access channel' available on a first-come, first-served basis. The cable operator would be required to provide equipment and training so that public-access users, discussed in Chapter 10, would have the technical capacity to air their views or present their talent on cable.

Such minor innovations as the public-access channel aside, the notion of 'public interest' has become so tied to the idea of market economics that it has lost almost all independent meaning. The outstanding example of this depletion involved a Congressional charge to the FCC, in 1992, to redetermine whether so-called 'home-shopping' channels, channels that were predominantly commercial or used for the sale of products, met the 'public-interest' standard. Home-shopping channels had become the darling of the moment in the 1980s. On the screen, diamond-cut ten-carat gold necklaces were dangled before the eyes of millions of insomniacs and stay-at-homes, who initiated a small revolution in shopping patterns. Lineal descendant of the early fruit-and-vegetable slicing and grinding machines of the grainy black-and-white era, the new high-tech interconnected networks of desire sold billions of dollars worth of goods.

In the complex interplay between the regulation of broadcasting and the regulation of cable, Congress had tentatively determined to require that these channels be carried by the new technology. But the Congressional inquiry represented a doubt as to the soundness of this decision, in terms of the history of the public-interest standard. Could cable operators—already complaining about the constitutional problems implicit in forcing them to carry many broadcasters—be required to use a valuable slot for these dominantly commercial entities? The FCC gathered comments on questions that, in some ways, went to the heart of the issue of the public sphere. The agency construed the question as asking whether the fact that people, in large numbers, were watching these channels was sufficient to meet a public-interest test. It was difficult to fathom that the standard had sunk so low as to encompass programme-length commercials vaunting teeth-whiteners or twenty shades of lipstick or stick-proof pans with the merest figleaf of programme obligations. But now the rhetoric had changed. Where was it inscribed that *any* part of the broadcast day had to be given over to news and information or involvement in the matters of public controversy? The home-shopping inquiry demonstrated the end of the debate.

An FCC that a couple of decades before had found that over-commercialization—measured in minutes of commercials per hour—was inconsistent with the statutory standard now determined that current home-shopping channels, with upwards of 90 per cent commercial content per hour, met the licensees' obligation.[32] If people watched, that meant that a need was being met; the vision of the country contained in the 'public-interest' standard now hinged on the quantitative, not on an independent vision of the relationship between programming and the common good.

With a disappearing tradition of 'public interest', and no reservoir that could hold some sense of the relationship between television and national identity, the development of rationales and justifications for dealing with important questions affecting the society would become more difficult. Specific concerns—the improvement of children's television, the reduction of violence on television, representation of race or gender—serve as weak and misleading surrogates in the absence of an articulated, more enveloping ethic.[33] The consequence could be a crisis of social consciousness. In the absence of a general theory, one that has an acknowledged and acceptable role for mediating community interests, greater threats to the freedom of speech can arise. The language and methods of the age of broadcast television will not work in the age of new technologies. But that does not mean that the underlying problems of identity and participation have vanished.

Private Enforcers

The disappearance of the public-interest standard has not necessarily meant that the instruments of power can no longer be used to affect the structure of the market for loyalties in the United States. True, the First Amendment makes it difficult for those who try to bring a substantive vision of society to the electronic media if they wish to ingrain those values through the specific orders of a federal agency. The demise of the public-interest standard conceals how changed doctrine has merely pushed interest groups into different strategies for shaping national identity. The ideological battle for control of narrative that was a feature of war and honed in the McCarthy period continues, though the substance of that battle for control is more varied.

Set aside those clear government-mediated actions that have had important consequences for the narrative: the decision (notwithstanding the Establishment Clause) to grant religious organizations their own channels to proclaim, proselytize, and evangelize; the long war between the networks and the local stations, which can be reread as a struggle for alternative national identities, one based in Hollywood and New York and one that is somewhat more plural, less predictable and idiosyncratic; or President Richard Nixon's decision to immobilize public broadcasting, to force it to decentralize, a decision which arose out of an expressed conviction (one that ascends again) that it was in the hands of forces creating allegiances hostile to more conservative values. What has occurred since the 1970s—almost coincidental with the *laissez-faire* approach of the FCC—has been a guerrilla warfare approach to establishing national identities through television narratives.

Increasingly well-organized private groups, each with their own agenda, have established outposts in Hollywood, with the aim of influencing the content of programming, and using, or threatening to use, contacts with government if their objectives were not reached. Kathryn Montgomery has been the historian of this movement, attributing the expansion of tough and organized advocacy to television's power as 'the central storyteller for the culture'. Her survey of the activities of such groups as the Population Institute, the Solar Lobby, the Anti-Defamation League, Justicia, and others concluded that their lobbying efforts were recognition that 'fiction programming, even more than news and public affairs . . . most effectively embodies and reinforces the dominant values in American society'.[34] Or, as George Gerbner, communications scholar, drawing from Scottish patriot Andrew Fletcher, has concluded: 'If you can write a nation's stories, you needn't worry about who makes its laws.'[35]

The examples are legion. In a hundred newspapers across the United States, in early January 1992, a full-page advertisement, placed by the American Family Association (Reverend Donald Wildmon, Director), announced a new pressure campaign. The target would be members of the boards of entertainment companies.

> The reason for all the sex, violence, filth and profanity [said the broadsheet], is with the writers, directors, producers, singers, actors, etc. But they can be controlled. All it takes is for the Boards of Directors of their companies to order them to stop. Remember when movies were wholesome family entertainment? That's when people at the top set standards and enforced them. We're going to insist that happen again.

Wildmon was from the frequently vilified Christian Right, but he was far from alone and by no means a pioneer.[36]

The dozens of interest groups seeking to pressure the writers and producers whose stories now are global are part of a modern version of the public sphere. Using whatever leverage they can, through pressure on advertisers, on corporate boards, on Vice-Presidents and Members of Congress, these associational representatives establish an agenda for public discussion and help to determine the limits on the nature of the ensuing debate.[37] From all sides of the political spectrum, they are concerned with the handling of environmental issues, the depiction of gays and lesbians, the construction of narratives concerning race, the representation of Jews and Catholics, and the stories that affect the agenda of the Christian Right. They engage in the process of jawboning and friendly persuasion, often using links of friendship and peer pressure. So effective have these advocacy groups been that, by the 1990s, it had become the practice, where sensitive questions were raised, for producers to vet scripts and gain input from the relevant organizations before a progamme was even placed before the camera.[38]

Even when these efforts are collegial and not explicitly coercive, important ethical distinctions can be made. Alan Dershowitz has argued that 'it is more appropriate to boycott an advertiser who plays an active role in determining content than one who plays no role'.[39] Another analyst of the constitutionality of boycotts has suggested—without irony—that lines can be drawn between boycotts and advertising influences on behalf of conservative and anti-violence groups and boycotts and influences of behalf of 'social-activist and status-based interest groups'. The first group, in his view, restrict the public's viewing options (bringing pressure on producers to reject certain themes), while the second, concerned with lack of visibility for their views, wish greater access or 'increased speech and debate'.[40] Some groups have more favourable access to writers and producers than others, a consequence of wealth or ideology, or the familiar network of neighbourhood and club. Other groups imply not only the threat of consumer boycotts, but the intervention of the state (Congress or the courts). It is difficult to conceptualize an arena of passionate articulation of ideas by advocacy groups in which advantages of wealth or access to power are not invoked.

Deregulation and the Public Interest

In the era of deregulation, in a time when government plays less of a regulatory role, a newer form of the market for loyalties thus emerges, reliant on a new set of powers and constraints, more ephemeral, less visible, less subject to the old forms of analysis. Government pressure to change television's stories takes the shape of the bully pulpit, not the censorial stick. George Bush's Vice-President, Dan Quayle, and Bill Clinton's Secretary of Health and Human Services, Donna Shalala, can both descry the television character, Murphy Brown, for the too-romanticized depiction of single parenthood out of wedlock. Congress votes networks immunity so that it can negotiate an agreement to lessen violence during the hours of family viewing. The strengthening of community, the shaping of national identity, turn, increasingly, on subsidy, tax policy, private actions combined with public influence, the shaping of educational curricula, and the stocking of the libraries that provide the texts of everyday life. Television is part of a far wider context—beyond broadcasting as the major influence on civility—to include other sources of imagery, such as museums, the National Endowment for the Humanities and the National Endowment of the Arts, the daily struggle over words in the commercial production of modernity. How images are produced, regulated, censored, and approved involves an even more complex interplay between public pressure, government influence, and private action.

In some broad definition, every articulation, every movement, every human effort is a form of communication akin to speech, and there will always be constructions of the social fabric that make some images and some words objectionable to the point of sanction. Governmental appetite to shape national identity is universal, as is the similar need of competing interest groups. The state, even in a democratic society, even in the United States, necessarily has a positive role in reinforcing national culture and building a sense of community.[41] With the collapse of the 'public interest' as a doctrine unifying and justifying government concern for the impact of the media, it is likely that a new formula will emerge to link communication technology to those purposes of society not fully encompassed by the working of the economic market. A jurisprudence which is based on a stark contrast between censorship and free speech does not take into account the many intermediate roles that public entities play.

9 Regulating Imagery

To describe how society and the state purposely change the value and meaning of signs and signals is difficult: 'censorship' has a justifiably wicked connotation and propaganda does not suffice as a complement. A formula which claims merely that 'more speech' is an answer fits too easily into the lexicon of the First Amendment. An approach is necessary that describes more charitably the modes by which society evolves standards and establishes patterns limiting, channelling, and controlling imagery, as a matter of custom, if not of law.

If there is an acceptable approach, one that can be instructive in terms of public concern for the media, it must be found in the absence of the props of scarcity and ownership of the air waves, props no longer capable of carrying the weight of justification. In the many judicial decisions dealing with the social impact of broadcasting, only rarely have US courts had to deal directly with the power of the symbol.[1] Outside broadcasting, however, such disputes have been frequent. Images of hate have emerged in public places: swastika as graffiti and Ku-Klux-Klan crosses in urban squares. There have been decades of hard-fought ideological battles in which control over symbols became increasingly central to those seeking to maintain or achieve power. The combat zone for competing notions of the good America extended beyond the living-room. Political advertisements, as they became more compact, held the intensity and compression that mark the single stroke, the magic conjunction of words, the choice of image that alters consciousness. Vast popular movements, as an organizing principle, battled against perceived modern blasphemies, fighting what they saw as ubiquitous assaults on long-established or accepted norms. Control over language, itself, became a major preoccupation. Interest groups saw in the mass of images off and on television the capacity to reorganize public attitudes towards gender, crime, age, consumerism, and political beliefs. The censorial instinct, always strong, intensified.

In each of these areas, an old and haunting question became newly grave in the light of disarray and undercurrents of conflict in the United States: what should be the range of appropriate societal response to the brutal and sometimes inexplicable power of the image, to the use and impact of the word and picture? Approaches emerged, including the fostering of custom as a means of establishing standards, new patterns of forcing disclosure of content (labelling or rating), government reinforcement or encouragement of private regulation, and a contested jurisprudence of government as maker, patron, and preferrer of some images over others.[2] Throughout, government was implicated because advocates of particular forms of regulation (whether having to do with race, or gender, or any other aspect of a national identity) often felt a need, not only to speak, not only to persuade, but also to compel adherence. When persuasion was insufficient, they sought the power of the state to bring the force of law behind their points of view.

The Salute to the Flag

Arguments about the American flag can serve as a metaphor for the general question of state power, just as the flag often serves as a metaphor for the state. Besides, the flag, and its surrounding protections and ceremonies, have a history of litigation in the United States, including Supreme Court pronouncements, so that there exists a set of essays, including judicial essays on this particular symbol and the limitations on state power. With respect to a flag, countries (or states) have different attitudes: some leave the formation of a flag to chance and private action and some design and adopt an official flag; some respect pluralism, allowing any competing flag to fly. Sometimes, even when the general policy is tolerant, particular flags become symbols of exclusion so strong as to warrant extraordinary intervention.[3] Nations dictate how and where the flag may be flown; some, not now the United States, make it a crime to deface any flag. There is the etiquette, protocol, or law of respect: countries require that, when the flag comes into view, the citizenry take off their hats, bow, extend an arm, or place it over their heart, and there can be different rules for children and adults.[4]

In recent years, the debate, legislation, and judicial opinions in the United States have been primarily about 'desecration' and the right of citizens to express their dissent by burning, defacing, or ironically displaying the flag. Cases about flag desecration have had the most recent notoriety,[5] but they are not so relevant to the question of media and government as some of their predecessors. The desecration cases deal with the scope of private expressive speech critical of national symbols and clearly hold that, under free-speech principles, citizens have the fundamental and unabridgeable right to express a wide variety of views concerning their government.

The relevant battle over the relationship of flag to national identity arose on a now temporarily quiescent front, namely, the 'salute' cases, testing the constitutionality of state statutes compelling students to pledge allegiance to the flag. Think of the flag as one of the longest-running narratives—akin to a television show, or, better still, advertisements for ourselves—promoted by the government, aired in prime time, subsidized as a symbol of national unity. The flag-salute cases come as close as any to dealing with a compelled announcement of loyalty, the equivalent, in broadcasting, of requiring networks to carry a President's speech or forcing people to watch. The salute cases are the extension of the desecration cases: the energy and resources of the government are engaged not only in generating and protecting an idea, but in demanding acknowledgement and requiring an expression of faith and belief.

The arguments for and against the proper role of the government in commanding and promoting allegiance are nicely encapsulated in two decisions of the Supreme Court, decided in virtually opposite ways, each written by a distinguished and eloquent Justice. The first, *Gobitis*, written by Felix Frankfurter J., was a paean to unity. The second, *Barnette*, authored by Robert Jackson J., overruling *Gobitis*, is a paean to the individual, redefining the state in the light of the lessons of the Second World War and totalitarianism.

In the late 1930s Lillian Gobitis, aged 12, and her brother, William, aged 10, were expelled from a public school in Minersville, Pennsylvania, for refusing, in violation of local law, to salute the national flag. They refused on the ground that this act of faith was inconsistent with their religious scruples, as Jehovah's Witnesses. In their interpretation of the scriptures, saluting the flag was a form of bowing down to other gods. When the case reached the Supreme Court in 1940,[6] Frankfurter J. treated it as raising a question of religious freedom, not freedom of speech, and decided that the statute was constitutional. His excursion into the stuff of national identity and the role of the state is worth quoting:

The ultimate foundation of a free society is the binding tie of cohesive sentiment. Such a sentiment is fostered by all those agencies of the mind and spirit which may serve to gather up the traditions of a people, transmit them from generation to generation, and thereby create that continuity of a treasured common life which constitutes a civilization. 'We live by symbols.' The flag is the symbol of our national unity, transcending all internal differences, however large, within the framework of the Constitution.[7]

Frankfurter J. also incorporated the pledge into a general view about the relationship between education and inculcation of values: 'The wisdom of training children in patriotic impulses by those compulsions which necessarily pervade so much of the educational process is not for our independent judgment.'[8] So the point would not be missed, Frankfurter elaborated:

A society which is dedicated to the preservation of these ultimate values of civilization may in self-protection utilize the educational process for inculcating those almost unconscious feelings which bind men together in a comprehending loyalty, whatever may be their lesser differences and difficulties. That is to say, the process may be utilized so long as men's right to believe as they please, to win others to their way of belief, and their right to assemble in their chosen places of worship for the devotional ceremonies of their faith, are all fully respected.[9]

The *Gobitis* decision lasted only three years. In *Board of Education* v. *Barnette,*[10] one of the most eloquent and most quoted opinions of the Court, Robert Jackson J. revisited the question of compulsory pledges of allegiance and, with the support of a surprising majority,[11] seemed forcefully to limit the power of government. For Jackson J., this case—coming to the Court in wartime America—presented a dramatic opportunity to describe the difference between the role of government under the US Constitution and the role of government in more repressive regimes. In an early footnote, Jackson J. subtly indicted the flag salute by quoting a comparison to a loathsome counterpart: 'In the Pledge to the Flag the right arm is extended and raised, palm UPWARD, whereas the Nazis extend the arm practically *straight to the front . . . palm* DOWNWARD, and the Fascists do the same except they raise the arm slightly higher.'[12]

'The sole conflict', Jackson J. said, 'is between authority and the rights of the individual':

Any credo of nationalism is likely to include what some disapprove or to omit what others think essential, and to give off different overtones as it takes on different accents or interpretations. If official power exists to coerce acceptance of any patriotic creed, what it shall contain cannot be decided by courts, but must be largely discretionary with the ordaining authority.[13]

Jackson J. triumphed in his rhetorical onslaught on the *Gobitis* decision. For him, it was not patriotism, but close to cowardice, to compel young children to assert their faith in icons of loyalty. In oft-cited words, inspiring admiration for his rhetoric, he intoned: 'If there is any fixed star in our constitutional constellation, it is that no official, high or petty, can prescribe what shall be orthodox in politics, nationalism, religion or other matters of opinion or force citizens to confess by word or act their faith therein.'[14]

Rhetoric aside, there is something confounding and ambiguous in Jackson J.'s opinion: precisely those elements of his logic that are closest to the intersection of media, culture, and national identity. Jackson J. drew his line between compulsion and persuasion and between coercion of belief and education in seeking to ascertain the role that government could play. For him, as for Frankfurter J. (and it could not be otherwise, especially in time of war), 'national unity' was a welcome and acceptable public goal. Indeed, 'national unity as an end which officials may foster by persuasion and example is not in question'. He deplored the fact that government officials were too lax and indolent; that they resorted to compulsion instead of the 'slow and easily neglected route to arouse loyalties'[15] that comes from education. Jackson J. was echoing the complaint, propounded by Stone J. dissenting in *Gobitis*, that the force of law is an acceptable tool of national identity as part of education, but not when used to compel a pledge to the flag. For Jackson J.: 'Without recourse to such compulsion the state is free to compel attendance at school and require teaching by instruction and study of all in our history and in the structure and organization of our government, including the guaranties of civil liberty which tend to inspire patriotism and love of country.'[16]

Master of the aphorism, Jackson J. used a phrase that had, within it, complexities of the democratic process, previews of the public sphere: 'Authority here [in the United States] is to be controlled by public opinion, not public opinion by authority.'[17] But one wonders about the internal contradictions, contradictions that would be most apparent in the new age of electronic propaganda. Indeed, behind Jackson's sermon on the flag salute, there may have been a hidden message about government and broadcasting.[18] If government could educate, and in so doing, could harness the instruments of forming public opinion,[19] the foundations of tremendous power existed, together with licence for its use.

The distinction between persuasion and compulsion seems compelling; so much of law is divided between what is voluntary and what is forced. But modern public relations, modern advertising, and the machinery of the modern state continue to draw persuasion and compulsion closer together. In this time of mass communications and information management, the two are closer still. Much the same could be said of the line between 'education', which government officials could influence under Jackson J.'s judicial essay, and 'public opinion', which presumably was supposed to exist, in some autonomous way, as free of government if not opposed to it. As noble as was Jackson J.'s rhetoric, and his defence of the individual against a state-forced faith, he did not define the limits on the power of the government to speak, to persuade, or to use the vast resources of the official machine. What is important about the opinion is not what *Barnette* prohibited, but what it permitted.

What makes the flag cases—Justice Jackson's opinion in *Barnette* in particular—so immediate and challenging is that they invoke the lessons of modern public relations and propaganda. The way to inculcate attitudes is not solely through the ancient forms of compulsion, but through the modern forms of persuasion. Compulsion may yield short-term loyalties, but persuasion, thoughtful inculcation, provides fealty over the longer run. The common sense that underlies this constitutional logic has its chilling side; it legitimates the power of the state to enter the market-place of ideas without a suitable guide to the limits on that power. In one other place in his opinion, Justice Jackson combined notions of education with compulsion, and it is not clear that he saw them always as opposites: 'Probably no deeper division of our people could proceed from any provocation than from finding it necessary to choose what doctrine and whose program public educational officals shall compel youth to unite in embracing.'[20]

But compulsion, in this sense, is extremely elastic. It certainly encompasses attendance for students who, for economic or legal reasons, must attend a set of schools with an official account of a national history tantamount to 'compelling youth to unite' in embracing that narrative. Here, in the area of education, technology has hardly touched government power; not here arises the question raised by technology whether governments can use the media to inculcate national identities at all.

Ordinarily, the residue of the flag-salute cases is not deemed relevant to the issue of government's role in television. But, from time to time, the constitutionality of a federally operated—or even federally funded—public broadcasting system has been questioned. The argument has not been that television is too cheap and lazy a way to gain allegiance, but that government ought not to be so heavily in the business of forging domestic loyalty. The Voice of America has a charter to broadcast throughout the world, but is forbidden from transmitting its product within the United States. Yet the Constitution outlaws only the establishment of a religion, not the establishment of a press. So long as the speech of others is not abridged, the speech of government may not only be constitutional, but a vital element in the shaping of community. In a future time of thousands of disparate channels of communication, when the central core of nationhood is fragmented, and certainly in times of war, the positive lesson of *Barnette* becomes even more important. The capacity of government to summon the community to its banner through propaganda may be steadily limited, but the legitimacy of the enterprise is established.

Official English

Statutory treatment of language—the English language in particular—provides another category of insight into the multiple capacity of the state. Regulation of official languages is a forum for adjusting, perpetuating, encoding, and reinforcing particular notions of national identity. The often fruitless search for a *lingua franca* that does not offend strong ethnic groups in a multi-lingual society is a commonplace. Much nineteenth-century history, especially the growth of nationalism, is explicable in terms of the relationship between language and boundary.[21] In the United States, the march for an official English has become a rallying-point for concern about unity and identity; and, like those who sought state intervention to control the flag, those who favour a particular view of national identity expressed through an official language have sought to place the coercive power of the state behind their view. Many American states have already made English their official language, an embodiment of values or a barrier against alien influences.[22]

Language protection as an instrument of forging national identity has a long US history. An Iowa proclamation, in the 1920s, forbade the use of foreign languages in public and private schools, in church services, in public places, and over the telephone.[23] In *Meyer* v. *Nebraska*,[24] the state had passed, also in the 1920s, a statute prohibiting the teaching of any subject in any school in a language other than English (dead languages exempted), and the study of modern languages itself could not commence until the eighth grade. Mr Meyer, a teacher at a school with a large German immigrant student body, brought suit against the state, claiming that his liberty interests had been infringed.

McReynolds J. recognized that the case was about the desire of Nebraska's legislature 'to foster a homogeneous people with American ideals', but, none the less, the Court held the effort unconstitutional. Writing for the Court, McReynolds J. spurned the power of government to shape what it considered ideal citizens, likening Nebraska's actions to those of ancient Sparta—to the assembly of 'males at seven into barracks and entrusting their subsequent education and training to official guardians'.[25] Interestingly, Holmes J. dissented. 'We all agree', he wrote (in a more collegial time), that 'all the citizens of the United States should speak a common tongue, and therefore that the end aimed at by the statute is a lawful and proper one'. That major premiss out of the way, Holmes J. recognized the legislative choice of childhood as the time and school as the place for such a common bond to be forged.

Disputes over language ('the shortcut from mind to mind', as McReynolds J. put it) incorporate conflicting aspirations for the American future. Because of what is at stake, the regulatory debates relating to language show an attempt at crystallizing competing notions of national identity. The official English movement seeks to maintain dominance for a particular set of narratives by limiting competition from other languages. Simultaneously, the forces for pluralism, based on non-discrimination principles, seek to compel the recognition of other languages as a means of empowering non-dominant cultures. Statutes concerning bilingualism in education favour the legitimation of a collection of alternate symbols.

Hate speech statutes are an illustration of intervention in the language-field to shape national identities. Generally, such statutes prohibit the invocation of certain symbols, certain key phrases, or certain images. It is not only that these symbols, phrases, and images can be used to mobilize passions, incite actions, or provide a sense of *malaise* that is inconsistent with a desired community identity. Hate-speech statutes exist to demobilize unwanted participants in the market for loyalties, as I have discussed in relation to the transition societies in

Chapter 7. Like official English statutes, they, too, are designed to limit the vocabulary of the public space. US courts, especially the Supreme Court, have been hostile to hate-speech statutes where they have singled out specific viewpoints for exclusion. Since it is in the essence of hate-speech statutes to single out particular activities (cross burnings, racial epithets) for special opprobrium, this application of the Constitution has the effect of expanding entry into the market of loyalties.[26]

But another phenomenon has occurred, important to our enquiry into the regulation of imagery. While a public definition and government ban on hate speech has been discouraged, the private or customary establishment of boundaries on acceptable language has proliferated. Colleges and workplaces have used the trappings of authority, including specially fashioned sanctions (like expulsion, suspension, or firing), to create new fields of speech behaviour.[27] These exercises of semi-official authority have been attacked as oppressive incidents of 'political correctness', but, more politely, they are forms of activity in the market for loyalties. Private rules which impose sanctions for impermissible speech act as a barrier to entry in the market for those with disfavoured views. Constitutional law acts as only a partial limitation on the meta-powers, whose impact on the evolution of attitudes can be quite substantial.

Government and Art

The tortured federal concern with art—visual arts, poetry, theatre, dance, and performance—the so-called 'culture wars' of the end of the 1980s which has continued into the 1990s—has been a struggle over the proper role of government in favouring one notion of national identity over another. In the debate over the tender future of a National Endowment of the Arts, rhetoric both exposed and deflected the nature of the underlying difficulties. Here, for example, were some Presidential statements about the Endowment:

> Government can seek to create conditions under which the arts can flourish: through recognition of achievements, through those who seek to enlarge creative understanding . . . through recognizing the arts as part of the pursuit of American greatness. (President Johnson)

> We don't want a state-directed culture . . . But our government does have an interest in a national culture to which all our people and institutions contribute. It should, within prudent limits, foster artistic and cultural expression

which stands close to the center of the American effort to nourish freedom in the world. (President Nixon)

The relationship between government and art must necessarily be a delicate one. It would not be appropriate for the government to try to define what is good or what is true or what is beautiful. But government can provide nourishment to the ground within which these ideas spring forth from the seeds of inspiration within the human mind. (President Carter)

[The arts] lie at the very core of the culture of which we're a part, and they provide the foundation from which we may reach out to other cultures so that the great heritage that is ours may be enriched by—as well as itself enrich—other enduring traditions. (President Reagan)

The arts . . . contain the signposts of civilization and provide the symbols and vocabularies of our national identity. (President Bush)[28]

These were political statements, not judicial opinions, and they can be the lyrics of freedom or, in a more chilling society, the prelude to an official art. Together they contained nuances of recognition that, when government coerces revenue from its citizens through taxation and then undertakes to expend it, some agenda, stated or unstated, is likely to be present. They are reminders of how complex the social adjustment to the regulation of imagery since the 1960s has been.

President Johnson's is the comment of process and neutrality: government merely creates the conditions for the flourishing of culture. Activity takes place, as it were, independently. Recognition of the arts is put as a given, not a matter of disputation. For President Carter, metaphor realizes a similar result. Funding provides 'nourishment to the ground' without any choice as to what is good or what is not. The squib from President Reagan has its soft blanket of ambiguity: what is, after all, 'the culture' of which 'we're a part', from which a reaching-out to 'other cultures' can proceed? Is this a reaching-out within, pluralizing the national identity, or a reaching-out externally from an already complex national tradition? The excerpt from President Nixon raises and then distances the idea of a 'state-directed culture', one that should be avoided at all costs; yet there is as well the tie between the fostering of cultural expression and some instrumental purpose, 'to nourish freedom in the world'. Here, as in the flag cases, is the link between government action and a cohesion that serves a national purpose. Beneath platitudes is the complex relationship between government and the nourishment of custom, between overt government ordering of imagery and a reshaping of the public sphere.

These statements were the polite overlay to disputes concerning the role of the federal government and the arts. Throughout the 1980s and beyond, funding policies of the National Endowment of the Arts became one of the most vigorous focuses for arguments over the role of law and the state in generating or shaping imagery.[29] For those concerned with the health of American culture, the need for funding for the arts was always clearer than the criteria by which grant applications should be judged. Whether there should be any criteria, and whether acceptable criteria could be more stringent than the standards of the First Amendment, became the subjects of debate, legislation, and litigation. Frequently, controversy was triggered by charges of indecency or obscenity, or the performance or exhibition of objects that shocked a local conscience or its national equivalent. Similar to the historic debate about television (whether indecent material could be constitutionally excluded), one question put was whether the Endowment could be precluded from funding 'indecent' as well as obscene material in its pursuit of fortifying American culture. After the report of a Commission established under the leadership of former Congressman John Brademas, the Endowment's authority was limited by a general prescription vaguely encouraging that principles of general decency be observed.[30]

The pitched battles, over a crucifix dipped in urine, or an exhibition catalogue which criticized the Roman Catholic Church, or an artist who smeared her naked body with chocolate, was, in its starkness, an aspect of the market for loyalties. The National Endowment for the Arts, like the regulation of television, could be seen (and was seen) as an instrument for strengthening one or another collection of narratives about US identity with consequences for the nature and ordering of society. Quite properly, those who established the policy of the Endowment wanted to fulfil the aphorism of President Nixon that 'our government [has] . . . an interest in a national culture to which all our people and institutions contribute'. As the debate evolved, this directive came to mean that the narrative of American art, especially if supported by federal funds, should contain, within it, reflections of excluded cultures (whether regional, or craft-related, or gender, race, and ethnicity). Indecency may have been the articulated category for exclusion. At stake, though, was a more than usually visible circumstance in which the nature of the national identity was being assessed and its content consciously altered.

That patronage of the arts is part of the market for loyalties renders it hard to harmonize with notions of neutrality. Yet within every funding decision is a small commitment to reinforcement or altering identities. Most members of the art community who wished to support the Endowment were not willing to acknowledge that selection mechanisms inevitably had significance in the shaping of identity. They considered the question of choice resolved by the establishment of 'peer review panels' in each category of giving, who would render independent decisions, borrowing from the ideology of the jury. By using these juries, the Endowment sought to shift the debate over choice and identity to considerations of process, not substance. Delegation provided the basis for its Director to argue that he or she was avoiding too great a reliance on substantive criteria. Suppressing the articulation of the way decisions are actually made could avoid, in President Nixon's term, 'a state-directed culture'.

Peer review panels were not, and are not, exactly like juries, nor were they like lotteries. The decision as to who was a peer—who had sufficient experience and sense of the world of painting to select grants in the area of the visual arts—was not made by picking from voting lists, or even randomly from a list of self-identified American artists. Peers, themselves, were carefully chosen, fairly and broadly, but with concern about the implications of choice for broad inclusion in the narratives of identity. Questions of responsibility and criteria could not be easily avoided. Samuel Lipman, for example, has challenged commonly accepted approaches by doubting whether the agency, 'because it relied entirely on peer-panel review, in fact exercised no control over its grant-making'.[31] Lipman characterized this view as 'weak, and ultimately . . . lacking in philosophical weight'.

In the early 1990s, acting on the recommendations of the Brademas Commission and reauthorizing the National Endowment for the Arts, Congress modified the process by requiring the highest officials of the Endowment to take personal responsibility for decisions, rather than ratify, without review, the results of peer review panels. Among the messages contained in the Congressional reauthorization was one central to the market for loyalties: however the standards were articulated, there were competitors for shaping identity who should not be encouraged, nor be subsidized, nor be legitimated by a federal grant. No precise formula of words could capture who ought to be entered in this category of exclusion (sometimes those using art, actively, to alter perceptions of gender roles, sometimes those using the arts to make points deemed racist or otherwise destabilizing); but Senators would stand guard to make certain that Endowment officials personally determined that the category existed and was meaningful.

As difficult, and often reprehensible, as is the enforcement of this category of exclusion, there is something vapid about the familiar, but dubious argument that taxpayers (or their representatives) should have no direct voice in determining how their money is spent in the arts. Otherwise, it is said, 'many would have forbidden their taxes to be spent supporting Star Wars, the stealth bomber, and the Gulf War'.[32] The analogy is not quite apposite. Taxpayers certainly can and do complain about such expenditures and campaign against the election of Congressional representatives who support policies they do not like. Taxpayers who oppose certain defence expenditures can and do organize boycotts against companies that benefit from them; Congress can limit the Defense Department in its spending practices so as to cut funding for a particular weapons system. Certainly, the government has no constitutional obligation to encourage the work of artists and writers, though society would be poorer if it did not. Certainly, government should not be able to choose the individual artists or arts institutions to be supported if the discrimination is on the basis of 'images or ideas that are controversial or that criticize or attack, however violently, politicians, religious figures, government officials, and even religion and government itself',[33] though, in the low-visibility enforcement of a harsh Congressional directive, that is what may occur. What is doubtful is the conclusion that 'the only constitutionally valid grounds for grantee selection and denial are ones exclusively related to artistic values such as "merit", "quality", and "promise"'. Congress can favour grants to institutions over grants to artists, or small-business artists over institutions; it can favour public art over private; it can establish mechanisms for grant-making that virtually assure conservative, or liberal taste; it can, through the design of review, encourage multiculturalism or preserve the *status quo*. All these things occur and have important implications for national identity. Rather than denying the role of government, explicit aspects of choice in federal patronage should be tolerated, providing guidance to agencies that are involved in subsidizing the production of images.[34]

Custom and Coercion

The interaction between government and competitors for national identity can approach neutrality, but it is impossible wholly to be neutral. Part of an answer to the dilemma of having a market for loyalties without having a state-directed culture is recognizing that choices must be made, and focusing on the discourse that surrounds them. Government action is tied, especially in a democratic society, to the reinforcement of private custom. But custom itself alters.

Consider the implications of an exhibition that occurred in the image-dangerous days of 1990 in the classical precincts of the Brooklyn Museum: 'The Play of the Unmentionable', installed by the conceptual artist Joseph Kosuth. The exhibition of once-unshowable paintings and sculptures sought to bring historical and anthropological insights to age-old controversies concerning art and sexuality, art and race, and art and subversion. The exhibition had the requisite boldness, purposely using a grant from the National Endowment for the Arts as part of the process of demonstrating a history of censorship. Included were works prohibited in ancient times, or works in the nineteenth century that, through acceptable conventions, encrypted their sexual or political subversion. There were works whose superficial blandness rendered it difficult to believe that, in an earlier or different setting, the art would have been provocative. As an anthropologist, or an incorporator of anthropological and psychoanalytical truths, Kosuth seemed to reiterate and render more comprehensible the ubiquity of the subconscious, providing further insight, if more was necessary, into the relationship between history and desire.

The text and paintings together, though, could lead one to a surprising syllogism, undoubtedly not Kosuth's: (1) for centuries, artists have made works about sexuality, or race, or other subjects, possibly subversive, though the intent is not totally clear from the work itself; (2) during the same centuries, varying kinds of images, for reasons that are rarely clear in retrospect, have been discouraged, or banned (and the artist sometimes punished for making them); and (3) that anthropologists, philosophers, and psychoanalysts provide many reasons why these acts of suppression have occurred. Finally, the United States in the twentieth century, like any of its predecessors, has its own peculiar code of what imagery should be encouraged and what discouraged, and this code changes as well. The urge to control, to shape, indeed to censor—on a wide variety of grounds—is so deeply ingrained that it would be amazing to find a government that did not have some agenda that it was furthering. The exhibition was suggestive, more positively, of a dialogic process, in which interest groups and government participate as government power, affecting the narratives of art, is deployed in a multiplicity of ways. These include outright censorship, the patronage of artists, the choice of what museums to build and sponsor, whom to admit to the academies of privilege. Private forces, who are themselves a constant pressure on the levers of official power, make constant choices that affect the community's taboos. The government becomes a forum for the playing-out of the unmentionable, its suppression or its conversion to the quotidian.

There are thousands of examples of this interaction between the official and the unofficial. In 1983 Mary Washington College, in Virginia, accepted for an alumni exhibition[35] a work by Mary Cate Carroll, 'American Liberty Upside Down', a mixed-media work that contained 'the actual remains [in formaldehyde] of a saline abortion; a tiny, greenish fetus, its arms, legs and head well-formed and curled up in a jar'. Before the exhibition opened, the college asked Ms Carroll to remove it, because of complaints received or anticipated. What facts are important in judging the outcome, and establishing a label for it? Does it matter that the work was 'accepted', at an earlier point, rather than rejected? Must a curator provide a reason why a work is excluded? Should the artist receive precedence because the work concerns a public issue of controversial importance? Should it matter (and how much) whether Mary Washington College is a state college or state supported or that its gallery receives funding from a state or federal arts agency?

One self-styled guardian of the First Amendment characterized the incident as 'plain old straight-armed censorship'. If the intervention was arbitrary, clumsy, unthinking, and undiscussed—as it probably was—then the criticism may be wholly supportable, at least as to administrative style. Rather, one can see in the hard-scrabble decision-making in Virginia an ordinary day-to-day evolution: what images are permissible in what environment and under what conditions. To be sure, the dispute over Ms Carrol's work of art was, in its incremental way, about the redefinition of the role of women in society and attitudes towards reproduction as elements of national identity. Dialogue, in the sense of a series of decisions to produce, exhibit, fund, exclude, has a tendency to be resistant to standards. Mary Washington College should be able to adopt a standard that would vest a curator with enough authority that he or she could decide to exclude works of art incorporating a foetus (or some other speech-implying symbol) or even, as a bow toward professionalization, empower curators to mediate taboos themselves even without a specific guide. More important is how, over time, the narratives of inclusion or exclusion are defined.

Negotiated Standards

The dialogic process among government, producers of imagery, and citizens was illustrated in 1994 with respect to a cruder form of imagery: the narratives of video-games as they proliferated in the malls and homes of teenage America. Senator Joseph Lieberman opened a Congressional hearing to call upon Nintendo, Sega, and other elements of the video-game industry to exercise 'self-restraint and self-regulation'. Do more, he exhorted, to remove violent and sexual images from the games. He argued that the leading cause of death among teenagers was gunshot wounds and that the link between violence in popular entertainment and violence in society 'has been proven in more than 3,000 scientific studies'. He quoted a letter from a constituent, one Tara Geist of Norwich, Connecticut, writing of young children passing pictures of Mortal Kombat figures ripping off heads. 'These games', she wrote, 'are repulsive . . . When younger and older kids thinking that blood and violence is "cool", that's a bad sign.'

Senator Lieberman did more than exhort. He introduced legislation that would establish an Interactive Entertainment Rating Commission which would 'evaluate whether any voluntary standards proposed by the video game industry are adequate to warn purchasers and users about the violence or sexually explicit content of video games'. The Commission would have a life of one year, during which it would report on the voluntary actions of the industry to see if they were sufficient. Left ambiguous was whether the sufficiency would be measured only in terms of the exhaustiveness of disclosure, or some measurable difference in the narratives available to those, like the young, considered particularly vulnerable.

The hearings on video games involved a now familiar dance: faced with the prospect of government intervention, the industry itself established its own rating committee. Executive after executive paraded before the Senators, expressing concern about the future of the society and sincerity in being co-operative. The threat of government action yielded a change of custom in the industry. The first change would be in the custom of presentation, with the flowering of icons signifying levels and degrees of problematic material. A second change, undoubtedly, would come in terms of pressures on susceptible department-store chains and malls as to what rated material would or would not be sold or displayed.

If customs and standards develop in a dialogic manner in modern society, it is as a result of an ongoing set of conversations among institutions and interest groups. Censorship, in the narrow legal sense, is the explicit support of the preferences of one or another of these groups through the force of law. I have written about the evolution of custom in the early time of AIDS when, during the long march to find vaccine and cure, government became a partner in the process of mass education, distribution of information, and the changing of behaviour to assure safer sexual practices.[36] The process of change in the national consciousness took place gradually, but noticeably, an arresting combination of voluntary actions of committed interest groups, those who guided media, the forces of economics, and the subtle pressures of government and public opinion.

The government, at all levels, was and is involved, in the AIDS era, in the process of altering, modifying, or repudiating the messages of popular culture. The role of government in educating children in the risks of imprudent sexual behaviour is almost universally recognized, even though the nature of the message is vigorously contested. In New York's subways, the City once provided a running comic strip designed to raise the sophistication of its inhabitants. Government provides funds for community groups to educate their members and tax incentives for those who contribute to charities that furnish additional information and guidance. It is too simple to say that the state shapes opinion; but it is too simple, as well, to say that it does, or should, stand aside. The society withstands direct censorship because individuals, engaged in the free exchange of ideas, are subject to influence by compensating and competing forces each promoting values they believe likely to guarantee the community's survival. Television, as a licensed medium of mass communications, stands specially subject to the process of dialogue and community involvement in its representation of AIDS. Though we think of the medium as largely escapist, it is blatantly instructionist (even in its escapism), and perceived to be so. From mini-series to documentary, television has been the locus for a negotiated message, in the AIDS crisis, much as I have described in Chapter 8.

Art, like television, has been seen, anew, to percolate through and to influence the masses and the mass media, to accomplish, in fact, some of the most democratic objectives claimed by supporters of culture who seek federal subsidy. With this understanding, the philistine impulse to judge and censor has become enlivened. If federal support for the arts is important because of its impact on identity and community, then the nature of that impact becomes a matter for public debate and determination.

Yet the animus towards art may be a form of displacement. Without the capacity to affect the mass media themselves, Congress becomes preoccupied with a minor performance in Minneapolis, a painting in Chicago, or a sculpture in North Carolina. Carole S. Vance, writing about censorship and the arts, has pointed out that the 'desire to eliminate symbols, images and ideas they do not like from public space' arises particularly from those who see a loss of social control over much of their lives and the lives of others. It is not the introduction of censorship, but the enriching of the public zone of discussion that should be the civic goal for community well-being. 'Diversity in images and expression in the public sector nurtures and sustains diversity in private life.'[37] A society impoverished in imagery yields a population likewise demoralized and isolated. Its representatives resort, increasingly, to controlling the proxy, such as the art and writings about disfavoured and threatening behaviour.

The Language of Television

It is doubtful that mass alienation and struggle have reached a peak or that the energy to control is waning. The battle over imagery may revert to a more subdued level. Artists may associate themselves, more readily, with a refurbished, 1990s idea of progress and government as a positive force, so that the arts, especially the avant-garde arts, move from a place of almost automatic opposition to a place that is more associated with the mainstream and with legitimated power. The major political parties have converged to the extent that formerly divisive symbols (crime, patriotism, fiscal prudence) become common property. The hardest edges of insulting epithets have been smoothed by increased consciousness and sensitivities. But new issues will arise; the power of images and the influence of government to affect the tone and mood and values of the society will persist. What will change is the agenda, not the fundamental tie between a modern state and the belief patterns of its citizens. From this relationship, an affirmative theory of a state role in the generation of images can emerge, encompassing government patronage, built on the idea that simple acts of censorship are not the only measures of freedom or its absence, nor the sole gauge of how ideas are nourished and society strengthened.

In a dreamland of cultural improbability, the American public expends vast sums for the formal education of its children, only to see its impact swept aside by the overwhelming force of a media world of fantasy and diversion. Mandatory school attendance is virtually taken for granted, but the power of the society to protect the resulting investment from the culture at large is minimal, uncertain, undeveloped. Congress has enacted legislation designed to benefit children by imposing requirements for beneficial television programming on US stations, but the law is so mild and toothless that it is a monument to hypocrisy.[38] A jurisprudence of youth protection has developed, obsessed with indecency, and, at Congressional direction, spreading throughout the radio dial, furnishing a tougher standard for programming where children may be listening or reading or watching.[39] This new jurisprudence speaks of a solution, but is merely a symbol of a shift from a society in which a prime responsibility was the training of youth (an investment in regeneration) to one in which that responsibility seems unlikely to be fulfilled.

To use the words of Jackson J. in *Barnette*, there is something of the cheap and lazy in much of government intervention to shape national identities. Those groups who wish to fence out other shapers of national identity do so, too frequently, by coercion and exclusion. Speech is so dynamic, so explosive, that no momentary definition of what is permitted and what is excluded can endure. As with hate speech, those who propound an official language undoubtedly know that dominance cannot be assured and frozen into place. Hate-speech ordinances are most productive if they are accompanied by educational efforts that reinforce more positive practices.

I return here to what, in an earlier chapter, I called the Kapuściński theorem—namely, that throughout the world, a narrative of modernity and progress is used to deflect (what is perceived as) the roiling alternative of disorder and change. In the United States, diversity and pluralism embody the decline of the old hegemonies as new ones take their place. English as an official language contains a vision of society in which the primacy and dominance of the common language is unquestioned. In the world of the advocates—as in the group, founded by the philosopher S. I. Hayakawa, 'US English'—bilingual education is suspect, the swearing-in of new citizens in Spanish is shocking, and the provision of ballot information in alternative tongues is a step towards the loss of the sense of nation. These groups, advocating aggressive language intervention, are like forces in the West seeking a narrative of modernity that provides an alternative to the narratives of decline and loss of empire. Language guarantees provide reassurance, backed by the force of law, against the threat of a changed balance of power.

The set of images we call television-programming can be taken as yet another language. The images, words, and impulses that are imbibed by its habitual users and reflected to television's writers and producers contain, like all languages, particular world-views and social structures.[40] The language of American commercial television is a language of power, but power first and primarily for a vision in which modernity and progress are defended against the ubiquitous forces of dissolution. Those who are the speakers and have substantial control of the forum naturally seek to fend off threats to their relative monopoly of imagery, as well as threats to their control of the channels in which the imagery, or language, is expressed.

Government has an approach to television language as subtle and complex as it does to language in general. In the analogy to language and the arts, government acts by subsidy and positive intervention. Public broadcasting could be defined as a 'language' of television that is an alternative to the dominant advertising supported mode. Government has fostered minority ownership of broadcasting licences to gain more plural images on television on the premiss that the current collection of images, words, and symbols is a carrier of an imperfect version of the national identity. Most reincarnations of the public interest—rules concerning over-commercialization, fairness, improvement of children's television, the abatement of violence or indecency—are an oblique attack on the special language that is, as it were, the current dominant language of American television. As in the debate over federal financing of the arts, the effort is to find ways of making the governmental role as neutral as possible. The use of 'access' to the narratives of television has been the mechanism designed to accomplish that task, and it is to that doctrine that I now turn.

10 A Taxonomy of Access

NATIONAL identity claims automatically raise conflicts over content: whose identity, whose balance or perspective on race or gender or violence, will prevail and how will the narrative of the media change. In the US setting, there has been profound discomfort, as we have seen, with any explicit government role in affecting content. To circumvent this unease, but yet to address problems of great significance, government has sought, often, to shift to a focus on process, on the rules of the game, and to divert attention from outcome to the opportunities that competing speakers in the society have to tell their story. In this circumvention, the doctrine called 'access', an intriguing and fugitive element torn between democratic theory and notions of representation, serves as an umbrella, a catch-all term for the determination of who can use the electronic media to speak, when, and under what conditions.

Deeply imbedded in the idea of access are fundamental notions connecting communications technology, democratic discourse, and the public sphere. The notion of access, even the word itself, brings forth echoes of easement, the right of one person to cross the property of another. We speak of the right of a land-locked nation to have access to the sea. Access sometimes implies an extraordinary right, a situation in which the property involved is in the control of another but circumstances require that the perquisites of ownership be modified. In a highly romantic form, access suggests a search to replicate mythic conditions of the imagined village by the use of high technology, fulfilling a desire to recreate a world wherein any person can talk to any other person on a non-hierarchical basis. Access doctrines become an index of ways to reconstruct the mass media so that the predominant mode is no longer the few speaking to the many, but the many speaking to the many.

Gaining access has come to mean not mere representation, but assurance of fair representation among those who control the electronic media, preventing monopolies of the narrative. 'Providing access', as a political agenda, has become a euphemism for locating those who have been excluded from the community's dominant dialogue and providing them with the opportunity to speak to the whole, thus making more equitable the distribution of opportunities for one citizen or group to address others. Explicitly furnishing access to specified groups may seem antithetical to a US legal tradition of non-differentiation based on race, class, gender, or political perspective, but a mass media perceived as exclusionary by large segments of the population could have a destabilizing impact, and widening 'access' is a means of forestalling perceptions of political injustice. Providing access can mean creating gateways to sources of information for listeners who have been deprived of such sources in the past or, conversely, providing access for speakers to an audience which has not adequately heard them. Access can also mean allowing the marginalized to speak to the marginalized through internal communications networks for those who deem themselves otherwise disenfranchised. More cynically, concepts of access may mean constructing a set of artificial decorations, a false mosaic, a means of legitimating the dominant voices by showing a toleration of difference and dissent.

Since enhancing access may prove one of the grounds for government affirmatively to intervene in the field of speech, a window into its complexity and confusion is valuable. Access is now in vogue as new technologies spring forth, transforming the entire structure of television. The plea for universal access by all households to a new information infrastructure turns patterns of data distribution into the very essence of citizenship. Alternative proposals for a new communications infrastructure are evaluated in terms of 'how much' opportunity they provide for access to communicate and to whom. Activists for access, techno-versions of their public-interest predecessors, seize the moment: through the imposition of access requirements they aspire, Sisyphus-like, to eliminate the massness of the mass media with its structure in which the powerful few engage the distributed many. 'Access' is the term of choice because it has the ring of neutrality, though what structure is neutral, in comparison to its alternatives, is a conundrum yet unsolved.

While there has been increasing access talk in the United States and elsewhere, and much concern over access doctrines within Congress, the FCC, and the courts, the different historic responses have not been analytically organized and justified in terms of their relationship to democratic theory. The history of access regulation in the United States reveals a public inability or unwillingness to be explicit about the relationship of narrative to social context and of ownership structures to the nature of narrative. The importance of access is often premised on the dangers inherent in a monopoly over the instruments of mass communication and the implications of substantial imbalances in access to pedestals of influence. Consequently, American legal doctrine has hinged the right to access on notions of 'scarcity' and bottlenecks in the distribution of information; the existence of scarcity is often put as a *sine qua non* for anchoring the power of government to regulate. But the function, implications, and justification for access regulations are far broader than the existence of scarcity.

In what follows, I try to establish a taxonomy of access as an aid to understanding how, in the US context, questions of discourse and identity traverse competing definitions of free speech and press. From this taxonomy, I try to demonstrate that doctrines of access—dependent on a particular model of speech—are examples both of the operation of the market for loyalties (national identity) and the search for a public sphere. I have taken some liberties and recharacterized much of communications policy so that efforts not thought of as conferring access in the ordinary sense of the term are here brought under the canopy of a more expansive doctrine. The purpose of the broader characterization is to present a coherent picture of the circumstances in which society looks to government to provide ground rules for the better conduct of a democratic society.

Ownership and Content

If there is to be democratic discourse, it is important who controls the forum. A fairly universal belief exists in the link between ownership of media and the social narrative of their content. Ownership is not everything: government regulation can impose harsh restrictions on the most private of systems and a publicly owned forum can be democratically run. Ownership is a factor, however, and the commitment to privatize the media in the transition societies has, as one of its premisses, this bond between ownership and content. Diversifying ownership has a seeming advantage. Access solutions seem most objectionable if they require a government official to determine whether the range of stories told and pictures shown properly represent some desired or actual reality; therefore, a more process-oriented approach, regulating the composition of proprietors, has seemed preferable. Thus, what might be called 'ownership access'—forcing diversity among owners to achieve diversity in content—has been a favoured technique of Congress and the FCC.

Implicit in the preference for ownership access are ragged, seldom-articulated assumptions about a public sphere. These include the notion that a multiplicity of owners will lead to competition that will in turn produce a robust, open discussion. The history of US broadcast regulation is riddled with rules about control of licences based on assumptions that the characteristics of the owner—and the profile of all owners as a group—have important effects on the content of broadcasts. A group of now-liberalized FCC and Congressional policies, including rules limiting the number of stations one entity can own, and limiting the number to be owned in a single place, assumed that expanding the range of owners would lead to expanding the range of views or social narratives, rendering the community of listeners more content with the responsiveness of the system. Ensuring that there are private as well as public owners (or determining, in the US experience, that owners will be almost exclusively private) assumes better service of the 'checking function' of the First Amendment, the function of serving as a curb on abuse of official power.[1]

Early manifestations of 'ownership-access' considerations were important determinations about spectrum allocation—between governmental and private uses—and statutory requirements that radio licences be geographically distributed throughout the nation. In the 1940s extensive enquiries into 'chain broadcasting' and the emergence of networks reflected concern that binding contractual relationships made the national programmers, and not the local licensees, the true owners, thereby defeating stated Congressional policies. The hypothesized nature of discourse, a society in which local voices were to be reflected, would be disrupted.

Rules governing the networks, including limitations on the number of licences that one entity could control and prohibitions on cross-ownership made possible a full-blown articulation of the relationship of ownership to public discourse. In a surprisingly large number of communities, the surviving newspaper, the radio station, and the television station were under common ownership. The situation presented itself because the publishing entrepreneur in town—usually the newspaper owner—applied for a radio-station licence in the pioneering days of radio and then for a television licence in the pioneering days of video. The FCC determined that this concentration of ownership was inconsistent with its assumptions about democratic discourse. In a ruling that embodied ownership concerns, the FCC required divestment, over time, by newspapers that owned co-located radio and television stations, having already adopted a rule that no licensee could have more than one licence in a given community. The Commission also limited the aggregate size of audience which could be controlled through a group of commonly controlled licences.[2] In *FCC* v. *National Citizens Committee for Broadcasting*,[3] the Supreme Court upheld the Commission cross-ownership ruling because of fears that joint operations would monopolize local news. The Court concluded that the Commission policy contributed to a First Amendment goal of 'achieving the widest possible dissemination of information from diverse and antagonistic sources'.[4]

Rules that provide certain groups with special opportunities to become owners are based on related assumptions concerning access and democratic discourse. The most marked recent example of ownership access—and the example that makes the most interesting assumptions about the relationship of ownership to narrative—is the effort (now declining) of the Commission to encourage disadvantaged groups (including black, female, Hispanic, Native American, and Asian) to gain ownership of radio and television stations. These rules, leading to gender and racial diversity in ownership, can also be viewed as providing marginalized groups with an enhanced opportunity to compete in the market for loyalties, as described in Chapter 4. In the 1970s the FCC adopted a policy that provided tax incentives and advantages in comparative hearings that would result in the transfer of some existing radio and television licences to minority owners or businesses controlled by members of minority groups.[5]

When the FCC announced its ownership policies, it made it clear that the programme was intended to alter the social narrative. At the same time, the Commission constantly admitted the existence of constitutional limitations precluding government from affecting the stories told on the screen in a way that would entail establishing categories of content. Affecting ownership patterns was the solution. In a decision upholding the constitutionality of the minority preference,[6] the Supreme Court accepted the assumption that minority ownership would produce more diversified speech.[7] The evidence to support this vital assumption was fragile, as O'Connor J. argued in dissent, though, according to FCC findings, it was sufficient.[8] The Commission, and the Court, skirted a fine, perhaps non-existent line. Critical to constitutionality was the fact that no effort had been made to assign frequencies to a group because of its point of view or specifically because it promised programming of interest to a particular community. That would have smacked of the now-fatal sin of selecting licensees based on content or even viewpoint. On the other hand, for the decision to have integrity, the presumed link between ownership and narrative had to be plausible.[9]

'Ownership-access' rules, of the kind I have described, have a mechanical truth to them. More owners, rather than fewer, seem likely to diversify speech. It would be wrong, under this view, to have a single owner, in a major city, of all newspapers, or of the daily newspaper, the television station, and the radio station (the way in which markets were once constructed). The FCC has never been tolerant of the argument, made for so long by the BBC, that a single manager of frequencies would maximize audience by purposely and rationally diversifying, playing to small segments, in the way only a monopolist can.[10] Most licensees do seek an affiliation with one of the national networks, however, and, if successful, adopt or 'clear' most of the network's programme offering.[11] Even if the programming that the local licensee selects is from non-network offerings, there are patterns of great similarity, based on what will maximize audience or advertising revenues. Seldom does ownership diversity—except in specific market circumstances—lead to the kind of programme diversity that has overtones important in furthering pluralist goals. At the very margin, stations owned by minority groups are somewhat more sensitive to minority issues; perhaps they have better affirmative action records. But there has not been a convincing showing that, in a system where licensees, by dint of a relationship to banks or shareholders or because of general desire, are committed to maximizing profit, the identity of the owner makes a great deal of difference.

Political Parties and Preferred Speakers

Another technique for approaching the ideal public sphere is to provide, regardless of ownership, greater equality of access to the forum of discourse by all potential speakers. Much of the regulation of the broadcasting era has been designed to ensure that a carrier or transmitter of speech (a television station or a cable operator, for example) is obliged to make its facilities available to certain speakers, viewpoints, producers, or categories of programmes. 'Speaker access', an awkward term for this *melange*, includes a wide variety of mechanisms, each of which shares the characteristic of asserting that the focusing is on process and opportunity rather than on the substance.[12] This granting of access to particular speakers or makers of programmes presupposes some imbalance in output, some imperfection in the market, or some need, basic to the democratic enterprise, that a particular speaker or organization of speakers gains an opening in the forum. In particular, 'producer-access' rules deny the owner full power over the forum.[13]

The most familiar and accepted speaker-access rules in the United States are those specifically related to the political process. These rules, in conjunction with many other campaign-structuring provisions, help ensure that recognized or qualified political candidates are entitled to time at a regulated price or rate that is non-discriminatory among political candidates. Federal law assures candidates access to television and radio stations at the lowest available rates and gives one candidate equal time whenever another candidate receives time, under prescribed circumstances.[14] There are no rules, in US law, that set aside time for political parties at no charge or require televised debates, but such arrangements, often proposed, would fit within this category. Political-access rules also do not apply to newspapers or magazines in the United States.[15]

An early access rule, section 18 of the Radio Act of 1927, established the 'equal-opportunities' standard and also exhibits the ambivalence that US law has always displayed towards access provisions. The successor statute provides that, if any television licensee permits a legally qualified candidate for a public office to use the station, equal opportunities must be provided to other candidates. On the other hand, there is no obligation, based on the equal-opportunities law, to provide access to any candidate. Owners cannot discriminate, but neither are they obliged, under this provision, to provide a forum. They can prevent access, but, if candidates take advantage of the statutory-access opportunity, the owner is forbidden from controlling the material that the candidates broadcast.[16]

The complex evolution of the equal-opportunities statute demonstrates the perils of state administration of the public sphere. The rule originally jeopardized national presidential debates between major candidates, because of the rights of minor or fragment parties. Demonstrating the power of law to determine the nature of the forum, Congress suspended the equal-opportunities rule in 1960 to permit

John F. Kennedy and Richard Nixon to face each other alone. After a 1975 Commission ruling, 'coverage' of a debate, sponsored, for example, by the League of Women Voters, was exempted from the equal-opportunities rule as a category-of-news event, and later even the rule requiring a sponsor was weakened. After 1975, negotiations, backed by the possibility of resort to law, determined who among candidates would be given favoured access to the national television forum of presidential debates.[17] In a related complexity, the Commission and the courts have had to decide whether an incumbent official's use of the medium—as when President Eisenhower obtained time to discuss the Suez crisis in 1956—triggered equal time opportunities for a political opponent.[18]

While the equal-opportunities rule provided no absolute access to the televised forum, another law, passed in 1971, does. Section 312 (*a*) (7) of the Communications Act permits the Commission to revoke a licence if a television station repeatedly fails to permit candidates for federal office 'reasonable access' to free time or the right to purchase time (at a somewhat favourable advertising rate).[19] Here, access took a peculiarly American turn. The broadcaster had the discretion to decide whether the candidate's access should be satisfied by the ability to buy advertising or, rather, the provision of time. In its operation, the law has been confusing, often increasing the impact of wealth differentials rather than diminishing them.[20] In upholding the constitutionality of this access provision, the Supreme Court used high-minded language underscoring the importance of public speech, despite the arbitrary and limited impact of the statute. Access to the forum was important so that 'the electorate may intelligently evaluate the candidates' personal qualities and their positions on vital public issues before choosing among them on election day'; and because 'speech concerning public affairs is . . . the essence of self-government'.[21] In a passage which wallows in the ambiguity of the access provision, the Court admitted that it had 'never approved a *general* right of access to the media'. Substituting italics for reasoning, Chief Justice Burger continued: 'Nor do we do so today. Section 312 (*a*) (7) creates a *limited* right . . . [and] does not impair the discretion of broadcasters to present their views on any issue or to carry any particular type of programming.'[22]

Almost all access provisions concerning political access to the television forum are rendered absurd by a Supreme Court decision on campaign financing. The Court has held that neither federal nor state law can restrict how much money a candidate spends on his or her own campaign.[23] The result has been a distinct advantage, even surpassing traditional opportunities, for those with great personal wealth to gain political office. The 1992 presidential campaign demonstrated this 'Perotist' access, in which it is individual fortune, rather than other criteria, that triumphs over clumsy and often-biased attempts to control access to the medium. Access rules that relate to the political process could serve pluralistic ends, encouraging less entrenched parties. They could be drawn so as to provide excluded groups with greater opportunities to participate. But because of the caricatural relationship between money, constitutional determinations, and legal rules, US political access fails to reflect pluralist tendencies or further equitable access.

The most famous 'speaker-access' rule involves the Fairness Doctrine and its tributaries. The government surely cannot pick and choose among viewpoints in determining the access of speakers to a public sphere. But vital to understanding the history of communications regulation is the power of government to provide conditional access, a regulatory pattern which provides a given speaker or producer the right of access under certain circumstances. A well-known example of this in the United States is the personal-attack rule or the reply to editorial rule. If a licensed broadcaster airs a personal attack, its subject has the right to respond. If an editorial is aired, parties with competing views have some right to respond.

These rules are aspects of the Fairness Doctrine, long seen as the chief tool by which the FCC could promote a rich and robust discourse on radio and television. Under the Doctrine, which I have referred to in Chapter 8, broadcasters were obliged (1) to present controversial issues of public importance and (2) to ensure that, if one side of such an issue was presented, other sides were presented as well. Like the equal-opportunities rule, the regulation incorporated an ambivalence towards invasions of the broadcaster's 'rights'. The Fairness Doctrine provided no specific speaker (except under the personal-attack and right-of-reply rules) with direct access. The obligation was on the broadcaster to ensure coverage, with no individual holding a correlative right. The broadcaster became the keeper of the public sphere.

In the famous *Red Lion* case,[24] the Court upheld the FCC's conditional-access rules, using language which underscored the power of government to enhance a public sphere. The authority to regulate was related to the still-considered scarcity of broadcast frequencies, but scarcity was not the genius of White J.'s analysis. Nor was the Court's language, justifying FCC action, based on the power of the medium as it had been in *Pacifica*.[25] Instead, the Court was articulating a political theory and the role that the medium could play in its application. The idea was radical: Congress and the FCC could, compatibly with the First Amendment—indeed, in the service of the First Amendment—design the broadcasting system as an infrastructure for political discourse. Free speech would be better served by a system which provides speakers with unencumbered time than one which promotes 'fairness' solely by relying on broadcasters to select themes and, uncoerced, assure balanced presentations.

The fundamental assumptions, however, underlying the Fairness Doctrine were flawed. The Doctrine can be seen as a symbol of the complexity of government involvement in enhancing the public sphere. Under the Doctrine, government was involved too much and too little. Broadcasters were almost never penalized for failing to become carriers of important public issues, as required by the first prong of the Doctrine. Moreover, during its decline, the Fairness Doctrine was heavily clotted by procedural and substantive paraphernalia. At times, fairness was measured by stopwatch: the staff of the FCC would look to the number of minutes given to one side and the number to be given to others. It examined whether the original position was given in prime time and the balancing position in fringe. Intricate disputes raged over whether the balancing period had to be immediate or could extend over time, even over the period of the licence. Detailed rules were developed to determine, among many other details, the duty of broadcasters to seek out champions of contrasting views, and the measures to be taken when no such champions could be found.[26] The mechanism of the Fairness Doctrine, with its *in terrorem* impact on broadcasters, was used by several Administrations (particularly the Nixon Administration) to harass and intimidate those managing news programmes for broadcast licensees.[27] Bureaucratized, the clumsy product of vying angry forces, the Doctrine became virtually extinct, unable, like the dodo bird, to fly when necessary.[28]

Public Access

With the coming of cable television, a new form of speaker access occurred: the establishment of public-access channels as part of local cable franchises. This was a radical form of access, since the idea, unlike the Fairness Doctrine or most forms of political access, was that speakers would have unalloyed, unmediated opportunities to use the medium. This was the access channel of populist dreams, a romantic, fantasy version of the public sphere. For almost twenty years, some, though not all, cable systems in the United States have had a form of these channels, a technological mirror of the aggressive individual speech typified by a soap-box in a corner of Hyde Park. Public-access channels are animated by the notion that everyone ought to have a space in which to release passion, show talent, or articulate a point of view. The channels are designed for use by individuals or community groups, and often provide time on a first-come, first-served basis. In many communities, the owner of the franchise is obliged to provide production facilities for groups or individuals to make videos. Public-access channels provide a public pathway, an echo of the streets as they have been used from time immemorial, to hector, to implore, and to transform the nature of the debate and its participants. A soap-box in a small village, though, is different from a soap-box in a global village, which could be no more than a mechanism for shouting into the void. Public-access channels may become an unkempt corner of the public sphere, a place of disarray and margin, rather than significant contributors to public debate. Cable operators have argued that forcing them to carry the programming of this grab-bag of producers violates their speech rights.

The jurisprudence of public-access channels provides an important window into the hesitation to provide unencumbered opportunities to speak on television. When Congress passed its first cable statute, in 1984, one of its goals was to assure that the medium provide 'the widest possible diversity of information sources and services to the public'.[29] Among other ways of accomplishing this goal, the Congress authorized local governments to require cable operators to provide these public-access channels, and also to provide 'leased-access' channels for commercial use for entities not affiliated with the cable operator.

As a means of enlarging the opportunity for public-access and leased-access channels to enjoy exuberant free speech, Congress precluded cable operators from exercising any editorial control over them. But, simultaneously, cautions and barriers were imposed. Congress required cable operators to supply subscribers with a so-called 'lock box' with which, presumably, parents could prohibit the viewing of offensive material. In addition, Congress declared—ambiguously, since it was unclear how enforcement would occur—that programming unprotected by constitutional rights of free speech (obscene, and perhaps indecent programming) would not be entitled to the access rights.

This balance between mediated and unmediated access was not a satisfactory equilibrium. Between the passage of the 1984 Act and the early 1990s, lurid stories appeared about the content of these public-access channels. When extremist views were propounded, cities and others sued to censor them, as occurred with a Ku-Klux-Klan use of public-access channels in Missouri.[30] But 'indecent' programmes, even more than programmes that were politically inciting, caused legislative concern. In 1992 Congress passed the Cable Television Consumer Protection and Competition Act and, in its labyrinthine provisions, reduced the unmediated nature of the public-access channels.[31] As a result, the cable operator, as well as the franchising authority, would have the power to regulate transmission of specific categories of speech (obscene, indecent, or otherwise not constitutionally protected). A cable operator was encouraged to enforce a published policy that would prohibit programming that described or depicted 'sexual or excretory activities or organs in a patently offensive manner as measured by contemporary community standards'.[32]

In the years since passage of the 1992 legislation, there has been litigation galore over the constitutionality of the provisions giving the cable operators more authority over speakers on the public-access and leased-access channels to control specified categories of offensive speech. Cable operators argued that, because they are 'speakers', they should not be required to provide the channels at all. To do so is to force speech. The users complained that, despite the pretence that it is the private operator determining what programming should be permitted, the true censor was the government. Finally, those who use leased channels or public-access channels complain that law cannot impose special controls on them. To avoid discrimination, similar standards would have to be imposed across all channels of the cable universe.[33]

Cable Carriage of Broadcasters

The public-access channels are the most radical of the innovations that accompany cable and the new technologies, and the innovation that most implicates national-identity and public-sphere concerns. But other legislative steps underscore the relationship of government to the organization of speech. The access rules that were the most important from an economic perspective, and therefore gave rise to the most focused deliberation, were the 'must-carry' rules, already briefly discussed in Chapter 8. These rules, which gave over-the-air broadcasters (both public and private) access to homes through cable systems, reflect a long history in which, for economic and social reasons, the FCC provided a protected transition. Cable operators, who bitterly opposed these rules, reinvented themselves as 'speakers' themselves, not mere conduits, so that they could claim the benefits of the First Amendment. The argument, which has been accepted by the Supreme Court, provides them with a status that limits the power of government to regulate them.

From an access and public-sphere perspective, the problem of distinguishing the speaker from the means to speak is an important one. Access rules are easier to justify if cable operators are not social communicators, but merely passive providers of a conduit or highway. One reading of the 1992 Cable Act is that it was designed to preserve a certain stock of discourse in a mode of delivery that is 'free'—that is, advertiser supported rather than viewer supported. This programming, now delivered by over-the-air broadcasters, includes local news, carries important elements of the political debate, and transmits federally funded public, cultural, and instructional presentations. The 'must-carry' rules have the side-effect of reorienting the way in which commercial broadcasters perceive their public responsibilities. The US Supreme Court, in holding that the 'must-carry' rules might be constitutional, recognized Congressional interest in maintaining 'free' or over-the-air television as an important aspect of the structure of speech. The Court seemed anxious, again reflecting the ambivalence that characterizes access and content, to determine that 'free' television was being favoured, not for its content, not for the viewpoint of those who used it, but rather because of qualities it had of providing more universal service. Still, the requirement that broadcast channels be preferred in terms of carriage over other providers of programming may ultimately be justifiable only if they serve goals relating to the enrichment of the public sphere.

Other forms of access, in the broad sense I use it, are relevant to the discussion of the public sphere. In the 1950s the FCC first established its Table of Allocations for the distribution of television broadcast licences, reserving channels for educational purposes. These rules provided access to spectrum, not access across broadcast licences reserved to others. It was out of that reservation that the public broadcasting system emerged. The reservation can be seen as a wholesale act of providing access, first for colleges and municipalities that wanted to use the new medium to fulfil their public responsibilities, and then for a far broader range of cultural institutions. The reservation was a fundamental decision about the architecture of the electronic public sphere. Twenty years later, many local governments, as part of a highly competitive system for awarding local cable franchises, required that cable operators set aside a certain amount of channel time for governmental, educational, and public uses. In early cable television rules during the 1970s, the FCC mandated that local franchises set aside channels for educational and governmental purposes, and in later legislation, the Cable Act of 1984, Congress authorized, but did not compel, these reservations. The FCC, in the past, has required network stations to provide access to their channels to producers other than the large networks, and given special priority to those who produce programming for children. During a brief and unforgettable period, an active Commission, applying the Fairness Doctrine with unexpected rigor, required stations that provided cigarette advertising with the obligation to air anti-smoking ads as well.[34]

Access and the Public Sphere

Common-carrier theology—the imposition of common-carrier standards on portions of the media—is the refuge for those who oppose the access provisions I have described. Ideas of access are intrinsic to the aesthetic of the common-carrier model. The common carrier establishes the fair and non-discriminatory use of an instrument which is essential to the conduct of the society. A common carrier for transportation allows, within limits, assurance concerning travel. Common carriers, providing transit at a set rate and without preference, have been the model for ferrying across rivers since time out of mind. In the twentieth century, the telephone has been the common carrier first for voice, and now for data, and video.

Some think of the common-carrier model as the perfect mechanism for a free-market society dedicated to unencumbered speech and access to modes of distribution of that speech. Multi-channel common-carrier systems, the *deus ex machina* of the new technology, avoid the need for intrusive government intervention. But common carriers provide equal opportunity, not equal access. The introduction of a common-carrier system may change the social narratives, but its introduction will not necessarily create a more pluralistic collection of stories, one that reflects historically excluded racial and ethnic groups. Of course, a common-carrier model can include features that promote universal access and diversified programming: subsidies to preferred groups, specifically mandated reductions in fees for such groups, and similar methods.

The common-carrier model for video and press applications represents, in its full embodiment, an architectural decision that some distribution modes, such as cable or optical fibre should be like the telephone, with published non-discriminatory rates and ownership separated from control of content. Access would be much eased; one might say there would be no gatekeeper. Common-carrier access is appealing because it has the aura of eliminating government intervention to choose among speakers. The 1934 Communications Act precluded the FCC from treating broadcasters as common carriers, and the 1984 and 1992 Cable Acts substantially restricted the regulation of cable by local governments and the FCC. There is a limited treatment of the cable operator as a common carrier, at least imposing an obligation to carry existing broadcast stations and certain specialized carriers which the local franchising authority requires.[35] The intense US debate about whether to allow telephone companies to compete with or absorb cable television companies, for the next generation of broadband video distribution, is precisely about these access questions. Broadening the number of channels should, in theory, reduce the cost of access (though there will always be preferable channels and the access cost will be low relative to the cost of production). An additional step, permitting full switching and digital compression, may mean that the concept of channels themselves will become obsolete, replaced by new marketing, storage, and pricing strategies that give each person access to whatever message or programme he or she wants and can afford (though not necessarily the right of each producer of a message to have automatic access to the desired homes).

To impose a common-carrier model may, however, be the most dramatic form of intervention possible. Cable television companies and telephone companies resist efforts to shape the way they can determine who can use their services. They have emerged as the new speakers and the new press lords. They assert that their determination of the market-place should decide questions of access. Technology, in this way, is creating massive new structures that undermine the old, antiquated ideas of access. It is yet unclear whether improved modes of access will result.

Beneath the romance of access doctrines, there are analytic moments that suggest why government has the power, in some settings, to affect the infrastructure of speech. Throughout the cases and decisions there is the fleeting idea hinted at in the *Pacifica* case discussed in Chapter 8: access rules are premised on a view of speech, in an age of modern mass media, in which a confined theatre of discourse contains powerful narratives that affect the society. Because of the narrowness and powerfulness of that theatre, some rules are necessary to assure that particular groups have access to the narrative. Because the theatre of this speech is ever-present, almost imposed, special rules—rules concerning lock-boxes and indecency, for example—are necessary, separate from the standard constitutional immunities protecting speech from government intervention. Speech practices that are more private, negotiated between provider and consumer, have a different status, and are less susceptible to government control. The theatre of public speech—the mass speech that dominates the political system—is, however, what animates ideas of access. New technologies, new practices, alter these assumptions, however, as Chapter 11 explores.

Access claims in the US broadcasting experience have not been sufficiently grounded in theory. Access doctrines reflect a search for an ersatz politics of pluralism; a surface architecture of free speech that combines the trappings of government non-interference with the illusion that narratives—the stories of the good life—are fairly distributed among its tellers. US communications policy has not produced the ideal public sphere. The efforts to produce diversity of ownership or ownership access did not, during the broadcasting era, produce meaningful diversity of content or necessarily alter the paths of entry into the halls of discourse. Special steps to create ownership by minority licensees were apparently accepted as a way to avoid harsher pressures for programming changes among the industry at large. There is a kind of hubris in the fashioning of access doctrine—the shaping, and taming, and channelling of the massive and unruly forces of opinion and difference in society. Talk of assuring unencumbered access may be a luxury of societies like the United States, where dissent, for the moment, is not perceived as sedition. In transition societies, where the very existence and composition of sovereignty is in a kind of armed equipoise, broadcasting statutes tend to exclude material that would stir up racial and national hatreds.

To the extent that there is greater programme diversity and a greater breadth of narratives now on American television, government intervention through the making of law was not the primary reason. The satellite enabled the efficient delivery of competing programming sources to land-based multi-channel ground distribution sources. The marketing potential of increased channels produced increased diversity for a simple reason: after mainstream subscribers were enrolled, cable entrepreneurs and some broadcasters dependent on cable had an incentive to present programming at the margin that would attract additional subscribers and viewers. In some large—and small—cities, one can now receive the Black Entertainment Network, several Spanish-language channels, the news from Russia and Poland, programming from Italy, Taiwan, India, Korea, and elsewhere around the world. Splintered direct programming, virtually private networks, begin to be introduced because they make economic sense within the present regulatory framework. The new potential of pay-per-view may enable previously ignored audiences to demonstrate the intensity of their desire for special-interest programming through collective bidding for time.

Because most elements of access regulation have been halting, half-way, and under-theorized, the yield has been relatively unproductive in terms of contribution to democratic dialogue: what we have achieved in the United States is a defunct Fairness Doctrine, a clumsy effort to harmonize the growth of cable with the coexistence of broadcasting (through 'must-carry' legislation), and a badly conceived and damaging set of rules concerning the political process (with many built-in irrationalities). It is important to determine, anew, how the structure of television relates to democratic values and citizenship as a grounding for considering public intervention.

Some argue that modern television—not as an instrument of news and information, but as a blanket aspect of culture and education—is antithetical to citizenship and democratic values. The approach to reform with the most integrity might be the abolition of television as we know it. But resurrecting print as the dominant mode of communication is a fantasy. The behemoth of television, with its massive impact, can be seen as having belittled treasured differences, mauled history, and subverted belief patterns. Provision of access by minorities to their constituencies, or to a larger whole, may merely be a counterfeit counterweight to such an overarching tendency. Modern television does not pay its own way, one could argue. It eats away at qualities of citizenship, at the capacity to read and analyse, without having those who consume it pay for the costs to society.

Access must be rethought as a way of groping towards a public sphere: searching not for ethnic and minority representation, but for assurances that there exist the conditions of supervision, involvement, and discourse necessary for a modern democracy. If elements of the principal agenda of access are to be building blocks of the public sphere, then mechanisms beyond traditional modes of political access must be reviewed. A combination of telephony, new communications technologies such as the fax machine, forms of participatory broadcasting such as the radio phone-in, and new ventures, taken together, seems to be part of a new electronic zone of discourse.

Modern-access doctrines must be adapted, interpreted, or evaluated as successors to historical developments of the eighteenth century. This was the period, as Michael Warner has written, of the Republic of Letters, novel ways of using print to provide intercommunication among citizens and the growth of a public sphere. It was not exactly free speech that made modern democracy possible, nor was it solely the existence of the technology of print. Some magical combination of changed industrial practice and technology was at the heart of the new democratic possibilities. Studying the organization of television against the backdrop of the organization of print in the eighteenth century offers us a different way of examining the relationship of technology to culture. We can harken back to the literature relating the history of print (and its technology and organization) to democracy and transfer that learning to the study of television capitalism.[36]

We can hardly reinvent the eighteenth century, and we certainly cannot transplant it into the twentieth. The question is what elements of emerging processes with respect to television create a kind of public sphere, the Republic of Letters. To situate radio and television in this discussion of the public sphere is problematic, since these instruments of communication are late developments of democratic societies. Radio was not necessarily the descendant of the newspaper, as opposed to vaudeville and the music hall, though it claims the mantle of succession today. Indeed, there is something about the emergence and history of radio (and later television) that is almost antithetical to the idealized notions of the public sphere. Almost from the beginning, radio was a vehicle of entertainment, a toy, a soother or organizer of the masses rather than a locus for interpersonal rational discourse among individuals dedicated to the public welfare. In too many places, in the 1930s, radio, and television after it, became instruments for rearranging loyalties rather than more perfect tools for debating the public good. These technologies have been too useful a weapon for the sale of goods (or of ideas) for them to be conceptualized, automatically, as a neutral forum for public discourse.

The public sphere in the twentieth century cannot be described without thinking about the role of radio and television, indeed the altered states of the serial changes in communications technology. Over time the electronic media have become so pervasive, so linked to political institutions, so seized with importance, that the public sphere cannot be imagined without them. Our immediate impulse is to think that reformed electronic media must be at the core of a healthy public sphere in modern society. But simply to assert that is to avoid the analysis that may shed light on how debate is conducted. We have yet to see whether the new broadcasting, at least with respect to the public sphere, is more than another cheap technological illusion.

11 The Open and Closed Terrain of Speech

EACH communications technology, in the convoluted jurisprudence of the US Supreme Court, gives birth to a different test for the permissible regulatory capacity of government. Newspapers are virtually immune. Broadcast television warrants oversight so long as frequencies are scarce. Cable television is susceptible to federal governance because it presents a bottleneck between programmers and the household. These are the oft-criticized justifications for judicial decision. There are, however, other hidden distinctions that explain the Court's preoccupation with differences among the media, distinctions based on the relationship between each technology and the social geography it generates.

Early in this book I emphasized how the footprint of the satellite—the surface reach of its celestial signals—can have a stronger future role in defining the identity of a people than such natural boundaries as rivers or mountains, or the artificial boundaries of empires and the residue of wars. New technologies, including the National Information Infrastructure (the so-called information superhighway), break down borders in other ways. These developments require public consideration because, as the British scholar, Kevin Robins, has written, the 'issues around the politics of communication converge with the politics of space and place: questions of communication are also about the nature and scope of community'.[1]

Most of the access rules outlined in the last chapter, and much of American media regulation, has been based on a given mix of technologies, and, as a consequence, a particular politics of space and place. Over time, however, 'the open terrain' of speech, as I term it, the dominant idiom of communication during the broadcasting era, is giving way to a different mix of technologies and a closing of the public forum. In this chapter I examine the process of change, its implications for the political process, and its consequences for free speech and government regulation.

The Geography of Communications

The next generation of transformations in the United States—the converging technologies of cable, satellite, and telephone—continue to move the society further away from dependence on existing traditions of physical geography as a central means of self-definition. The geography of signals has always organized audiences, whether through the impact of the coaxial cable on creating a national audience for television, through negotiation of radio and television frequencies on the Canadian–United States border to assuage national feelings, or through the long and frustrating search by an individual state, like New Jersey, squeezed between the identities of New York and those of Pennsylvania, for its own VHF television outlet. During an unusual moment in the history of US cable regulation, when only some neighbourhoods in San Diego were permitted to receive television signals imported from Los Angeles and New York, house prices reflected sensitivity to such information changes.

The United States long ago underwent its transition from local media to regional and national services, an internalization of uniformity. John Carey has called the United States a product of 'literacy, cheap paper, rapid and inexpensive transportation and the mechanical reproduction of words'. These technologies transported 'not only people but a complex culture and civilisation from one place to another . . . eclipsing time and space'.[2] Although local-broadcast stations continue to exist, as perhaps the most decentralized model of broadcasting in any country, there is a certain camouflage to the structure. The progress of Constitutional interpretation which extended the federal constraints on the states was an important step in the creation of a common market for information within the United States.[3] What Europeans have dreamt of and worked towards—through the 'Television Without Frontiers Directive'—has, within the United States, long existed. Internal borders have become irrelevant and linguistic differences seem (perhaps erroneously) to have been surmounted. In broadcasting and then in cable television, the doctrine of federal pre-emption—which permits Congressional legislation to trump state law—helped clear the field of state-imposed obstacles. Much of twentieth-century law concerning speech in the United States can be interpreted as a means of creating this market, a prerequisite for the development of a powerful national industry of imagination.[4]

The overpowering strength of the great national television networks, during their golden years, is testimony to the interaction of technology, regulation, and culture. The idea of the 'local' has, historically, been the antithesis of the national in US broadcasting law. Congress and the FCC long emphasized the opportunity for local broadcasters to programme differently from the networks, to strive for diversity and local voices. Licences were and are issued on a community-to-community basis; elements of the community spirit were to be reflected in station operations. An emphasis on local ownership, on determining local needs, on the integration of ownership and management—all of these were designed to reinforce a vision of American life and imagination in which the geographical community had dignity. The skeletal arrangement for localism persists, though the reality is hardly present.

A second transformation of the geography of communications comes through the support of intense and exclusive diasporic communities.[5] The characteristic of 1950s television was the limpid, pleasantly amorphous, broadly assimilating, homogenous, 'Leave It To Beaver' picture of society. Contrast that with the new capacity to have highly tailored modes of communications today; and, more than that, the increased desire that these particularist modes of forming communities be activated. Satellite-delivered channels gather and unite a Spanish-speaking audience. Similar channels or national programmes provide narrowcasting for born-again Christians, members of Chabad Lubavitch (a Hasidic Jewish sect), and groups with special interests (sometimes sports, sometimes political or economic issues). This process will accelerate as the number of channels becomes greater, the interconnection easier, and the method of self-identification more convenient.

What makes these groups diasporic is that the members are physically, though not spiritually, disassociated from one another; what will make them intense is the strength of loyalty to the group fostered by the communications technology itself. There is nothing novel in the idea of shifting loyalties and newly formulated groups. The heart of the United States, in the nineteenth century, was filled with utopian communities. But, given sufficient intensity, the cumulative impact on aspects of national identity will be profound. Television channels will mirror the other new technologies, as, across the Internet, using the new technologies of rapid and private communications, groups establish new allegiances and diminish old ones.

A third geography that emerges from technologies is the reduction to irrelevance of specific place. The convergent technologies so increasingly familiar—telephone, computer, fax, the information infrastructure—reduce the constraint of place as a condition of interaction.[6] Not enough is known about ways in which electronic media have altered or destroyed common notions of the tie between place and person. Even in an earlier time, now nostalgically remembered, a writer observed of the impact of technology that 'millions of Americans who watch TV every evening . . . are in a "location" that is not defined by walls, streets or neighbourhoods but by evanescent "experience" . . . More and more, people are living in a national information-system rather than [in] a local town or city.'[7] This is not exactly the 'global village' predicted by Marshall McLuhan. Rather it is a kind of placelessness, a 'generalised elsewhere' so that 'places are increasingly like one another and . . . the singularity . . . and importance of . . . locality is diminished'.[8] While it is popular to regard expansions of freedom as the consequence of increased choice, and to think of choice as the archetypal prerequisite for increased liberty, this 'emergent placelessness'[9] represents deprivation as well as growth for both democratic processes and notions of identity, a geography of anomie as well as a geography of opportunity.

Defining Open and Closed Terrain

A final shift in the geography of communication is the least well understood and least discussed. It is the geography that reconfigures the balance between broadly available, publicly accessible speech and closed channels of communication. The open terrain of speech includes the soap-box in the park, the streets themselves, so used from time immemorial, and radio and television, open to all to hear. The open terrain of speech creates common experience, or at least its possibility, for all within its purview. Inversely, the 'closed terrain' of speech involves those channels that interconnect individuals privately or serve as dedicated networks committed to the protected use by groups.

To use these terms—open and closed—is not to imply that one mode is better than the other, though openness is generally considered a virtue. A society is not truly free if it fails to protect communications made privately. We bristle at eavesdropping and the suspicion that the right to send and receive letters securely has been invaded. A well-operating civil society depends on the opportunity for individuals to associate, to choose with whom they speak and to whom they listen. Association implies a degree of exclusiveness, privacy, and even secrecy. At the heart of the right to associate is the opportunity to shape a community for protected and shielded speech, and this right is as important as the right to speak at large.

Just as an increase in 'gated communities' may be a danger sign for cities, the communications equivalent may bode ill for a sense of democracy. What is in the open terrain—the space for images available to all—becomes more contested, more valuable, because of its increased scarcity. As the open stage contracts, its text for the encouragement or discouragement of violence, for models of sexual behaviour, for the way the society idealizes children and the family, becomes more intensely examined. Open terrain is intensified as an area of increased sensitivity, a place where public patronage comes under greater scrutiny. Closing the terrain redefines the way space, communities, and human relationships are conceptualized. Reducing the extent of common speech may fracture society, and, conversely, a fractured society has less tolerance for public space.

Our current ideas of free speech are based on an unarticulated relationship between these open and private forms. One could hypothesize that each society has its own balance between channels of communication which are transparent, commonly received, pervasive, and everywhere available, and channels of communication for which people must pay, or, through some special mechanism, elect to hear, read, or watch. A society might be characterized by how much of its speech life takes place in public (in coffee-houses or bookshops) and how much access everyone has to a common pool of political debate and discussion (as through C-SPAN or the nightly network news). A society rich in these opportunities—the life of the village square—can be contrasted with one where the patterns of communication are more selective, hierarchical, open only on the permission of the monitor. These two societies—even with similarly restrained governments—are quite different in terms of the speech experience and the nature of political activity.

This distinction is important because something striking is happening, not only in broadcasting, but throughout society, to the balance between these two forms. Because of new technology, changed attitudes, and the reorganization of the communications industry, much of the traditional open terrain is tending to close and corridors of discourse are becoming more private and more selective. This does not mean that there is less speech; indeed there may be more. The balance changes, with implications that are not yet clearly fathomable. The broadcasting exemplar of this phenomenon is the shift in audience from the over-the-air networks—ABC, NBC, CBS—to channels for which one pays or subscribes: Home Box Office, pay-per-view services and cable television generally. The trend towards self-definition and self-ghettoization, into the intense diasporic communities described above, is another example. The transformation is from spaces for communication that are ubiquitous and commonly available to corridors of expression available for the payment of a fee. In the future, the channels may be available only to those with specific credentials, to groups of common bond.

It is not only in the electronic media that the shift towards the private is taking place; far beyond broadcasting disputes exist over the power to regulate images that are open, accessible, and pervasive. The curriculum of the US public schools is an example of a similar transition, instructive even though the arena is so dissimilar. Public education can be reconceived as open terrain in which children are mandatorily exposed to a set of messages, the purpose of which is training in the art of citizenship. Much of the curriculum is required by law.[10] This terrain is so valuable that an elaborate mode of public involvement exists; formally or informally, machinery has been established in every state for citizens and interest groups who seek to fashion or limit the curriculum. The depiction of subjects about which there are sharp differences becomes a matter of mediated, negotiated conclusion in which governmental involvement is central. State commissions exist to determine which textbooks should be approved.[11] Departures from consensus—no matter how justified—lead to a reduction in the enrolment of children in the public schools (withdrawing them from the open terrain). Similarly, the vanishing of traditional common areas occurs with respect to public parks, public swimming pools, and public libraries.[12]

The very conflict over the use of this open zone leads to its abandonment. The push for consensus, for a lowest common denominator of conflict, robs the curriculum of its vital punch; the highest quality of education is siphoned off to other sites. Lack of quality leads to a spiral of decline. In the extreme, if a society cannot agree on the curriculum for a public school, one choice is to allow common education to dwindle and then disappear. The voucher system, in this reading of events, is tied to the weakening of the open terrain. Under a plan to provide individual students with tuition funds for schools of their choice, the fierce struggle for a consensual curriculum no longer needs to be faced. What remains of the public zone—public schools—

can become, especially in urban areas, education for those on welfare, the poor, those for whom the debate over content can continue without harm to those who control the zone of imagery and discourse.

The parallel to broadcasting is not so difficult to devise. Precisely because the open terrain there has become so contested, the alternative of private channels, a 'voucher system' for television, becomes attractive. Broadcasting has become an arena for contesting the narrative of national identity, with constraints concerning indecency, depictions of gender and race and violence. The private channels are unencumbered and, as a result, can compete unimpeded. Broadcast channels become weaker as their audiences diminish, but, because of their continuing site as the remaining open terrain, the debate over content continues.

Passionate disputes over art in public places is akin to disputes over school curriculum and broadcast offerings. What makes art 'public', in this sense, is precisely what makes broadcasting 'open terrain', in the sense that I have defined it. In addition to being publicly financed (like the education example), it is situated in a place where viewers come across it accidently (as in broadcasting), necessarily, but without intention. Though it has been difficult to articulate, the fact that art is 'public', in this specific audience-related sense, has justified greater mediation and the assertion of competing claims of right. The controversy over Richard Serra's 'Tilted Arc', a brooding and massive vertical sheet of rusting steel, exemplifies the similarities. The sculpture, placed in front of the federal court-house in New York's Foley Square, caused intense (though orchestrated) public outcry. Powerful judges and others who passed the sculpture daily called for its removal.

Serra claimed that his speech rights would be abridged by any action which took the sculpture from the site for which it had been commissioned by the General Services Administration of the federal government. As the dispute matured, the issue of rights shifted from Serra's claims as the sculptor to the concerns of the viewers or passers-by. Foley Square was an essentially public space, a nicely geographical version of the open terrain of speech and ideas. A few years after the height of the Serra debate, David Antin, a poet and critic who, among other unusual things, had produced projects of poetic sky-writing, raised questions about the ethical propriety and the cogency of Serra's arguments based on First Amendment rights. 'Think of it this way: the nice thing about [sky-writing] is it goes away fast, if you don't like it. And if you do like it, you remember it. But it takes an awful lot of energy to get rid of *Tilted Arc*.'[13] For Antin, adapting his argument to the issues here presented, duration of message is a variable which helps determine problems of abuse and occasions for mediation in the open terrain:

> We would probably have very much better public art if everybody wasn't afraid of disturbing people, because they knew you could eventually wheel the art away. I would like to suggest that you could make the most disturbing public art in the world and nobody would give a damn, because you would know that after some limited time it would go away. The way all good discourse goes away. I don't think public art installations should be permanent. I think they should be wreckable. I think we should have a ceremony of destruction and remove them regularly. I think works like Serra's works should after some specifically limited time have been publicly destroyed in an honorable fashion. . . . There was no reason for Serra to iterate his single utterance forever. Perhaps the right to repeat yourself endlessly in a given space is not freedom of speech. It may become a form of tyranny.[14]

Each aspect of the shifting balance in the geographies of speech has important consequences for the political process—and its relationship to the regulation of the media. The shift from the local to the national is the most obvious, since, among other things, it was accompanied by (in a not wholly unrelated manner) the growth in the power in the United States of the presidency and has been the subject of the most writing and analysis. Placelessness may contribute to the dissatisfaction with the relationship between television and politics, as now configured. The political scientist Michael Sandel argues that 'the moral and political institutional scheme of liberal democracy no longer fits the moral and political aspirations of its citizens' because of 'a sense of disempowerment and loss of self-government' and a related loss of community: 'public life is no longer an arena for expression of larger meaning, or a collective identity of the common good.'[15]

The evolution of intense diasporic communities, reinforced by the media, also follows well-documented lines, in which fractioning of constituencies occurs. Major political parties, just like the major national networks, lose the capacity to control a vast, almost universal middle. Just as splinter channels are established to take advantage of intense affinities, the same process takes place for political parties. This diasporic communications geography has implications, too, for the structure of representation in the US democratic system. If individuals are linked, politically, ethnically, and culturally, through television and technology, that undermines traditions of drawing election-related boundaries. Gerrymander, a much-ridiculed concept, has characterized the design of Congressional districts in ways far from the compact and contiguous. Political parties, protecting vulnerable districts, have so contorted boundaries as to override any geometrical rationality.[16] If technology replaces land-related geography as the significant binding mechanism, it is not clear why any physical contiguity should be constitutionally required.

The most important consequence of the shift in the infrastructure of communications is its impact on the machinery of representative democracy. The balance between open and closed terrain manifests itself significantly in the meaning of the First Amendment for the political system. The shift towards abundance brings choice, but shifts in the use of the new technologies mean further evolution in the system of candidate selection, polling, campaigning, and party structure. The current machinery of campaign regulation relating to the media is based, in large part, on the existing balance between open and closed. Elaborate practices concerning advertising, fairness, and access by parties and candidates have developed because of the importance of broadcast television in US electoral politics. Congress, the FCC, and the courts have served as arbiters of access because of the valuable quality of this scarce open terrain. As channels become abundant and audiences splinter, the existence of these traditional common spaces during political campaigns will diminish. Already, national networks, in the face of competition, and seeing their public function diminish, no longer necessarily carry political conventions, or presidential addresses, or other moments of national political significance.

Among the responses to this shift has been the desire to emulate the common and open speech of the New England village, to consider ways of using new technologies—interactivity, abundant channels, and satellite—to foster electronic town meetings.[17] Town meetings were a forum for civic education, and constituted a way to empower ordinary citizens and, within historical limits, promote access and equality. 'To attend a town meeting', Jeffrey Abramson has written,

> was to participate in a potentially transforming process of open debate that was different in kind from the more isolated way individuals participate in voting and elections. Town meeting members might eventually vote; they might agree to disagree and settle their differences only by outvoting one another. But first the members *deliberated*; they stood up, in the presence of their neighbors, and exchanged claims about the town's best interests.

Much romanticized, the town meetings were, in Toqueville's phrase, 'to liberty what primary schools are to science; they bring it within the people's reach, they teach men how to use and how to enjoy it'.[18] They provided, perhaps in fact, but certainly in perception, a sense that government was in the hands of ordinary citizens. As Emerson wrote, 'not a school house, a public pew, a bridge, a pound, a mill-dam, hath been set up, or pulled down, or altered, or bought or sold, without the whole population of this town having a voice in the affair'.[19]

The traditional face-to-face town meeting has declined, even in the picture-perfect New England villages where the tradition has had its longest course; capturing its elements, its genius, its essence, using the new electronic media is filled with conceptual and practical barriers. Abramson has defined the obstacles to easy transformation and the preconditions that need to be met before the virtues of the ancient form can be replicated in a modern teledemocracy: too often the electronic town meeting models avoid the preparation, the immersion in the issues, that characterized the idealized original. Too often, there is no real empowerment. The electronic town meeting should not become a push-button democracy with authoritarian overtones; but the consequences of consensus must be a meaningful influence on government action. And for electronic town meetings to be faithful to their origin, there must be an absence of manipulation, a representative participation in the outcome, and a sense of equality of access.[20] The electronic-town-meeting movement is part of an effort positively to affect the social geography of the new technologies, a technique to establish a new instrument for democracy by controlling the shift from the open to closed terrain of speech.

Apart from the town-meeting experiment, the new technologies present the illusion that, by providing an abundance of channels and greater choice of modes of linking speaker and listener, they will avoid some of the past problems of cost and campaigning. Ironically, the open, common zone will become more scarce, not less so, more subject to rationing, either on the basis of price or by regulation. The consequence will not be cheaper and more available access. Intervention, by law or by agreement, will be necessary to determine how much of a campaign has to be on the open channels rather than the closed one, whether, for example, campaigns will have orchestrated television debates as a legislated requisite.

It may be that the 'basic tier', an invented category from cable that includes the fundamental television service that most households receive, should include some central elements of the political system. Congress and the FCC have worried about the siphoning of valuable programming—such as the World Series—to the closed terrain from historic open broadcasting availability.[21] A similar concern should affect the availability of a forum for campaigns. The technologies of addressability and encryption mean an increase in the coded differentiated messages sent by a single campaign to various constituencies, and the implication of that phenomenon for cost, financing, and disclosure cannot yet be determined.

Political processes have altered with each new broadcast technology. Because of broadcast television itself, efficient large-scale campaign expenditures became more useful. The more complex the technological environment, the more opportunities to tailor messages, to move among media, the more useful vast expenditure advantages will continue to be. The weaker the political parties and the stronger the tie between individual candidate and constituency, the more Jeffersonian the political system will become. The electronic media of the future could fragment the public space or enlarge it and provide the genesis for wholesale changes in the organization of the political system (as in terms of direct democracy or changed patterns of representation).[22] Congress could conceivably carve out, on the electronic highway, campaigning space for Presidential, Senatorial, and Congressional elections. The possibility of dedicated channels for political parties is on the horizon.

Government Role in Preserving Balance

The search for the proper role for government in the architecture of the media, clumsy enough in the era of broadcasting, thus alters direction as the transition to the information superhighway takes place. New challenges arise in mediating access to the open terrain. The commonly held view sees increased technology as a unifying force, leading to one great, intercommunicative culture, a state of economic, political, and social equality. The optimism is based on the notion that abundant channels and increasing choice, almost by definition, reinforce democratic values. As new technological possibilities shape patterns of communication, this vision may come true, but not in the evolutionary way implied. New technologies will irretrievably alter the current structure of speech, politics, and law, as each other technology has in its turn.

The problem of finding the right balance between the open and closed terrain of speech is useful in explaining the difficult problem of differential federal jurisdiction over various media technologies. In a famous pair of cases, *Red Lion* and *Tornillo*, the Supreme Court held that regulation of broadcasters could be more rigorous than regulation of newspaper content.[23] Requirements of 'fairness', or a kind of access, could be imposed upon television licensees but not upon newspaper publishers. The Supreme Court, ruling on the power of Congress to regulate cable television, found that there, too, Congress could engage in forms of regulation not permitted with respect to newspapers, though not so comprehensively as might be warranted by scarce television frequencies.[24] Many commentators have criticized these decisions, arguing that broadcasters and cable operators are speakers—or part of the press—entitled to the same freedom from governmental regulation that newspaper publishers enjoy.

Differing treatment of the three modes of distributing information can be explained in terms of the open and closed terrain of public discourse. In its description of varying treatment of the three technologies, the Supreme Court has fastened on scarcity (for broadcasting) and bottlenecks (for cable) as articulated bases for forms of regulation. These arguments, so familiar, mask a more complex and deeper justification: the more intrusive or invasive a medium, the more involuntarily it is received, the more government regulation of some sort is warranted or justifiable.[25] In this scale, broadcasting is the most invasive and openly and broadly available, newspapers can be described as partaking most of the quality of private transaction between buyer and seller, and cable is in the middle. The distinction is based not on the persuasiveness of advocacy, but on pervasiveness in a sense not usually acknowledged.[26]

I have already mentioned the Supreme Court case reviewing legislation and FCC rules that would require cable systems to carry the signals of local commercial and non-commercial broadcast channels.[27] In its infancy, cable television needed to deliver improved broadcast signals to attract subscribers. Cable systems fought for the right to carry the local television stations, arguing that they were performing a public service by doing so. By the mid-1980s, with the coming of the satellite and the proliferation of new networks (like HBO and MTV), cable had many other products to sell (including motion picture channels, news channels, and sports channels). In some instances, with limited space available, cable systems wanted to discard local broadcasting stations to make room for the specially created programme services. Cable operators certainly wanted the unregulated authority to decide what arrangement of programming should be selected, from all sources available, and delivered to subscribers.

In response to intense pressure from broadcasters and from Congress, the FCC stepped in: the agency drafted a series of regulations, the afore-mentioned 'must-carry' rules, that limited the freedom of cable operators. In part, the FCC was acting to protect the economic interests of an industry—broadcasting—that it had long regulated. Fearing that, over time, services that had generally and 'without cost' been made available to the mass of American viewers would diminish on free, 'over-the-air' television, the FCC told cable operators what signals they were obliged to carry and, at an early stage in the rules, what kinds of programmes should not be available for cable programming services. The FCC tried to keep, for the established broadcasters, a competitive advantage, with the most important athletic events (like the World Series), dramas, and films, partly to provide an economic basis for public service uses of television.

The Court of Appeals for the District of Columbia, a distinguished federal tribunal, consistently rejected these rules, using a traditional free-speech analysis. The court upheld the right of the cable operator to choose what signals it wished to carry. The FCC's justification for the rules—preserving local news and information and a universal free television service—might have been an adequate ground for regulation, but the rules were so crudely drawn, so broadly inclusive, that the nature of the restrictions was beyond what was necessary to achieve even the constitutionally doubtful goals. In a famous shorthand phrase, the court said that the FCC was unconstitutionally protecting broad*casters*, not broadcast*ing*.

After the FCC had failed, twice, in its adopted 'must-carry' rules, Congress included a complex scheme in its 1992 Cable Act. One could read those rules as establishing a zone of open terrain on the cable, a regime that assured the continued viability of the licensed television broadcast stations. Those rules could be interpreted as a tribute to 'free television', including public broadcasting, as a carrier of America's national identity (though the term would not be used). Cable television may be wonderful; it brings an abundance of channels into the home, new opportunities for access, new realms for producers of speech. Most cable channels, however, will be largely private. There is a need, Congress's seemed to be saying, for a residual system of conventional over-the-air broadcasting stations, available to all, with public-service obligations, carriage of local news, and a mechanism for traditional forms of advertising and consumer access.

In June 1994 the US Supreme Court demonstrated its state of confusion over the power of the Congress to preserve the 'open terrain' of free broadcasting. Splitting 5–4, the Court determined that Congress could (under limited circumstances, not yet demonstrated to judicial satisfaction) require cable systems to carry local commercial and noncommercial broadcasters. The Court went out of its way to demonstrate that Congress could do so only—oddly—if it did so for reasons indifferent to what was carried on these channels. Congressional efforts to sustain public broadcasting because of its educational content, or local broadcasters because of their contribution to localism and news and public-affairs coverage, were harshly resisted. 'Free television', some version of what I have called the 'open terrain of speech', could be preserved. What the Court could not admit, not even the narrow majority gathered for the result, was that anything like national identity or strengthening of the public sphere—anything having to do with substance or content or the nature of American society—had any influence on its decision at all.

Content, Scarcity, and Open Terrain

The Supreme Court's sterile and aloof approach to content was in studied contradistinction to debates, raging throughout America, about imagery, narrative, and their relation to television, radio, and culture. As the last years of the century approached, the content of the open terrain, the shape of national identity, and the nature of the public sphere were constant aspects of the social agenda. In the 1990s the threatened reinstatement by Congress of the Fairness Doctrine (requiring competing views on public issues to be broadcast) was a symbolic mark of concern about public debate. The Television Improvement Act—a legislated cease-fire in the dispute over television violence—was passed to exempt networks from the antitrust laws, so that they could convene, free from fear of retaliation,[28] to achieve a less objectionable common broadcasting terrain. The 1990 Children's Television Act was passed as a modest protest to popular fears about the nation's youth.[29] Federal cable legislation imposed obscenity rules on channels that were made generally available (as opposed to those, on the more closed terrain, solicited by the viewer by special charge).

Proposed legislation dealing with the National Information Infrastructure sought to cope with universal access and uses by schools, public broadcasting, and the growing popular television community. Piecemeal, often coming from different motives and different groups, these steps remained fitful and incoherent—a condition inevitable in a society so fearful of abridging free speech.

The authority of society to intervene, in this reading, declines with the tailoring of communication. In the private transaction to buy the viewing of a movie, the recipient has expressed his or her desire, and, apart from the frontiers of hate, violence, and obscenity, the function of the state seems minimal.[30] In contradistinction, 'free television', a category recognized by the US Supreme Court as a justifiable institution for Congress to protect, has qualities of openness, since its content flows, unimpeded and unmediated (except for the weak resistance of the off–on button), into the living-rooms of the citizenry.[31] Broadcast television is more open; pay television is more closed.

In the world of the Internet and the switched communications systems of the future, these distinctions become more pervasive and more meaningful. Except for the greatest dramas of the day, moonwalks and coronations, audiences will be carved up, redefined, and enter into transactional relationships with each other and with providers of information. Far from being sinister, this transition can be productive and efficient in terms of the distribution of information. Yet, without intervention, the inevitable consequence will be greater divisions between those who have and those who do not have relevant information (because information will now be priced and wealth will be an ever more reliable criterion for distribution). The ability to distinguish, so remarkably, in terms of intensity and passion for information, will mean that the closed channels of the future will divide groups and render the messages more centrifugal than they have ever been before.

The new technologies, replete with addressability, are heralded for putting the viewer in charge of choice. But the patterns of interactivity that emerge will not necessarily be those enthusiastically projected as signs of a restored autonomy for the individual. Newspapers are filled with diagrams explaining the frontiers of the information world of the future. Within the forest of charts and metaphors, something important is obfuscated: contrary to what might be anticipated, the very abundance of channels may mean more, not fewer, calls for government intervention to ensure that something remains of the public space.

It is possible that remaining open space, the broadcast channels of our past, will wither and decline, like an abandoned park or a theatre no longer attended. Increasingly, quality programming will continue to migrate to the channels where viewer choice will be expressed through individual paid experience. The highest quality news, the important films, and great sporting events will be delivered along the channels of the closed and privatized terrain. Advertising will adjust to the opportunities provided by the interactive technologies. While the open terrain retains value, consumer and other interest groups will find sophisticated techniques to control or affect its narratives; and the contraction of the open forum means that these contests, at least in the short run, will become even more bitter. As consensus on what should be the content of the open channels becomes more elusive, regulation will broaden in scope and increase in intensity; this, perversely, will contribute to the process by which information and entertainment providers will switch to unregulated alternatives. Ultimately, resort to government will continue, in the long run, if open pathways for speech remain valuable, and speech there becomes even more influential because of its capacity to sustain a general reach. Then, what is left of the open terrain will be even more carefully negotiated, more subject to compromise.

A thousand factors will converge to determine the impact on the balance between the open and the closed. These include how the system is organized, who exercises control, what entities have access on what terms, whether there are incentives or subsidies for public users (such as public television), how they are priced, how they are secured (in terms of the privacy of the message), and what mechanisms, if any, exist for their policing as to content. Scarcity as a traditional justification of intervention can re-emerge: as the shift from open to closed terrain occurs, instead of vanishing, the scarcity of common space becomes a cause for disputation and government involvement.

A mechanism must be fashioned so that some speakers, at some times, have an opportunity to broadcast views generally, to invade the space necessary to reach even those for whom a transaction greater than pushing the off–on button would be a barrier. The market may automatically produce such an opportunity, at least for the grand occasions of social life, but for those occasions significant to identity and the public sphere, such as in the organization of political life, the common openness of public celebration needs nourishing. Granted, the right of the listener not to be bombarded, to have refuge from the onslaught of modern technology, must be respected.[32] Defining the appropriate place for refuge—an important problem in the past so as to avoid an Orwellian universe—will continue into the future. A related problem in a world of closing terrain is fashioning a greater right of access by listeners to speech the speaker wishes to withhold. In that zone called cyberspace, for example, some keepers of the new morality contend that there should be a limit on anonymous messages—that there is an obligation for a speaker to self-identify. Just as law now provides that some government meetings must be open and some government information available, constraints may be imposed on how much secrecy in communications between organizations and individuals is tolerable.

Akhil Reed Amar has written movingly of the problem of captivity and the closing of the speech terrain. Early in a June morning in 1990, young Robert A. Viktora and several teenage friends assembled a crude cross, made from broken chair legs, and set it afire within the fenced yard of a black family in St Paul, Minnesota. The malefactors were arrested under a city ordinance that made it a misdemeanour to use certain symbols, including a burning cross, that would likely arouse anger, alarm, or resentment on grounds of race, colour, creed, religion, or gender. In a much-noted opinion restricting the power of states to proscribe categories of expression, the Supreme Court struck down the St Paul ordinance on the grounds that the statutory scheme improperly singled out certain speech, on the basis of content, to be criminalized as hateful.[33] Amar offers a sympathetic reading of the now-discredited law: the statute was aimed at preventing 'the intentional trapping of a captive audience of blacks, in order to subject them to face-to-face degradation and dehumanisation', which constitute circumstances engendering a badge of servitude.[34] In these circumstances, forced speech which is race-based raises Thirteenth Amendment issues even beyond the contention that 'there simply is no right to force speech into the home of an unwilling listener'.[35]

The two rights—the right to gain the theatre of the open terrain and the right to resist speech—must be separated, however; they have different justifications and different historical bases. The right of speaker and listener to form a closed community is akin to the right of association asserted by organizations like the National Association for the Advancement of Colored People, when membership lists were demanded by ill-motivated state governments.[36] The speaker's right to send a message solely to an intended recipient is similar to the right of the user of the mail to be sure that only the addressee receives it. But the right of a speaker to choose listeners is not absolute. Congress has enacted compulsory licence legislation which allowed cable operators to replay programming without the permission of the copyright owner. Perhaps there are limits, having to do with race or other matters, that would justify legislation governing the power of speakers and listeners to establish their own community. In the recent past, listeners have pushed through federal legislation that protects them from unwanted junk phone calls. In mail regulation, Congress established rate structures, such as second-class postage, which encourage particular patterns of distribution of information and provide addressees the right to stop letters found offensive 'because of their lewd and salacious character'.[37]

The hope—always the hope in a time of change—is that technology will render irrelevant the crises of identity and democracy that have marred the past and clouded the future. New technology, however, cannot remove the dilemmas of race and gender, the distinctions of poverty and wealth, the problems of education, and the challenge of creating an effective and fair political process. Technology alters the relationship of imagery and power, but it does not erase its divisive sting. The problem—or it may be the saving grace—of the society is that there has never been an explicit and comprehensive vision in the United States linking the broadcast media, national character, and US democracy.

Part Four

Conclusion

12 Globalism, Television, and Society

ANY essay on imagery in these times is a journey through the crumbling ideological monuments and scarred political landscapes of the late twentieth century: national dreams in tatters as 'ancient states vanish like morning mists';[1] the shaky founding of new countries searching for old identities; the trash heaps of articulated principles and statutory formulations; the ravages of modern popular culture; the recurring dreams connected to new technologies; and, everywhere, the unnerving, unpredictable competition between cohesion and dispersal, universal and local, modern and fundamental. The great transformations in media emerge against a field of hulking wrecks—warring civilizations, vanishing habits, the rusting machinery of old technology —from which vast changes emerge. Such a moment couples the sadness of obsolescence with the possibilities of hope.

Two themes dominate: the importance of perfecting a public sphere and the necessity to rethink the relationship of media to community, cohesion, and national identities. The theoretical danger is that the achievement of one is put in jeopardy by the strengthening of the other. A re-engineered communications system which enhances the closed terrain of the public sphere stands a chance of loosening the traditional bonds of cohesion. And a system in which the government can too effectively underwrite its version of a national identity jeopardizes the movement to a more effective zone for autonomous popular discussion and debate. The task is finding ways in which the two themes can yield harmonization not conflict. There is nothing particularly new in this tension but the technology.

National Identity

I have emphasized that every state holds a conversation with its subjects as to the legitimacy of its existence. In this conversation, the state is engaged in self-justification, in making the case for the loyalty of its citizens. Some states may have so weak a franchise without the use of force or fiction that the creation and propagation of a narrative of legitimacy is all-consuming, pervasive, and devastatingly revealing of the regime. Even in democratic societies, however, the necessity for generating and maintaining a narrative of community is a universal occupation. What is important is that these ideas and images are part of every state's definition. Governments are virtually compelled to generate or favour images that reinforce the relationship between their subjects and themselves. The state may claim to intervene in the market-place of ideas out of defence of its culture, a valid and relevant ground for intervention, or, more ambitiously, to encourage a world outlook that extends its dominion. National identity, so theatrical and compelling a concept, becomes, as I have argued, the often elegant collection of images that the government (or a series of interest groups) manufactures or encourages to keep itself in power.

In the face of global competition, the articulation of national identity, and its connection to language and the arts, to writing, film, and television, must be doubly nourished. For the state's competition to be effective in the tempestuous market for loyalties, far more is necessary than a wholly privatized system in which contractual standards are imposed on licensees to create obligations to carry cultural programming and perform other communal tasks, such as the distribution of news and information. Those licensees, faced with an inner mandate to build audiences, are obliged to their shareholders to interpret public-interest duties as narrowly as possible; consequently, these clauses become hollow and mocking. That is the lesson of the US experience, and it comes, quietly packed, in the model of broadcasting in which the lesson was learnt.

To be effective, the state must reform and enliven the often rigid, overstaffed, sometimes corrupt, and cynical public-service broadcasting organizations. Everywhere these organizations are under threat and, often, in decline. They must, instead, become to television what the great national orchestras are to music, or a great university to education in general. They must seize the opportunities presented by the new technologies rather than collapse in the face of a relatively fictive new abundance. Revisiting old approaches, such as reimposing a Fairness Doctrine, controlling the extent of advertising, or restoring other forms of the 'public interest', is insufficient. The old agenda is somewhat threadbare, conceived in another era, with another set of competitors, another technology, another audience. Even at the US high-water mark of broadcast regulation there was precious little to indicate a strong correlation between intervention and positive contributions to democratic objectives. What is necessary, rather, is a reformulation of the public interest in terms of the new technology. The role of government as patron—as funder of television programming—is part of that analysis. Mark Yudof put the role of government well:

democratic governments . . . cannot decline to teach or lead or persuade; they are democratic to the extent to which they convey democratic values. To put the matter differently, government advertising, government publication, and government programs that consciously seek to reinforce notions of tolerance, electoral participation, government by consent, and the like need not be feared. They contribute to the establishment of a framework in which government indoctrination to 'objectionable' values—there is no better way to describe them—is rendered more difficult. Thus what seems at first blush a paradox or antinomy . . . may really be a question of balance. The self-controlled citizen is the foundation of representative democracy, but a product of socialization.[2]

In Kiev, in the early 1990s there was a crude characterization of the government's own broadcasting reminder of its cultural past: 'short-pants' television, so-named because of the costumes worn by accordion-playing men. 'Short-pants' television is hardly sufficient. Public-service television must find a new national role as the vehicle of patronage in the market for loyalties and must strengthen its links with other forms of patronage in the arts. Establishing this role is hardly easy, but it must remind a nation what is best about itself, about its association with excellence (not only within its borders but from around the world). We have seen that the United States, in its financial support of the transition societies, through government and foundations, and by its fervent and understandable commitment to free enterprise, has had a tendency to build up the vehicles that tinselize society, sometimes at the expense of those that reinforce it. The general effort to finance an independent sector in broadcasting through Western aid is laudable, but equal attention should be given to the wholesome reform of the public broadcasting sector.

When the Berlin Wall fell, when the Soviet empire was in its days of collapse, globalization seemed to imply, rather rosily, a celebration of openness, the broadcasting equivalent of the end of history. Notions of cultural imperialism were momentarily cast aside and the inconsistencies between the building of new nations and the destruction of old communications systems were avoided. Now, shifts of momentous significance include contests over communication spheres of interest.

As the difficulties of maintaining stability in a post-Soviet or post-Communist period begin to emerge, it becomes necessary to question whether the nation-state can survive in a world in which the boundaries of culture, faith, and imagination do not.

Long ago now, Marie Brenner, the critic, called television the 'plug-in drug', and in a wildly implausible book, Jerry Mander wrote of 'Four Arguments for the Elimination of Television'. Elimination of television is neither possible nor wholly desirable, but the extent of watching and its relationship to education and civic participation ought to be a matter of national concern. Television-watching should be considered, like cigarette-smoking, an activity that has dangerous consequences, so dangerous that an effective strategy should be adopted to reduce or modify it. With a number of aspects of such behaviour, including unprotected sexual practices in the light of AIDS, and the use of drugs, it is increasingly the case that the role of government is to educate, to use imagery and information to alter the customs of the community. In each of these areas, a government role has been established not to restrict freedom, either of action or of speech, but rather to affect the environment in which people make decisions. In the case of smoking, the most encumbered and elaborate intervention has taken place, involving not only official warnings, but tax policies, limitations on the capacity to advertise, restrictions on the location of points of sale, and restrictions on the age of those who can buy. In the instance of AIDS, affecting behaviour has been far more exclusively a matter of education, a kind of collective responsibility to help inform individuals—particularly the young—of the risk of casual unprotected sexual activity.

No Western society has yet come to the explicit conclusion that too extensive viewing is harmful, not only to the viewer, but to society itself. There is no visible impact, as there is with cigarettes, no physical equivalent of abused lungs. Indeed, for some, heavy viewing is a benefit, a source of information, and, for others, a diversion from otherwise cruel, narrow, impoverished lives. But it is fairly obvious that what might be called virulent television is the enemy of contemplation, of reading and the arduous process of citizenship. It is not that violence on television necessarily yields violence, or that supposed indecency yields alleged immorality; but rather that excessive mindless watching of television affects the quality of citizenry, the sense of responsibility, even the capacity to compete. Popular culture, transmitted through the new technologies, constitutes the most effective, most influential, most technically proficient curriculum throughout the West and the transition states. Rather than deny the fact, or engage in the impossible fantasy of censorship, societies must consider how to provide critical understanding of the alternatives they face. This does not mean lessons, as of old, in which young comrades read of the virtues of collective enterprises. Squaring the life of the screen with the life of one's existence is no new problem; neither is learning how to decide between the attractions of the market and the necessities of home. As these dichotomies and similar ones increase, they require attention or lead to despair, and worse.

The Public Sphere

Concerns about education, the very core of the means of maintaining community, bring together national-identity questions and those relating to the public sphere. Without attention to the best virtues of a national identity, the public sphere cannot function. Those who are to participate within a public sphere will fail to have the tools necessary for deliberative democracy. For that reason, the debate over who and what is protected by limitations on state intervention in the field of speech is perpetual. The debate, however, cannot be limited merely to content, to the familiar issues that represent, as I have tried to demonstrate, aspects of national identity. More attention must be paid to the infrastructure of speech, the balance between the open and closed terrain, the question of cost and access, the issue of what entities in the society receive the privileged status of speaker. Increasingly, the questions include how specially to treat multinational corporations, in terms of their capacity to envelop the culture; whether there is a difference, in terms of the regulation of communication, between the stuff of immediate political discourse (news, information, debate) and the stuff of popular culture (entertainment, advertising, and other commercial speech), whether there is a difference between establishing the architecture of communications (addressing monopoly concerns and assuring competition) and controlling speech itself.

The future sanity of a society may rest on its capacity to make meaningful, principled, honourable distinctions in addressing these questions. As we have seen, historic approaches that justified state intervention are eroding and enhanced discourse and freedom are not the only result. Technology combines with altered legal doctrine to reduce government's nominal capacity to affect national identity and enhance the public sphere. In the United States, cable television corporations and telephone companies, successfully arguing that they are 'speakers', rather than instruments for other speakers and listeners to use, have depleted the power of the Congress (or of the states) to impose regulatory standards. This technique is employed to deny government, at a time of technological change, the power to influence the design of the electronic highway. Historic separations between those who use the highways of speech and those who operate them—as in the evolution of telephone—are virtually undone. Whether it is convergence of technologies, disappearance of editorial categories, the elimination of scarcity of frequencies as a justification, or a more libertarian hostility to the state, increased immunity from government intervention means that a rethinking of the relationship of state to speech becomes more pressing.

In this environment, interpretations of the First Amendment, and equivalent doctrines throughout the world, can become not an instrument for the realization of democratic values, but a severe and significant block to vision. Those who benefit from the expansion of the US free-speech jurisprudence find it advantageous to couch the question of state power in terms of process and law rather than in terms of a substantive idea of the relationship of popular imagery to the course of history. Prevailing metaphors, encapsulating directions in regulation, demonstrate the law-related mentality. The first is government as 'traffic cop', in which the state is little more than a facilitator of movement among competing private interests. The second, which implies minor remedial activism, ascribes to government the task of 'levelling the playing field', with the levelling function usually limited to overcoming advantages earlier conferred on some competitors rather than others. The champion of all metaphors is 'the market', the market economy, the free market, the market-place of ideas. The market is, by definition, a place of no intrinsic loyalties except to the market itself. In all these formulations, orchestrated neutrality is vaunted as a means of denying a positive role to the official decision-maker.

But what appears to be a form of non-intervention may be merely the reconfiguring and reconfirming of the collection of American and other myths. In the transnational arena, extended and unbounded concepts of human rights and free speech are the forward guard of narratives of the West arriving on commercial wings. A new sense of concern must emerge, new structures of thinking, if there is to be hope of cultural, educational, and civic redemption. At the least, alternative conceptions of the role of government and society are needed so that we, collectively, are not powerless to adjust to shifting circumstances in the circulation of images. Cass Sunstein, the noted University of Chicago legal scholar, has called for 'a new understanding of freedom of expression . . . [that] would draw a sharp distinction between a "marketplace of ideas" and a system of democratic deliberation'. Such an understanding would 'be more self-consciously focused on our constitutional aspirations to democracy'. Sunstein has argued that the market-place of ideas is not a thing found in nature, but 'itself a system of regulation, not an untrammeled intellectual bazaar'. The choice is not between regulation and laissez-faire, in Sunstein's view, but 'deciding among different systems of regulation, some of which serve the aims of democratic deliberation better than others'.[3]

Especially within the United States, there is the stretching-out of free-speech principles, the conversion of the First Amendment into a doctrine that, in a broad fashion, hampers the capacity of the community to deal with the infrastructure of speech and its impact on national identity and the public sphere. The issue is the power to determine large-scale industrial questions: the relationship of broadcasting services to cable, the extent of permissible access, the changing role of the telephone companies, the scale and architecture of the information highway. As technology alters, the existing relationship between state and the media must undergo radical change. While these changes redetermine the environment for speech, they do not require a shut-down of efforts to think through how media can be used, consistent with democratic values, for purposes of enhancing the public sphere. New communications technologies, massive and expensive, have always depended on government subsidy, favourable regulation, special privileges, and, often, protection from competition. There is nothing inherent in the air waves or the inert wire or the optical fibre that dictates the social organization or business and legal structure that accompanies it as the service is delivered. Physics controls what occurs in the wire. Law and social organization determine what occurs before and after. These elements of organization are open to a realm of public definition and legislation without 'abridging freedom of speech'.

There are novel aspects as a consequence of change. The design of emerging technologies, for example, will affect demand and patterns of viewing and use. Ever since the rise of cable television, what is obtained in the home (primarily in the form of entertainment at present) is priced and repriced, with, increasingly, direct payments from home to supplier. Just as viewers now pay for television on a more accountable basis, rather than indirectly through advertising, information itself will soon be more finely metred. As a precursor of things to come, US courts and Congress debate how to preserve the option of 'free' or advertiser-supported television.[4] Congress has commissioned a study of the migration of sports programming from traditional broadcasting to channels available only on cable or on a pay-per-programme basis; implicit was a sense that the availability of certain events to a national audience was an important aspect of citizenship.

At the close of the twentieth century in Europe and the United States, the emerging symbol of a new future is the electronic superhighway—the vision of five hundred channels (or a single switched channel of access to a universe of information), unlimited interactivity, and the capacity for heightened consumer choice and apparent control. The vision is full of promise, freedom, and choice. It is the hope for a life of ultimate choice without externally imposed boundaries. But most expressions of the vision, for all the industrial excitement, tell little or nothing about its impact.

Five hundred channels—or the more likely fully switched network—can be like five hundred flavours of chewing gum, or models of automobiles; they can provide the illusion of choice or actual diversity. Five hundred channels can contribute to the balkanization of community, or they can create new concepts of cohesiveness. Their content can reinforce national identities or destroy them. Public debate can be enhanced or diminished. Five hundred channels can mean more news, as is often assumed, or, without care, they can mean less, including the disappearance of newspapers as we know them. The new abundance can mean a multiplication of channels that increase the openness of government, or the undermining of those experiments in access that now exist. Five hundred channels can be organized to provide lifeline service to the poor and the aged, or they can mean a two-tiered system of access to information and entertainment, increasing the gap between haves and have-nots. Five hundred channels can mean a healthier political system with greater access by political parties and more substantive discourse by candidates, or they can mean unmediated, non-critical cleaving perspectives and an acceleration in the relationship between wealth and access to voters. Five hundred channels can provide room for more public broadcasting, but they can also mean the end of the public-service role as it has historically developed in the twentieth century. New technologies can provide the infrastructure that makes existing polities more efficient, or they can be the web of their undoing.

The political dimensions of these vast changes in technology and delivery of systems have drowned in fanciful enticements: more is better, motion equals freedom. In terms of technological plenty, more is not only good, it is inevitable. Abundance equals choice equals liberty. Progress is measured by the move to higher planes of availability. But more can be less: more pollution, more violence, more distance of individual both from self and from community. Indeed, the bleak prospect exists that more channels can mean less speech, endless variations on the same themes, or time-switching as a figleaf of choice. The vocabulary of change provides insight into the social outcomes. The concept, for example, of an electronic highway helps define the probable government role as minimal, limited to planning, to some traffic-cop functions, and the minor collection of tolls. But thinking of change in another way—say in terms of its impact on education, or literacy, or the competitiveness of labour—might yield a different definition of the government's authority.[5] The rush towards the electronic highway with its portrayal of the autonomous individual is an important aspect of the debate in the most developed societies. But it can also be a distraction from the geopolitical implications of the new technologies.

In this environment, governments, never loathe to censor, will be surprisingly resilient. And those passionate enough to press for general conformity to their views will employ the machinery of the state to aid them in their crusade. The more concentrated the press (and other aspects of the entertainment and information industry), the easier it is for the government to affect, sometimes subtly, their behaviour. If there is concentration at a bottleneck, it will not matter how many sources there are that feed into the yaw; unless there is a common carrier, the possibility of control will be sufficient for the exercise of government influence. A highly decentralized press, with hundreds and thousands of independent publishers of newspapers, or owners of television stations can be a greater mark of a free society than a market-place dominated by a few multinational corporations. But if the thousands have to pass through the eye of a single needle, the effect may be similar.

This book has been an effort to rediscover and redefine justifications for public intervention in the market-place of ideas. The answer for the transition societies cannot be a closing-down, a look inward, a stony, faith-based rejection of programming from abroad. These societies, like their counterparts in Western Europe and the United States, must now enhance free speech, reinforce markets which ensure competition, and, simultaneously, build and maintain legitimate democratic institutions.

The task is the formulation of a legal structure which best serves the aims of democratic deliberation; and it is a task that plagues most contemporary societies, whether they are in transition to a post-Soviet society—in Eastern and Central Europe and the former Soviet Union—or in the European Union or the United States. The great media revolutions—radio, television, cable, satellite—though they expanded the potential instruments of discourse, have not necessarily contributed to an improved realization of political participation. To say that the new technologies seem more friendly to democratic processes is hardly a response. We have seen that here, as before, the fruits of the channels of abundance are sometimes illusory, and often bitter.

Promoting democratic processes can be merely a slogan, and one that does not provide an indication of the nature and stability of the political entity that is, itself, the organizer and collective fulfilment of all the communicative capacities in the state. A society is in grave difficulty if the promotion of a robust zone of debate and discourse leads to a dissipation of cohesion and a destruction of dominant ideas of national identity. But more and more societies seem to face the kind of fissures that this adverse juxtaposition implies. The open terrain of dialogue has, traditionally, required some notion of common ground, some point of joint aspiration. As these ideas of common ground diminish, fractious, first competitive and then destructive national identities emerge.

Encoding, legal systems send messages that accompany and contribute to what is on the screen; the formal structure, unseen, is part of the visible text. David Morley has written that properly to consider the 'meaning' of a television programme, one must understand the conditions of its production, the word and picture text itself (the 'media artefact'), and the interrelationship between the text and audience.[6] Law has traditionally had its impact on all aspects of this stream. Throughout the world, governments, through subsidy, antitrust law, and the establishment of state monopolies, have dealt with the circumstances in which the media are produced. Through censorship, whether of the velvet or the more intrusive kind, government has affected the word and picture text. Historic patterns of regulation have determined how text is delivered to audience, including how programmes are packaged and surrounded and how much choice the viewer has. In a time of global change, however, the power of government in each of these areas is no longer so strong, depriving law, in its deepest sense, of its impact on the very circumstances of production and the dwelling-house of presentation.

Indeed, the sudden tentativeness of political arrangements and the epidemic of national disintegration owe something to the transformation of networks of communications. I have reviewed how Radio Free Europe, Radio Liberty, the Voice of America, and the BBC take some credit for the collapse of the *ancien régime*. Whether all they claim is warranted will never be known; but governments act on the belief that altered patterns of the sending and receiving of messages has fundamental importance. Because of networks which are both more global and more local, what each individual imagines as a destination for loyalties and a matter of concern will alter. This is what I referred to as the geography of the mind, a geography that shifts with the reorientation of centres for the production of stories, organizations for their distribution, and modes established for interconnection.

What should be no surprise is that sermons to others are really sermons to ourselves. The issues that face Poland and Russia and Hungary also face the European Union and the United States and, in different ways and to different extents, the rest of the world. It is not even clear that there will be vast differences in the diffusion of new technologies—at least within these countries—though the gap seems major now. The essence of globalization is this common quality to the communications questions presented: while media developments have had global implications throughout history, there is the risk of a greatly altered role for the state in monitoring and affecting structure and content, and therefore in shaping national identity and the democratic process. Globalism is tied to a loss of control and an important loss in terms of maintaining the bundle of loyalties that constitute any particular national identity.

Great global contests have emerged between narratives of modernity and narratives of tradition. While much is written about these struggles for the soul, far less is said about the contests over media structure and openness that make these contestations possible. The United States and others export not only their television programmes, but, as a necessary adherent, the regulatory structure and business organizations that undergird them. New laws regulating mass media seem to function, purposely, to provide the appearance of change and movement towards social responsibility just when these goals are not in the offing. Laws incorporate hypocrisies, proscribing indecency or the curbing of violence in a culture in which pornography and images of brutality are ever-increasing. Law provides comfort; formal notions that things are under control when they are not. In the transition societies, mass-media laws incorporate not realities, but aspirations. At their best, they reflect hopes concerning diversity, the possibility of multiple national identities, the incorporation of fairness in the use of language, and the striving for objectivity. Mass-media laws, in context, signify a society's attitude towards speech and the public sphere and provide some formal insight into the construction of political discourse. These structures are understood, often, by those who watch the news, who must interpret its relationship to truth, to objectivity, and to their lives.

Conclusions

It is hardly sufficient to demonstrate, Cassandra-like, the ills that are to befall us. A notion of reconstruction, repair, and healing, necessary in a time of geopolitical change, requires a guide for the proper role of the institutions of society. These propositions emerge from this study.

As to national identity:

1. There is a market for loyalties both globally and within each state. A principal function of the state has been to mediate among the competitors within its own market; and media law is the vehicle for the organization and regulation of this market.

2. Governments participate in the global market for loyalties through the direct export of views by subsidizing or encouraging enterprises that, privately, achieve similar objectives. Governments seek global regulatory arrangements and media laws in third countries that favour their position in the market for loyalties.

3. Within a state, national identity consists of a set of ideas, myths, and narratives used by the dominant group or coalition to maintain power (and, as a corollary, by other groups to challenge or obtain power). Governments can, and almost always do, compete in their

internal market for loyalties by putting forward an internally mediated idea of national identity. In a properly operating market for loyalties, government does not act as censor, but interacts with other interest groups in a dialogic evolution of custom, definition of standards, and construction of appropriate limits or taboos.

4. Censorship is a short cut, condemned and, increasingly, technologically difficult, for policing the market for loyalties. To compensate for its justified rejection as a regulatory tool, alternative modes for government participation in the market for loyalties become indispensable for maintaining its authority (and sometimes for asserting the state's continued legitimacy). These modes include support of a competing public broadcasting service, patronage and subsidy patterns that enrich the national identity, and a recognition of the government, itself, as a forceful speaker.

As to public sphere and the infrastructure of communications:

5. Democratic processes, including the functioning of a civil society and a robust public sphere, are not natural phenomena and can no longer function (if they ever did) independently of government intervention and support. Television, as it evolves in the 'free market', does not necessarily contribute to, and often detracts from, a public forum in which citizens have equitable access, where wealth and power diminish as requisites for entry, and where opinions can be formed that serve as a check and influence on the activities of the state.

6. If the state has a legitimate stake in the machinery of democracy, and if the new technologies of speech have a substantial impact on the operation of political processes, then there is a public interest in establishing the infrastructure of communication. It should not be a violation of constitutional or human-rights principles for a government to establish an infrastructure that advances democratic processes and helps achieve an idealized public sphere.

7. As new technologies and new methods of organizing old delivery systems emerge, governments must concern themselves with the balance between what I have called the open terrain and the closed terrain of speech. Space must be preserved for common discourse and the development of common identity. Here, too, the state is called upon to make decisions about the infrastructure of a democratic society.

8. The very mechanics of the democratic process, candidacies, voting, and electoral debate, all require specific legislation that often constrains

the media. The state is called upon to make decisions about the role of advertising in the political process, the financing of campaigns, and, among other matters, the use of broadcasting and rules of access for candidates.

9. The impact of television on the education and acculturation of the young—universally a concern of society and the state—requires special attention if a healthy public sphere is to flourish and endure. The idea of government as *parens patriae* is unfashionable; but one aspect of an image-packed modernity is that historic values which reinforce community and strengthen political processes are destroyed by popular culture.

Notes

Chapter 1

1. W. H. Auden, 'Criticism in a Mass Society', *Mint* 2 (1948), 3–4.
2. There is always a problem of nomenclature in terms of differentiating among 'the state', 'the government', and interest groups or élites that, as part of society, affect power. Governments and their competitors vigorously assert versions of national identity, usually making their relationship to power by claiming fidelity to a historical truth, or by claiming to defend a culture or belief, or to protect a way of life. To draw a distinction, what is at issue for the state is its sovereignty; what is at stake for governments and contestants for authority is power.
3. Asa Briggs, *The Birth of Broadcasting* (New York: Oxford University Press, 1961), 37. The director, Arthur Burrows, was later the first secretary of the International Broadcasting Union.
4. See Rowland F. Pocock, *The Early British Radio Industry* (Manchester: Manchester University Press, 1988). In Canada, radio licences were granted by the Department of Marine and Fisheries. See Marc Raboy, *Missed Opportunities: The Story of Canada's Broadcasting Policy* (Buffalo: McGill-Queens, 1990).
5. For a general review, see Ernest Eugster, *Television Programming across National Boundaries: The EBU and OIRT Experience* (Dedham, Mass.: Artech House, 1983); and Monroe E. Price, 'The First Amendment and Television Broadcasting by Satellite', *UCLA Law Review* 23 (1976), 879.
6. Raboy, *Missed Opportunities*, 21.
7. Erik Barnouw, *A Tower in Babel* (New York: Oxford University Press, 1966),
8. *Sykes Committee Report*, United Kingdom Committee of Enquiry (London: King's Printer, 1923), 6.
9. Ronald H. Coase, *British Broadcasting: A Study in Monopoly* (London: Longmans, Green & Co., 1950). See particularly ch. 5, 'Foreign Commercial Broadcasting'.
10. Coase, *British Broadcasting*, 104–9. The determination that the BBC would not take advertising protected this market for newspapers; furthermore, at the outset, under the initial licence, the BBC agreed not to have an independent news-gathering entity but rather to take news reports from pre-existing newspaper sources and not to broadcast them except at limited times.

    Fifty years later, the Dutch government issued cable regulations which prohibited domestic cable networks from distributing foreign programmes containing commercial advertisements specifically directed at the Dutch market or containing Dutch-language subtitles. These regulations were invalidated by the Decision of the Court in *Stichting Collectieve Antennevoorziening Gouda* v. *Commissariaat Voor de Media*, case 288/89, EC Court of Justice, 25 July 1991, I-4007.

11. This history is explored in greater detail in Ch. 8.
12. Eli M. Noam, 'Beyond Territoriality: Economics and Politics in Telesociety', Columbia Institute for Tele-Information, Working Paper No. 690 (1994), 2.
13. In Nazi Germany, the government mandated the manufacture of People's Radio Receivers, which were engineered to receive the official programmes of the Third Reich. See Ernst K. Bramsted, *Goebbels and National Socialist Propaganda 1925–1945* (London: Cresset Press, 1965), 74–5.
14. Anthony Smith, 'Licenses and Liberty', in Colin McCabe and Olivia Stewart (eds.), *The BBC and Public Service Broadcasting* (Manchester: Manchester University Press, 1986), 233.
15. See Erik Barnouw, *The Golden Web* (New York: Oxford University Press, 1968), 155–68.
16. Ibid. 174–81, 246–57, 261–83; Erik Barnouw, *The Image Empire* (New York: Oxford University Press, 1970), 8–21, 46–55.
17. Among others, see Noam Chomsky and Edward S. Herman, *Manufacturing Consent: The Political Economy of the Mass Media* (New York: Pantheon Books, 1988); Walter M. Brasch and Dana R. Ulloth, *The Press and the State* (Lanham: University Press of America, 1986); Barnouw, *A Tower in Babel*; Barnouw, *The Golden Web*; and Barnouw, *The Image Empire*.
18. In 1947 the FCC published the Blue Book, a collection of regulations for radio-station managers, which told them of their duty to act as a mouthpiece of the community, to feature local original talent, to ascertain local problems, and to ensure that they were fairly covered.
19. See Daniel Dayan and Elihu Katz, *Media Events: The Live Broadcasting of History* (Cambridge, Mass.: Harvard University Press, 1992) and Daniel Dayan and Elihu Katz, 'Performing Media Events', in James Curran, Anthony Smith, and Pauline Wingate (eds.), *Impacts and Influences: Essays on Media Power in the Twentieth Century* (New York: Methuen, 1987), 174–97.
20. Barnouw, *The Image Empire*, 85–108; Robert E. Elder, *The United States Information Agency and American Foreign Policy* (Syracuse, NY: Syracuse University, Press 1968); and Fred Fejes, *Imperialism, Media and the Good Neighbor: New Deal Foreign Policy and United States Shortwave Broadcasting to Latin America* (Norwood: Ablex, 1986).
21. See K. R. M. Short (ed.), *Western Broadcasting over the Iron Curtain* (London: Croom Helm, 1986).
22. For example, on the vigour of the American debate in 1934 concerning commercialization and licence allocation, see Barnouw, *The Golden Web*, 23–6.
23. For the history of Radio Luxemburg before the Second World War, see Asa Briggs, *The Golden Age of Wireless* (New York: Oxford University Press, 1965).
24. See Robert Chapman, *Selling the Sixties: The Pirates and Pop Music Radio* (London: Routledge, 1992).

25. Herbert I. Schiller, *Mass Communications and the American Empire* (Boulder, Colo.: Westview Press, 1992).
26. Much of this work is cited in Tamar Liebes and Elihu Katz, *The Export of Meaning: Cross Cultural Readings of 'Dallas'* (New York: Oxford University Press, 1990).
27. See Ralph Negrine and Stylianos Papathanassopoulos, *The Internationalization of Television* (New York: Pinter Publishers, 1990), and Preben Sepstrup, *Transnationalization of Television in Western Europe* (London: J. Libbey, 1990).
28. See Eli Noam, 'National Culture and the Iron Law of Hollywood Dominance: An Economic Critique', ch. 2 in his *Television in Europe* (New York: Oxford University Press, 1992), 11–27.
29. See *FCC Cable Television Report & Order*, 36 FCC 2d 143, 37 Fed. Reg. 3252 (1972); *Memorandum Opinion & Order on Reconsideration of the Cable Television Report & Order*, 36 FCC 2d 326, 25 Rad. Reg. 2d (P & F) 1501 (1972). Some of these interventions were held illegal. See *Home Box Office, Inc.* v. *FCC*, 567 F. 2d 9 (DC Cir. 1977) (per curiam), cert. denied, 434 US 829 (1977). But the actions of government, and the continuous role of Congress, were not atypical for the activity of the state in connection with this technology.
30. ITU is the oldest operating intergovernmental organization and the principal co-ordinator of international telecommunications.
31. It is noteworthy in this respect that the US Constitution precludes Congress from establishing a religion.
32. Denis McQuail calls television the least revolutionary medium ever created (*Mass Communication Theory: An Introduction* (London: Sage Publications, 2nd edn., 1987)).
33. Compounded, of course, by the introduction of computers, improvements in telephony, and the communications changes that have come with them.
34. Ithiel de Sola Pool, *Technologies of Freedom* (Harvard, Mass.: Belknap Press, 1983).
35. A more standard meaning of global relates primarily to content. See Marjorie Ferguson, 'The Mythology about Globalization', *European Journal of Communications* 7 (1992), 69.
36. 'Local' television in terms of these definitions is just a subset of national television.
37. The former Soviet Union, or part of it, may turn into a 'region' with the devolution of control over television accompanied by some pan-Republic television signal or co-operative policy. See Chs. 6 and 7.
38. See also Elihu Katz and George Wedell, *Broadcasting in the Third World: Promise and Performance* (Cambridge, Mass: Harvard University Press, 1977), and Liebes and Katz, *The Export of Meaning*.

Chapter 2

1. See Ellen Propper Mickiewicz and Charles Firestone, *Television and Elections* (Queenstown: Aspen Institute, 1992).

2. American Enterprise Institute's Conference, 'The New Global Popular Culture: Is it American? Is it Good for America? Is it Good for the World?' 10 Mar. 1992, Washington, Organized by Ben Wattenberg, Senior Fellow.
3. Much of this discussion draws on Nicholas Garnham's article, 'The Media and the Public Sphere', in Peter Golding, Graham Murdock, and Philip Schlesinger (eds.), *Communicating Politics: Mass Communications and the Political Process* (New York: Holmes & Meier, 1986). An article by Garnham of the same title appears in Craig Calhoun (ed.), *Habermas and the Public Sphere* (Cambridge, Mass.: MIT, 1992). Unless otherwise noted, citations will refer to the 1986 version. Garnham states: 'Changes in media structure and media policy, whether these stem from economic developments or from public intervention, are properly political questions of as much importance as . . . subsidies to political parties' (p. 39).
4. The key work is Jurgen Habermas, *The Structural Transformation of the Public Sphere: An Inquiry into a Category of Bourgeois Society*, trans. Thomas Burger (Cambridge, Mass.: MIT, 1989). See also Calhoun (ed.), *Habermas and the Public Sphere*, and Jean L. Cohen and Andrew Arato, *Civil Society and Political Theory* (Cambridge, Mass.: MIT, 1992). Habermas, himself, has addressed the structure and functioning of the media in the public sphere. See ch. 8 of Jurgen Habermas, *Between Facts and Norms: Contributions to a Discourse Theory of Law and Democracy* (Cambridge, Mass.: MIT, forthcoming).
5. Garnham, 'The Media and the Public Sphere', 41. Garnham states the usual criticisms of the eighteenth-century public sphere among which, of course, was that access was restricted to bourgeois males and their class interests were coterminous with the discourse. Ibid. 44.
6. Habermas, quoted in Garnham, 'The Media and the Public Sphere', 42.
7. Indeed, sometimes, as we shall see, the legal and regulatory framework looks like efforts to rewarp speakers into a zone of ideal speech—in Habermasian terms—or to suggest to the audience that the speech they are witnessing follows those rules.
8. Jurgen Habermas, 'The Public Sphere', *New German Critique* 1/3 (autumn 1974), 49, 54.
9. Garnham, 'The Media and the Public Sphere', 41.
10. Michael Schudson, 'The "Public Sphere" and its Problems: Bringing the State (Back) In', *Notre Dame Journal of Law, Ethics and Public Policy* 8 (1994), 532.
11. Jean L. Cohen, 'The Public Sphere, the Media and Civil Society', in Andras Sajo and Monroe E. Price (eds.), *Rights of Media Access* (Dordrecht: Martinus Nijhoff, forthcoming), summarizing the argument of the 'older Frankfurt School'.
12. Ibid. Cohen quotes Habermas from *The Structural Transformation of the Public Sphere*, 188: 'According to the liberal model of the public sphere, the institutions of the public engaged in rational-critical debate were protected from interference by public authority by virtue of their being in the hands of private people. To the extent that they were commercialized and underwent economic, technological, and organizational concentration, however, they have turned during the last hundred years into complexes of societal power, so that

precisely their remaining in private hands in many ways threatened the critical functions of [these] institutions.' See also Robert M. Entman, *Democracy without Citizens: Media and the Decay of American Politics* (New York: Oxford University Press, 1989.)

13. A related aspect of the transformation of 'the public' or the audience is the idea of its representation as well as its access. The media, as public sphere, are deemed to be more successful, more comprehensive, if they 'represent' the audience, as if representation is a form of participation. Thus, a marker of success for Paddy Scannell is whether a broadcasting service comes 'to represent the whole of society in its programmes'. This is a complex and increasingly noticed definition of publicness. See Paddy Scannell, 'Public Service Broadcasting and Modern Public Life' in Paddy Scannell, Philip Schlesinger, and Colin Sparks (eds.), *Culture and Power: A Media, Culture and Society Reader* (London: Sage, 1992), 317–48.
14. Marc Raboy and Bernard Dagenais, *Media, Crisis, and Democracy: Mass Communication and the Disruption of Social Order* (London: Sage Publications, 1992), 4.
15. See Sandra J. Ball-Rokeach and Muriel G. Cantor (eds.), *Media, Audience and Social Structure* (London: Sage Publications, 1986), and David Chaney, 'Audience Research and the BBC in the 1930s: A Mass Media Comes into Being', in James Curran, Anthony Smith, and Pauline Wingate (eds.), *Impacts and Influences: Essays on Media Power in the Twentieth Century* (New York: Methuen, 1987), 259–77.
16. Ien Ang, *Desperately Seeking the Audience* (New York: Routledge, 1991), 105.
17. Lord Reith as quoted in Ang, *Desperately Seeking the Audience*, 109.
18. Ang, *Desperately Seeking the Audience*, 112.
19. Paddy Scannell and D. Cardiff, 'Serving the Nation: Public Service Broadcasting Before the War,' in Bernard Waites, Tony Bennett, and Graham Martin (eds.), *Popular Culture: Past and Present* (London: Croom Helm, 1982), 161–88.
20. Asa Briggs, *The BBC: The First Fifty Years* (Oxford: Oxford University Press, 1985): 331, quoted in Ang, *Desperately Seeking the Audience*, 115.
21. Ang, *Desperately Seeking the Audience*, 115–16.
22. Cohen, 'The Public Sphere, The Media, and Civil Society' (emphasis added). Cohen goes on to take a more optimistic view of the role of the media. By 'propaganda techniques', Cohen would include aspects of modern advertising. See also Susan Herbst, *Numbered Voices* (Chicago: University of Chicago Press, 1993).
23. Garnham, 'The Media and the Public Sphere', 46–7.
24. Habermas, himself, provides a credo that has some of the tone of a newspaper publisher's convention: 'the mass media ought to understand themselves as the agent of an enlightened public whose willingness to learn and capacity for criticism the media simultaneously presuppose, demand, and reinforce; like the judiciary, they ought to preserve their independence from political and social actors . . . to look after the public's concerns and proposals in an impartial manner and, in light of these topics and contributions, submit the political process to a course of legitimation and intensified critique' (Habermas, *Between Facts and Norms*, ch. 8).

25. This is a slightly exaggerated recreation and understates the BBC's role as an entertainment medium. Indeed, at first, the BBC was limited in its capacity even to broadcast news, constrained through an agreement with Britain's newspapers.
26. Anthony Smith (ed.), *British Broadcasting* (London: Newton Abbot, 1974), 56.
27. Ulrich Preuss, 'The Constitutional Concept of the Public Sphere according to the German Basic Law,' in Andras Sajo and Monroe E. Price (eds.), *Rights of Media Access* (Dordrecht: Martinus Nijhoff, forthcoming).
28. Preuss points out that 'this institutional device has caused much dissatisfaction because it has developed into a kind of proportional representation of the three leading political parties . . . leaving the impression that, indeed, this system is state run' (ibid.).
29. Professor Cohen suggests that the necessary independence can best be gained by licensing frequencies to foundations, universities, and similar entities with a tradition of an arm's-length relationship with government (Cohen, 'The Public Sphere, the Media and Civil Society').
30. See Henry Geller *et al.*, 54 Rad. Reg. 2d (P & F) 1246 (1983).
31. See Smith, 'Licenses and Liberty'.
32. See *Council Directive* 89/552/EEC of 3 Oct. 1989.
33. *FCC* v. *League of Women Voters of California*, 468 US 364 (1984).
34. Howard A. White, 'Fine Tuning the Federal Government's Role in Public Broadcasting', *Federal Communications Law Journal* 46 (1994), 491.
35. William Maley called the BBC, at least the BBC of the early 1980s, a 'national church, an ideological state apparatus which most certainly serves its function of creating the illusion of social cohesion and political integration in the midst of difference and disintegration' (see William Maley, 'Centralization and Censorship', in Colin McCabe and Olivia Stewart (eds.), *The BBC and Public Service Broadcasting* (Manchester: Manchester University Press, 1986), 32–45).
36. Hon. Dieter Grimm, 'Freedom of the Mass Media', Paper delivered at 'Rights of Access to the Media' Conference, Central European University, Budapest, Hungary, 19–21 June 1993.
37. Robert M. Entman and Steven S. Wildman, 'Reconciling Economic and Non-Economic Perspectives on Media Policy', *Journal of Communication* 42 (Winter 1992), 5–19.
38. See Garnham, The Media and the Public Sphere', in Calhoun (ed.), *Habermas and the Public Sphere*, 359, 368.
39. See Jerry Mander, *Four Arguments for the Elimination of Television* (New York: William Morrow & Co., 1978).

Chapter 3

1. Note the difference between 'surrogate' radio operations, such as Radio Free Europe or Radio Liberty, and identity-spreading entities, such as the Voice of America. The surrogates are supposed to be true to the identity of the place to which they are broadcasting, while the VOA is the expression of the 'voices of America' and a general news operation.

2. Sect. 17 of the Broadcasting Authority Act 1960 as amended by sect. 13 of the amending Act of 1976.
3. Herbert I. Schiller, 'Fast Food, Fast Cars, Fast Political Rhetoric', *InterMedia* 20 (Aug. 1992), 21.
4. This is reflected in the scholarship. See e.g. Anthony D. Smith, *National Identity* (New York: Penguin Books, 1991); Ralph Negrine and Stylianos Papathanassopoulos, *The Internationalization of Television* (New York: Pinter Publishers, 1990); and Benedict Anderson, *Imagined Communities: Reflections on the Origin and Spread of Nationalism* (London: Verso, 1983).
5. Much of this work has its roots in the writings of Ronald H. Coase. See Ronald H. Coase, 'The Federal Communications Commission', *Journal of Law and Economics* 2 (1959), 1.
6. M. J. Edelman, *Constructing the Political Spectacle* (Chicago: University of Chicago Press, 1988).
7. James Donald, *Sentimental Education: Schooling, Popular Culture and the Regulation of Liberty* (New York: Verso, 1992), 155.
8. See Todd Gitlin, *The Whole World is Watching: Mass Media in the Making and Unmaking of the New Left* (Berkeley and Los Angeles: University of California Press, 1980).
9. Anderson, *Imagined Communities*, 6.
10. Hugh Seton-Watson, *Nations and States: An Inquiry into the Origins of Nations and the Politics of Nationalism* (Boulder, Colo.: Westview Press, 1977), 5.
11. Renata Salecl, *The Spoils of Freedom: Psychoanalysis and Feminism after the Fall of Socialism* (London: Routledge, 1994), 73.
12. Karolina Udovicki, 'Letter to the New Yorker', *New Yorker* 23 May 1994, 9, 11.
13. This was true for the Palestinians signing a Declaration of Principles with Israel, for whom provision had to be made for a Palestinian Broadacasting Authority, or for the Romanians seizing control of a transmission tower, or Ukraine, recently crossing from nation to nation-state, needing to ensure that the patina of sovereignty is nourished and guarded from attack.
14. Quoted in Patricia Mainardi, *The End of the Salon: Art and the State in the Early Third Republic* (New York: Cambridge University Press, 1993), 12.
15. Salecl, *The Spoils of Freedom*, 98.
16. Asu Aksoy and Nabi Avci, 'Spreading Turkish Identity', *InterMedia* 20 (Aug. 1992), 39–40.
17. Anderson, *Imagined Communities*, 44.
18. Jean Baudrillard, *The Ecstasy of Communication*, trans. Bernard and Caroline Schutze (New York: Autonomedia, 1988), 15–16, quoted in Timothy W. Luke, *Shows of Force: Power, Politics, and Ideology in Art Exhibitions* (Durham, NC: Duke University Press, 1992), 200.
19. Eli M. Noam, 'Beyond Territoriality: Economics and Politics in Telesociety', Columbia Institute for Tele-Information, Working Paper No. 690 (1994).
20. Karl Deutsch, *Nationalism and Social Communication* (Cambridge, Mass.: MIT Press, 1953), 70–1.
21. Anderson, *Imagined Communities*, 19.

22. Samuel P. Huntington, 'The Clash of Civilizations?' *Foreign Affairs* 72 (1993), 22.
23. Ryszard Kapuściński, *Shah of Shahs*, trans. William R. Brand and Katarzyna Mroczkowska-Brand (San Diego: Harcourt Brace Jovanovich, 1985), 113.
24. See William H. McNeill, 'Fundamentalism and the World of the 1990s', in Martin E. Marty and R. Scott Appleby (eds.), *Fundamentalisms and Society: Reclaiming the Sciences, the Family, and Education* (Chicago: University of Chicago Press, 1993), 558–73.
25. 'Since authority claims to represent progress and modernity, we will show that our values are different. . . . Only let life get better, and the old customs lose their emotional coloration to become again what they were—a ritual form' (Kapuściński, *Shah of Shahs*, 113).
26. Alan Rusbridger, 'The Moghul Invasion', *Guardian*, 8 Apr. 1994, p. T6.

Chapter 4

1. See *Abrams* v. *United States*, 250 US 616, 624 (1919) (Holmes J. dissenting). See also Mark A. Graber, *Transforming Free Speech: The Ambiguous Legacy of Civil Liberalism* (Berkeley and Los Angeles: University of California Press, 1991); and John Keane, *The Media and Democracy* (Cambridge, Mass.: Polity Press, 1991). For a criticism of the market-place metaphor, see Cass R. Sunstein, *Democracy and the Problem of Free Speech* (New York: The Free Press, 1993); and Owen M. Fiss, 'Free Speech and Social Structure', *Iowa Law Review* 71 (1986), 1405. See generally Monroe E. Price, 'The Market for Loyalties: Electronic Media and the Global Competition for Allegiances', *Yale Law Journal* 104 (1994), 667.
2. A controversial, north–south aspect of the market for loyalties was anticipated in the debate over the 'new world information order': see Anthony Smith, *The Geopolitics of Information: How Western Culture Dominates the World* (Boston: Faber & Faber, 1980), and Jeremy Tunstall, *The Media are American* (New York: Columbia University Press, 1977).
3. See Richard A. Posner, 'Free Speech in an Economic Perspective', *Suffolk University Law Review* 20 (1986), 1, 3–7.
4. See David Yassky's richly original account, 'Eras of the First Amendment', *Columbia Law Review* 91 (1991), 1699. See generally Leonard Williams Levy, *Emergence of a Free Press* (New York: Oxford University Press, 1985). Consider, for example, the specific protection of the right of religions to participate in the market for loyalties in the Free Exercise Clause. The clause, as interpreted, has both expanded and limited the range of techniques religions can utilize. See e.g. *Reynolds* v. *United States*, 98 US 145, 166 (1878). The Establishment Clause precludes Congress from following the British example of tying national identity to a single church. Yet there is no similar explicit prohibition against 'establishing' a press or set of speakers through subsidy.
5. See C. Edwin Baker, *Advertising and a Democratic Press* (Princeton: Princeton University Press, 1994), and Patrick M. Fahey, 'Comment: Advocacy Group

Boycotting of Network Television Advertisers and its Effects on Programming Content', *University of Pennsylvania Law Review* 140 (1991), 647.

6. See Monroe E. Price, 'Comparing Broadcast Structures: Transnational Perspectives and Post-Communist Examples', *Cardozo Arts and Entertainment Law Journal* 11 (1993), 275.
7. For efforts to relate economic analysis to speech issues, see Ronald H. Coase, 'The Market for Goods and the Market for Ideas', *American Economic Review, Papers and Proceedings* 64 (1974), 384; Ronald H. Coase, 'Advertising and Free Speech', *Journal of Legal Studies* 6 (1977): 1; Bruce M. Owen, *Economics and Freedom of Expression: Media Structure and the First Amendment* (Cambridge, Mass.: Ballinger Publishing Company, 1975). For a discussion of the market for speech, see Stephen A. Gardbaum, 'Broadcasting, Democracy, and the Market', *Georgetown Law Journal* 82 (1993), 373; and Paul G. Stern, 'Note: A Pluralistic Reading of the First Amendment and its Relation to Public Discourse', *Yale Law Journal* 99 (1990), 925.
8. See Anthony Downs, *An Economic Theory of Democracy* (New York: Harper & Brothers, 1957), 207–76; and Charles Lindblom, *Politics and Markets* (New York: Basic Books, 1977), 13. But contrast *Associated Press* v. *United States*, 326 US 1, 28 (1945) (Frankfurter, J., concurring) ('Truth and understanding are not wares like peanuts or potatoes.') Frankfurter contended that the constraints on the market for speech 'call . . . into play considerations very different from comparable restraints in a co-operative enterprise having merely a commercial aspect'.
9. Albert O. Hirschmann, *Exit, Voice, and Loyalty: Responses to Decline in Firms, Organizations, and States* (Cambridge, Mass.: Harvard University Press, 1970).
10. Jacques Ellul, *Propaganda: The Formation of Men's Attitudes* (New York: Alfred A. Knopf, 1965), 140–2.
11. See e.g. Zvi Gitelman, 'Exiting from the Soviet Union: Emigrés or Refugees?', *Michigan Yearbook of International Legal Studies* 3 (1982), 43; and Christopher Greenwood, 'Free Movement of Workers under EEC Law and English Law', *New Law Journal* 133 (1983), 933.
12. The effect of tax rates and regulatory costs on mobility is the subject of debate in a series of recent articles. See e.g. Richard Briffault, 'Our Localism: Part II—Localism and Legal Theory', *Columbia Law Review* 90 (1990), 346; and Vicki Been, 'Exit as a Constraint on Land Use Exactions: Rethinking the Unconstitutional Conditions Doctrine', *Columbia Law Review* 91 (1991), 473, 516–25. See, generally, Charles A. Tiebout, 'A Pure Theory of Local Expenditures', *Journal of Political Economics* 64 (1956), 416, 418, 420.
13. For a survey, see Richard H. Pildes, 'The New Public Law: The Unintended Cultural Consequences of Public Policy', *Michigan Law Review* 89 (1991), 936.
14. China is an interesting case study. See Zuo Liu Zhen, 'Broadcasting for the People, To the People', *InterMedia* 22 (Apr. 1994), 10. China has sought to limit outside signals, but, as of 1992, it was estimated that there were 700,000 TVRO receivers (satellite dishes) in China. Sun Lin, 'Foreign Capital and Equipment Fuel a Telecommunications Liftoff', *InterMedia* 22 (Apr. 1994), 22.

15. R. H. Coase lists some of the common assumptions that differentiate the market for ideas from the market for goods: see Coase, 'The Market for Goods and the Market for Ideas', 386.
16. Elasticity of demand comes into play here. Sellers of ordinary goods often want to know whether and how much an increase in price will decrease demand for their product. Manufacturers of national identities—including the state itself—must (in the economic model) ask the same question. Churchill put the issue, during the Second World War, in terms of sacrifice.
17. See Brian McNair, *Glasnost, Perestroika and the Soviet Media* (New York: Routledge, 1991), and Rochelle B. Price, 'Jamming and the Law of International Communications', *Michigan Yearbook of International Legal Studies* 5 (1984), 391.
18. See Ronald H. Coase, *British Broadcasting: A Study in Monopoly* (London: Longmans, Green & Co., 1950).
19. European Convention for the Protection of Human Rights and Fundamental Freedoms, 4 Nov. 1950, art. 10(1), 213 UNTS 221.
20. 12 Eur. Ct HR (ser. A) at 321 (1990).
21. Ibid. at 485.
22. See Barendt, *Broadcasting Law*, 223–25.
23. Council Directive 89/552 of 3 Oct. 1989 on Television Without Frontiers, 1989 O.J. (L 298) 23 [hereinafter Television Without Frontiers Directive].
24. European Convention on Transfrontier Television, 5 May 1989, Europ. TS No. 132; see also *Television Without Frontiers: Green Paper on the Establishment of the Common Market for Broadcasting Especially by Satellite and Cable*, COM (84) 300 final (hereinafter *Television Without Frontiers Green Paper*); and Barendt, *Broadcasting Law*, 222–36. See, generally, Kenneth Dyson and Peter Humphreys (eds.), *The Political Economy of Communications: International and European Dimensions* (New York: Routledge, 1990).
25. See Barendt, *Broadcasting Law*, 235.
26. Laurence G. C. Kaplan, 'The European Community's "Television Without Frontiers" Directive: Stimulating Europe to Regulate Culture', *Emory International Law Review* 8 (1994), 255, 341–5. Former European Commission President Jacques Delors has defended the EU's position by arguing 'that cultural goods are not like other merchandise' and deserve protection because '[c]ulture is there to reassure, it is part of our roots' (Hilary Clarke, 'EU Vows to "Move Forward"; Consensus on Maintaining Identity Sought as AV Confab Opens', *Hollywood Reporter*, 1 July 1994). For the American reaction, see 'Hollywood Urges End to Film War', *Guardian* (London), 6 Sept. 1994, 7.
27. See, generally, Eli M. Noam, *Television in Europe* (New York: Oxford University Press, 1992).
28. Willem F. Korthals Altes, 'European Law: A Case Study of Changes in National Broadcasting', *Cardozo Arts and Entertainment Law Journal* 11 (1993), 313, 318.
29. Joke J. A. Pelle and Piet W. C. Akkermans, 'The Dutch Broadcasting System: A Basic Right Caught between Dutch Constitutional Law and European Community Law', *RED/ERPL* 2/1 (1990), 39, 41.

30. Three European Court of Justice cases discuss the complexity resulting from Dutch efforts to regulate transfrontier advertising. See Case 353/89, *Commission* v. *Netherlands*, 1991 ECR I-4069; Case 288/89, *Stichting Collectieve Antennevoorziening Gouda* v. *Commissariaat Voor de Media*, 1991 ECR I-4007; Case 325/85, *Bond Van Adverteerders* v. *The State (Netherlands)*, 1988 ECR 2085. In *Commission* v. *Netherlands* the European Court of Justice held as violative of Article 59 of the EEC treaty a Dutch regulation that sought to impose on foreign broadcasters obligations similar to those required of Dutch broadcasters. Under the European Union's Broadcasting Directive, no member government is permitted, except under extremely unusual situations, to prohibit the transmission of programmes that are legally broadcast in a member country of origin. See Barendt, *Broadcasting Law*, 234.
31. See, generally, Aernout J. Nieuwenhuis, 'The Crumbling Pillars of Dutch TV', *InterMedia* 20 (Aug.–Sept. 1992), 37.
32. Asu Aksoy and Kevin Robins, 'Gecekondu-Style Broadcasting in Turkey: A Confrontation of Cultural Values', *InterMedia* 21 (June 1993), 15. See also Haluk Sahin and Asu Aksoy, 'Global Media and Cultural Identity in Turkey', *Journal of Communication* 43 (1992), 31.
33. Noam, *Television in Europe*, 258.
34. Ibid.
35. Aksoy and Robins, 'Gecekondu-Style Broadcasting in Turkey', 15.
36. Ibid.
37. See Christine De Keersmaeker, 'Organisation and Structure of Radio and Television Broadcasting in Belgium', *Entertainment Law Review* 3 (Sept.–Oct. 1992), 164–70.
38. See, generally, Ad van Loon, 'Pluralism, Concentration and Competition in the Media Sector', *CDMM (92) 8 Vol. I* (Strasburg: Council of Europe, 1991), 81. Van Loon is Legal Expert of the European Audiovisual Observatory of the Council of Europe.
39. European Court of Justice, *Commission of the European Communities* v. *Kingdom of Belgium, European Court of Justice*, Case C-211/91 (16 Dec. 1992).
40. See, generally, Vincent Porter and Suzanne Hasselbach, *Pluralism, Politics and the Marketplace: The Regulation of German Broadcasting* (New York: Routledge, 1991).
41. Ulrich Preuss, 'The Constitutional Concept of the Public Sphere according to the German Basic Law', in Andras Sajo and Monroe E. Price (eds.), *Rights of Media Access* (Dordrecht: Martinus Nijhoff, forthcoming).
42. See, generally, Stuart Ewen, *Captains of Consciousness: Advertising and the Social Roots of the Consumer Culture* (New York: McGraw-Hill, 1976); Michael Schudson, *Advertising, the Uneasy Persuasion: Its Dubious Impact on American Society* (New York: Basic Books, 1984). For a recent effort to rethink the relationship between advertising and free-speech doctrine, see C. Edwin Baker, *Advertising and a Democratic Press* (Princeton: Princeton University Press, 1994).
43. See, generally, Schudson, *Advertising, the Uneasy Persuasion*; and Cecilia Tichi, *Electronic Hearth: Creating an American Television Culture* (New York: Oxford University Press, 1991).

44. Certainly this is the view of the influence of Western television in Singapore, Malaysia, and much of the Islamic world. See e.g. Erhard U. Heidt, *Mass Media, Cultural Tradition and National Identity* (Fort Lauderdale, Fbr.: Breitenbach, 1987), 157, 160–3; James Lull, *China Turned On: Television, Reform, and Resistance* (New York: Routledge, 1991), 165–6. The BBC published excerpts of recorded prayer sermons at Tehran University on 16 Sept. 1994: 'Satellite transmission, broadcasting the programmes of foreign television networks, is not designed to increase the scientific knowledge of nations. Rather it has been developed to mislead the youth. . . . They sell obscene films either at a very low price or give it to you free of charge, whereas the scientific films are so expensive that one cannot afford to buy them. They [the West] do not transfer their knowledge . . . [or] their experience of modernizing technology. What they transfer is something which drags families into corruption. He [the Westerner] is planning to make the Islamic countries give up the ownership of their chastity. . . . he wishes to make our young people addicted to drugs . . . irresponsible towards their parents, spouses and their living conditions' (Emani-Kashani, West Interested in Transfer not of Technology but of Corruption, BBC Summary of World Broadcasts, available in LEXIS, News Library, BBCSWB File).
45. 'International satellite dissemination conducted by Western developed countries threatens the independence and identity of China's national culture . . . [which includes] loving the motherland, hard work, advocating industry and thrift . . . taking a keen interest in science, attaching importance to culture . . . and stressing moral courage. . . . Precisely because of this, we take seriously the infringement of overseas radio and television and the influence they bring which hampers the national spirit to expand. (Zhao Shuifu (Minister of Radio, Film and Television, People's Republic of China), 'Foreign Dominance of Chinese Broadcasting: Will Hearts and Minds Follow?', *InterMedia* 22 (Apr.–May 1994), 8, 9).
46. See President's Task Force on US Government International Broadcasting, *The Report of the President's Task Force on US Government International Broadcasting* (Washington: Department of State Publication 9925; Dec. 1991).
47. The effort in the United States to ensure increased minority ownership of broadcasting licences so as to encourage greater pluralism in the social narrative is an example. See *Metro Broadcasting, Inc.* v. *FCC*, 497 US 547 (1990).
48. But see *International Covenant on Civil and Political Rights*, art. 19, para. 2 (right to freedom of expression), entered into force 23 Mar. 1976. The full text of the *International Covenant* can be found in Richard B. Lillich (ed.), *International Human Rights, Documentary Supplement* (Boston: Little, Brown & Company, 1991).
49. See Steven H. Shiffrin, 'Government Speech', *UCLA Law Review* 27 (1980), 565, 571.
50. See Owen M. Fiss, 'State Activism and State Censorship', *Yale Law Journal* 100 (1992), 2087; and Owen M. Fiss, 'Essays Commemorating the One Hundredth Anniversary of the *Harvard Law Review*: Why the State?', *Harvard Law Review* 100 (1987), 781.

51. See Elizabeth A. Downey, 'A Historical Survey of the International Regulation of Propaganda', *Michigan Yearbook of International Legal Studies* 5 (1984), 341; Richard A. Falk, 'On Regulating International Propaganda: A Plea for Moderate Aims', *Law and Contemporary Problems* 31 (1966), 622, 623. The definitions of propaganda are myriad. Jacques Ellul's definition is 'a set of methods employed by an organized group that wants to bring about the active or passive participation in its actions of a mass of individuals, psychologically unified through psychological manipulations and incorporated in an organization' (Ellul, *Propaganda*, 61). See also L. John Martin, *International Propaganda* (Minneapolis: University of Minnesota, 1958), 10–20; Garth S. Jowett and Victoria O'Donnell, *Propaganda and Persuasion* (London: Sage, 1986).
52. Jacques Ellul is certainly of this school, as was Walter Lippmann. See Walter Lippmann, *Public Opinion* (London: Allen & Unwin, 1922). See also Kevin Robins, Frank Webster, and Michael Pickering, 'Propaganda, Information and Social Control', in Jeremy Hawthorn (ed.), *Propaganda, Persuasion and Polemic* (Baltimore, Md.: Edward Arnold, 1987), 1–18.
53. The destruction of European capacities to enforce barriers to entry (at least among European countries themselves) has been partly caused by the decisions of the European Court of Justice determining that broadcasting was a service to be, by and large, held to the same competition standards as other services. See e.g. Ad Van Loon, 'National Media Policies under EEC Law Taking into Account Fundamental Rights', *Media Law and Practice* 14 (1993), 17.
54. See Leonard Zeidenberg, 'President Pushes TV Marti; ITU Pushes Back', *Broadcasting* 118 (9 Apr. 1990), 37, reprinting message from International Frequency Registration Board (IFRB), an arm of the ITU, to the State Department concerning the legality of TV Marti, the American initiative to bring its television to Cuba. See also Steven Ruth, 'Comment: The Regulation of Spillover Transmissions from Direct Broadcast Satellites in Europe', *Federal Communications Law Journal* 42 (1989), 107.
55. *International Convention Concerning the Use of Broadcasting in the Cause of Peace*, 23 Sept. 1936, 186 LNTS 301, art. I. See also the *Litvinov Agreement* between the United States and the USSR, in which both countries promised not to spread propaganda hostile to the other and not to harbour groups working towards the overthrow of the other, and the 'Exchange of Communications between the President of the United States and Maxim M. Litvinov People's Commissar for Foreign Affairs of the Union of Soviet Socialist Republics', *American Journal of International Law* 28 Supp. (1934), 2.
56. Part of the reason is the move, in the rhetoric of international instruments, from multilateral sovereign expressions of rights of sovereigns to the rights of individuals irrespective of the actions of their sovereigns. Compare, for example, article I of the *Convention Concerning the Use of Broadcasting in the Cause of Peace*, drawn under the sponsorship of the League of Nations, with article 19 of the *Universal Declaration of Human Rights* and the *International Covenant on Civil and Political Rights*.
57. See Television Without Frontiers Directive. See also *Television Without Frontiers: Green Paper*.

58. Austrian radio cases II (*Informationsverein Lentia et al.* v. *Austria*), Council of Europe, European Commission of Human Rights, Report of the Commission (adopted on 9 Sept. 1992), para. 77.
59. This argument was fashioned to meet the standards provided by art. 10, para. 2, of the *European Convention on Human Rights. Convention for the Protection of Human Rights and Fundamental Freedoms*, 4 Nov. 1950.
60. Control over receiving technology to alter the structure of the markets is not new. In the United States, in the 1960s, Congress forced, through the All-Receiver Act, manufacturers of television sets to ensure that UHF as well as VHF channels were available (and with *détente* tuning, before *détente* was a Cold War-related word) so as to increase the possibility of competition and to help support public broadcasters.
61. Much of the regulation of broadcasting has rested on the scarcity rationale, see *Red Lion Broadcasting Co., Inc.* v. *FCC*, 395 US 367 (1969), but the manufactured nature of the shortage has caused this ground to be derided. See Owen, *Economics and Freedom of Expression: Media Structure and the First Amendment*. A dramatic example of a maintained scarcity was apartheid South Africa, which, by law, kept television out of the market for ideas altogether until 1976. The National Party considered that television would pose a threat to the Afrikaans language through overdependence on American and British programming and would undermine the 'multi-nationalism' of its bantustan system: Rob Nixon, 'Keeping Television Out: The South Africa Story', *InterMedia* 20 (Aug.–Sept. 1992), 35–6.
62. Jack M. McLeod and Lee B. Becker, 'Testing the Validity of Gratification Measures through Political Effects Analysis', in Jay G. Blumler and Elihu Katz (eds.), *The Uses of Mass Communications: Current Perspectives on Gratifications Research* (London: Sage Publications, 1974), 137.
63. See Jeri Laber, 'The Dictatorship Returns', *New York Review of Books*, 40/13 (15 July 1993), 42–4. Western countries, such as the United States, were not consistently using secondary economic tools, such as boycotts or refusals to deal, as a means of ensuring that competition in imagery occurred within the former Soviet Republic.
64. As an analogy, consider the impact of televangelism, made into a mass mechanism by multichannel cable television, on American politics.
65. William H. McNeill, 'Fundamentalism and the World of the 1990s', in Martin E. Marty and R. Scott Appleby (eds.), *Fundamentalisms and Society: Reclaiming the Sciences, the Family, and Education*, eds. (Chicago: University of Chicago Press, 1993), 558–73. See also Samuel P. Huntington, 'The Clash of Civilizations?', *Foreign Affairs* 72 (1993), 22; and above, Ch. 3.
66. Benedict Anderson, *Imagined Communities: Reflections on the Origin and Spread of Nationalism* (London: Verso, 1983), 175.

Chapter 5

1. Philip R. Schlesinger, 'Europe's Contradictory Communicative Space', *Daedalus* 123 (Mar. 1994), 25.

2. Robert K. Manoff, 'Independence and Mass Media in Transition', unpublished paper, Conference on Mass Media in Transition, American University, Washington, DC, 1994.
3. Commission on Radio and Television Policy, 'Report of the Working Group on Broadcaster Autonomy and the State', Prepared for the Aspen Institute Communications and Society Program, Queenstown, Md., 1994.
4. See Matthew Cullerne Bown, *Art under Stalin* (Oxford: Phaidon Press, 1991).
5. The Decree on the Press is reprinted in John Murray, *The Russian Press from Brezhnev to Yeltsin: Behind the Paper Curtain* (Aldershot: Edward Edgar Publishing Company, 1994), 2. The date adopted in the new calendar after the Bolshevik revolution is 9 Nov. 1917.
6. Lenin, quoted in Brian McNair, *Glasnost Perestroika and the Soviet Media* (New York: Routledge, 1991).
7. Much of this section is drawn from McNair, *Glasnost, Perestroika and the Soviet Media*. McNair's book, though written before the demise of the Soviet Union, is helpful in explaining problems of adjustment in the wake of Gorbachev and late-Soviet *glasnost*. See also Murray, *The Russian Press from Brezhnev to Yeltsin*; Ellen Propper Mickiewicz, *Split Signals: Television and Politics in the Soviet Union* (New York: Oxford University Press, 1988); Frances H. Foster, '*Izvestiia* as a Mirror of Russian Legal Reform: Press, Law, and Crisis in the Post-Soviet Era', *Vanderbilt Journal of Transnational Law* 26 (1993), 675; and Jamey Gambrell, 'Moscow: The Front Page', *New York Review of Books* 39/16 (8 Oct. 1992), 56.
8. See N. N. Lipovchenko, *Ocherk teorii zhurnalistiki* (Moscow, Mysl, 1985), 41, quoted in McNair, *Glasnost, Perestroika and the Soviet Media*, 19.
9. Lipovchenko, *Ocherk teorii zhurnalistiki*, 56, quoted in McNair, *Glasnost, Perestroika and the Soviet Media*, 23.
10. V. I. Lenin, *Lenin* v. *Pechati* (Moscow: Politizdat, 1958), 16, quoted in McNair, *Glasnost, Perestroika and the Soviet Media*, 24.
11. McNair, *Glasnost, Perestroika and the Soviet Media*, 24.
12. V. I. Lenin, *Lenin about the Press*, quoted in McNair, *Glasnost, Perestroika and the Soviet Media*, 29.
13. McNair, *Glasnost, Perestroika and the Soviet Media*, 90.

Chapter 6

1. As in Ch. 5, for a history of mass media in the Soviet Union, see Brian McNair, *Glasnost, Perestroika and the Soviet Media* (New York: Routledge, 1991); John Murray, *The Russian Press from Brezhnev to Yeltsin: Behind the Paper Curtain* (Aldershot: Edward Edgar Publishing Company, 1994); and Ellen Propper Mickiewicz, Split Signals: *Television and Politics in the Soviet Union* (New York: Oxford University Press, 1988).
2. The full text of the Russian Federation Law on Mass Media (hereinafter referred to as the 'Russian Mass Media Law'), signed by President Yeltsin on 27 Dec. 1991, can be found in the appendix to Monroe E. Price, 'Comparing Broadcast Structures: Transnational Perspectives and Post-Communist Examples', *Cardozo Arts and Entertainment Law Journal* 11 app. (1993), 625–55.

3. Art. 3 of the Russian Mass Media Law identifies 'censorship' as: (1) prepublication review of news media reports by state or other public agencies; and (2) the imposition of prior restraints on dissemination of news reports. In addition, the Law, perhaps revealing fears from the past, seeks in art. 25 to guarantee in some detail the freedom to distribute mass-media products. Specifically, art. 25 enjoins the government, unions, and citizens from harming the process of disseminating information.
4. The text to these documents can be found in Richard B. Lillich (ed.), *International Human Rights, Documentary Supplement* (Boston: Little, Brown & Company, 1991).
5. Russian Mass Media Law, arts. 43–6 (public remedies) and art. 60 (possible additional private remedies). Art. 15 renders registrations possibly 'invalid' if, among other reasons, the registration was obtained deceptively, or if the instrument of mass information has not been published for a year, or if the editorial charter has not been accepted.
6. See Ch. 4 and Price, 'Market for Loyalties'.
7. Art. 7, entitled 'Founder', reads as follows: 'The founder (cofounder) of a mass media outlet may be a citizen, an association of citizens, an enterprise, institution, organization, or state organ.'
8. See Peter Krug, 'The Abandonment of the State Radio–Television Monopoly in the Soviet Union: The First Step Toward Broadcasting Pluralism?', *Wisconsin International Law Journal* 9 (1991), 377.
9. Andrei Richter, 'Newspapers: Free to be Bankrupt', *Post-Soviet Media Law and Policy Newsletter*, no. 2 (Nov. 1993), 6; Andrei Richter, 'Direct Subsidies to the Press', *Post-Soviet Media Law and Policy Newsletter*, no. 4 (Jan. 1994), 2.
10. The Russian Mass Media Law presupposes a formal arrangement, at least for newspapers, with an 'editorship' that includes the editor-in-chief and the journalists' collective. Art. 19 states that the editorship performs its tasks 'on the basis of professional independence', and art. 18 prohibits the founder from interfering with the editorship except for pre-agreed conditions. A status agreement must exist between editorship and founder; and arts. 16 and 20 set forth components of such an agreement. These include setting forth the circumstances under which the founder may close the newspaper, and how the editor-in-chief is appointed and removed.
11. One additional important measure of a mass-media statute's treatment is the openness of a society to foreign sources of information. The Russian Mass Media Law demonstrates the desire for a state with permeable boundaries; art. 54 asserts that the citizens of the Russian Federation are 'guaranteed unhindered access to reports and materials of the foreign mass media'. But art. 53 authorizes 'interstate agreements' with respect to foreign mass media. The circumstances of distributing such foreign publications can be decided by 'interstate agreement', a phrase of complex ambiguity, which may include the right for bilateral decisions to limit transnational flows of information. In the 1950s and 1960s, the United States and the Soviet Union had an agreement in which the Soviet Union had the right to distribute a limited number of copies of *Soviet Life* in the United States, and the United States was permitted to

distribute limited numbers of like publications in the Soviet Union. For a discussion of these agreements and restrictions on the export and import of film, as well as other attributes of the Cold War, see Elizabeth Hull, *Taking Liberties: National Barriers to the Free Flow of Ideas* (New York: Praeger, 1990). See also Monroe E. Price, 'The First Amendment and Television Broadcasting by Satellite', *UCLA Law Review* 23 (1976), 879. Under art. 54 of the Russian Mass Media Law, where there is no such agreement, the foreign publication would apply to the Ministry of Press and Information. Art. 54 singles out direct television broadcasting for special protection. No limitations are allowed for such programmes except by prior inter-governmental treaties.

12. See Russian Mass Media Law, arts. 38, 39, 43–7, 49, 51, 59, and 62.
13. For the text of the 20 Mar. 1993 Decree 'On Protection of the Freedom of the Mass Media', see BBC Summary of World Broadcasts, 24 Mar. 1993 (reproduced in LEXIS, NEWS Library, CURNWS File).
14. See '*Sovetskaia Rossiia* To Be Closed, Too?', *Moskovskii Komsomolets*, 23 Apr. 1993 (reproduced in LEXIS, NEWS Library, CURNWS File).
15. See Celestine Bohlen, 'Home of First Revolution is Puzzling over This One', *New York Times*, 26 Mar. 1993 (reproduced in LEXIS, NEWS Library, CURNWS File).
16. For text of Resolution No. 4686–1 ('On Measures to Ensure Freedom of Speech in State Television and Radio Broadcasting and News Services'), signed by Supreme Soviet Chairman Khasbulatov on 29 Mar. 1993, see the BBC Summary of World Broadcasts, 7 Apr. 1993 (reproduced in LEXIS, NEWS Library, CURNWS File).
17. 'Heads of Radio and TV Companies Urge Yeltsin to Veto Amendment to Media Law', BBC Summary of World Broadcasts, 21 July 1993 (reproduced in LEXIS, NEWS Library, CURNWS File).
18. See BBC report, 'Eleven Opposition Newspapers to be Closed in Russia without Court Action', 16 Nov. 1993 (reproduced in LEXIS, NEWS Library, CURNWS File).
19. For text of the Council of Ministers Resolution 'On the Legal Succession of the Powers of the Supreme Soviet of the Russian Federation in Respect of the Mass Media', see BBC report entitled 'Government Adopts Resolution on Take-Over of the Supreme Soviet Media', 25 Sept. 1993.
20. *Post-Soviet Media Law and Policy Newsletter*, no. 1 (Oct. 1993), 4.
21. The text of the decree can be found in *Post-Soviet Media Law and Policy Newsletter*, no. 4 (Jan. 1994), 1 (supp.).
22. See BBC Summary of World Broadcasts, 'Tribunal Rejects Shumeiko Demand on Ban on Communists and Democrats', 2 Dec. 1993 (reproduced in LEXIS, NEWS Library, CURNWS File).
23. The texts of these decrees are found in *Post-Soviet Media Law and Policy Newsletter*, no. 4 (Jan. 1994), 1 (supp.).
24. A year later, in late 1994, the State Duma sought to establish a set of rules 'On the Procedure for State-Run Media to Cover the Activities of State Power' to assure more regular and more fixed coverage of legislative activities. A 'Parliamentary Hour' programme was reinstated.

25. The *Treaty of Civic Accord* was signed on 28 Apr. 1994. The first quote is from sect. 1, para. 5, of the Treaty; the second is from sect. 6, para. 1. Excerpts from the Treaty can be found in *Post-Soviet Media Law and Policy Newsletter*, no. 8 (June 1994), 3–6.
26. For the text, see *Post-Soviet Media Law and Policy Newsletter*, no. 12/13 (Dec. 1994), 9–11 (supp.).
27. Frances H. Foster, '*Izvestiia* as a Mirror of Russian Legal Reform: Press, Law, and Crisis in the Post-Soviet Era', *Vanderbilt Journal of Transnational Law* 26 (1993), 675.
28. Ibid.
29. Ibid.
30. Ibid.

Chapter 7

1. Eric Barendt, *Broadcasting Law: A Comparative Study* (New York: Oxford University Press, 1993), 41.
2. MK 48/1991 (X. 26) [Magyar Közlöny].
3. For a general discussion, see Wolfgang Kleinwächter, 'Out with the Cold, In with the New?', *InterMedia* 20 (May 1992), 12.
4. Art. 31, 'Law on Radio and Television Broadcasting', *Post-Soviet Media Law and Policy Newsletter*, no. 12/13 (Dec. 1994), 14 (supp.).
5. Art. 31, Draft Russian Statute on Radio and Television Broadcasting, *Post-Soviet Media Law and Policy Newsletter*, no. 12/13 (Dec. 1994), 6 (supp.).
6. Draft Media Act, Ministry of Justice, 20.053/1991 IM.VII (second draft), including alternate A and B versions.
7. Prior to Sept. 1989, Solidarity had obtained the right of opposition parties to broadcast weekly programmes on radio and television. The Roman Catholic Church also had rights to air time and to establish its own radio and television stations. In this early period, Solidarity also had its own department within Polish Radio and Television, but the office was dissolved upon Solidarity's ascendancy to power.
8. Karol Jakubowicz, 'The Restructuring of Television in East-Central Europe', Paper given at the CCIS, University of Westminster, May 1992.
9. In Romania, the National Council of Radio and Television consists of two members nominated by the President, three by the government, and six by the Parliament. The statute provides that the members of the Council 'shall be warrantors of the public interest in the audio-visual domain of radio and television, and they shall not represent the authority by which they have been appointed'. Romanian Law on Radio and Television Broadcasting, ch. 4, art. 25. The full text can be found in the appendix to Monroe E. Price, 'Comparing Broadcast Structures: Transnational Perspectives and Post-Communist Examples', *Cardozo Arts and Entertainment Law Journal* 11 app. (1993), 609–20.
10. The Slovenian law 'On Mass Media' was passed by the Slovenian Parliament on 25 Mar. 1994 and signed by President Milan Kucan on 2 Apr. 1994. The

Slovenian law 'On Slovenian Radio and Television' was passed by Parliament on 29 Mar. 1994 and signed by the President on 6 Apr. 1994.

11. Ibid., arts. 12, 13, and 15. The search for the public sphere is also evident in clauses—as are found in the radio and television law of the former Czech and Slovak Federative Republic—which required, in art. 4, that operators provide 'objective and balanced information necessary for the free development of ideas'. Certain broadcasters would have been required to 'contribute to the creation of a democratic society and reflect its pluralism in opinions, particularly by not one-sidedly paying regard to individual opinion orientations, individual religious affiliations or world outlooks, the interests of one political party, movement, group or part of society' (*Law on the Operation of Radio and Television Broadcasts*, Federal Assembly of the Czech and Slovak Federative Republic, 30 Oct. 1991).
12. Slovenia Draft Law on Public Media, 19 Dec. 1991, art. 16 (unpublished).
13. The full text of the 1992 Hungarian draft bill can be found in the appendix to Price, 'Comparing Broadcast Structures', 449–509.
14. *Post-Soviet Media Law and Policy Newsletter*, no. 12/13 (Dec. 1994) 13 (supp.) (reprint of Estonian Broadcasting Act).
15. *Post-Soviet Media Law and Policy Newsletter*, no. 3 (Dec. 1993), 7. For a general review and bibliographic summary of materials on national identity and broadcasting in Central and Eastern Europe, see Philip R. Schlesinger, 'Europe's Contradictory Communicative Space', *Daedalus* 123 (Mar. 1994), 25.
16. Andras Sajo, 'Hate Speech for Hostile Hungarians', *East European Constitutional Review* 3 (1994), 82.
17. A large number of European countries have similar provisions in their criminal codes or mass-media laws. The new Slovenian criminal code, passed by Parliament on 29 Sept. 1994, and signed into law in October, has a similar provision in art. 300. Art. 4 of the Russian Mass Media Law is discussed in Ch. 6. Regarding Germany's law making it a crime to publish denial of the Holocaust, see Eric Stein, 'History against Free Speech: The New German Law against the 'Auschwitz'—and other—'Lies', *Michigan Law Review* 85 (1986) 277.
18. Ibid.
19. *Beauharnais* v. *Illinois*, 343 US 250 (1952).
20. Most of the doubt as to whether *Beauharnais* remained valid doctrine was put to rest in the decision of the Supreme Court in *R.A.V.* v. *St. Paul*, 112 S. Ct. 2538 (1992). Speech considerations are sometimes overriden on national security grounds. Cf. *Snepp* v. *Snepp*, 444 US 507 (1980). See also Geoffrey R. Stone, 'Hate Speech and the US Constitution', *East European Constitutional Review* 3 (1994), 78, 79.
21. United Nations, *International Covenant on Civil and Political Rights*, GA Res. 2200, 21 UN GAOR, Supp. (No. 16) 52, UN Doc. A/6316 (1966), art. 20, sect. 2. The full text can be found in Richard B. Lillich (ed.), *International Human Rights, Documentary Supplement* (Boston: Little, Brown & Company, 1991), 52–71.

22. In Sept. 1994, the European Court of Human Rights decided the case of *Jersild* v. *Denmark*, ruling that Denmark's conviction of a broadcast journalist for airing interviews with a racist group was a violation of art. 10 of the European Human Rights Convention. In the opinion, the court suggested that prosecution of the persons making the racist statements themselves would perhaps not be a violation of the Convention.
23. Included in 'Committee of Experts on Media Concentrations and Pluralism, Study on Media Concentrations in Central and East-European Countries', MM-CM (94) 17 app. at 49.
24. Art. 22.
25. Law on Radio and Television Broadcasting, 19 May 1994, art. 25. The same provision also requires that 'transmissions must take into consideration the moral, political and religious beliefs of groups of the population and promote respect and dignity to all individuals . . .'
26. Constantin, '1993 Broadcasting Law in Romania', in W. Kleinwächter (ed.), *Broadcasting in Transition: The Changing Legal Framework in the Eastern Part of Europe* (Leipzig: Netcom Papers, 1993).
27. See Mickiewicz, *Split Signals*.
28. 'Newspapers: Free to be Bankrupt', *Post-Soviet Media Law and Policy Newsletter*, no. 2 (Nov. 1993), 6.
29. The Slovenian and Hungarian bills, for example. See also Breda Luthar, 'Slovenia Struggles with the Reithian Ethos', *InterMedia* 20 (Aug. 1992), 33; and Tomo Martelanc, 'Vulnerable Slovenia', *InterMedia* 20 (Aug. 1992), 34.
30. Eric J. Hobsbawn and Terence Ranger (eds.), *The Invention of Tradition* (New York: Cambridge University Press, 1983).
31. Benedict Anderson, *Imagined Communities: Reflections on the Origin and Spread of Nationalism* (London: Verso, 1983).
32. Austrian radio cases II (*Informationsverein Lentia et al.* v. *Austria*), Council of Europe, European Commission of Human Rights, Report of the Commission (adopted on 9 Sept. 1992), para. 77. The text of the European Court's ruling of 23 Nov. 1993 is in *Human Rights Law Journal* 15 (1994), 31.
33. In many of the transition societies, poverty meant a low demand for consumer goods and the supply was problematic. Developing a market for advertising was more difficult than acceding to the principle. Much advertising (off, more than on, television) is used to develop brand identification so that when the market matures particular competitors will have built a franchise for themselves.
34. US Department of Commerce, National Telecommunications and Information Administration, *Globalization of the Mass Media* (Washington: NTIA Special Publication 93–290, Jan. 1993).
35. See President's Task Force on US Government International Broadcasting, *Report of the President's Task Force on US Government International Broadcasting* (Washington: Department of State Publication 9925; Dec. 1991).
36. Michael Schudson, *Advertising, the Uneasy Persuasion: Its Dubious Impact on American Society* (New York: Basic Books, 1984), 210.
37. Information Commission for the Study of Communication Problems (MacBride Commission), *Many Voices, One World: Towards a New More Just and More*

Efficient World Information and Communication Order (London: Kogan Page, 1980), 110.

38. Schudson, *Advertising, The Uneasy Persuasion*, 214–15. Leo Bogart also discusses advertising as propaganda and compares it to Soviet propaganda in *Strategy in Advertising* (New York: Harcourt, Brace & World, 1967), 6–7. See also Caradog V. James, *Soviet Socialist Realism: Origins and Theory* (London: Macmillan, 1973); and Matthew Cullerne Bown, *Art under Stalin* (Oxford: Phaidon Press, 1991).
39. For additional reading about the ways media do or do not inculcate loyalty to capitalism, see Stuart Ewen, *Captains of Consciousness: Advertising and the Social Roots of the Consumer Culture* (New York: McGraw-Hill, 1976); David L. Paletz and Robert M. Entman, *Media Power Politics* (New York: Free Press, 1981); and John Fiske, *Television Culture* (London: Methuen, 1987).

Chapter 8

1. A recent treatment is Cass R. Sunstein, *Democracy and the Problem of Free Speech* (New York: The Free Press, 1993).
2. *Turner Broadcasting System Inc.* v. *FCC*, 114 S. Ct. 2445 (1994). Cf. *City of Cincinnati* v. *Discovery Networks*, 113 S. Ct. 1505 (1993).
3. 47 USC subsect. 303, 307(*a*). See its predecessor, *The Radio Act of 1927*, ch. 169, 44 stat. 1162 (1927).
4. For early accounts, see Merlin H. Aylesworth, 'Broadcasting in the Public Interest', *Annals of the American Academy of Political and Social Science* (Jan. 1935), 114; James Lawrence Fly, 'Regulation of Radio Broadcasting in the Public Interest', *Annals of the American Academy of Political and Social Science* (Jan. 1941), 102; and Jonathan Weinberg, 'Broadcasting and Speech', *Cailfornia Law Review* 81 (1993), 1103.
5. John J. O'Connor, 'Television View: Still Trapped in a Vast Wasteland', *New York Times*, 13 Dec. 1992, sect. 2, p. 1, col. 2.
6. See e.g. Kenneth L. Karst, 'Paths to Belonging: The Constitution and Cultural Identity', *North Carolina Law Review* 64 (1986), 303; Mari J. Matsuda, 'Voices of America: Accent, Antidiscrimination Law, and a Jurisprudence for the Last Reconstruction', *Yale Law Journal* 100 (1991), 1329; and Monroe E. Price, 'Controlling Imagery: The Fight over Using Art to Change Society', *American Art* (summer 1993), 2; see also Edward S. Herman and Noam Chomsky, *Manufacturing Consent: The Political Economy of the Mass Media* (New York: Pantheon Books, 1988), 16–18.
7. I have argued that the federal government has taken the position—though not explicitly—that the First Amendment protects the exercise of free speech only within the boundaries of the United States (a kind of common market of speech); and that the rights of Americans to gain speech from foreign sources or to communicate, free of intervention, from within the country to abroad is less bound by rule than one would presume from the wholesale tradition of First Amendment rhetoric. See Monroe E. Price, 'Comment', in Jack David and Robert McKay (eds.), *The Blessings of Liberty: An Enduring Constitution in a Changing World* (New York: Random House, 1989), 277.

8. The Sedition Act is at 1 Stat. 596 (Act of 14 July 1798). See Philip Kurland and Ralph Lerner (eds.), *The Founders' Constitution* (Chicago: University of Chicago Press, 1987), v.
9. Michael O'Boyle, 'Right to Speak and Associate under Strasbourg Case-Law with Reference to Eastern and Central Europe', *Connecticut Journal of International Law* 8 (1993), 263.
10. See *Second Interim Report by the Office of Network Study*, FCC Docket No. 12782, p. 114 (1965).
11. 67 Cong. Rec. 5558 (1926).
12. 67 Cong. Rec. 5479 (1926).
13. There is, of course, no question that scarcity was a factor in the thinking of the early Federal Radio Commission. In the *Great Lakes Broadcasting* case, the Commission, considering the standard it would use for the award of radio licences, called on applicants to provide 'ample play for the free and fair competition of opposing views'. One reason, which could be reduced to a concern for scarcity, was that 'There is not room in the broadcast band for every school of thought, religious, political, social and economic, each to have its separate broadcasting station, its mouthpiece in the ether' (FCC, *Third Annual Report* 33 (1929)). See also *Chicago Federation*, 3 FRC at 36 (labour union sought unsuccessfully for the extension of a licence dedicated wholly to the labour point of view).
14. In *Young People's Association*, the relatively new FCC denied an application for a construction permit because only those who agreed with the applicant's views would be permitted to use the proposed station: 6 FCC 178 (1938).
15. For a collection of such quotations, see Roscoe Barrow, 'The Equal Opportunities and Fairness Doctrines in Broadcasting: Pillars in the Forum of Democracy', *University of Cincinnati Law Review* 37 (1968), 447, 462. In a famous statement, in 1949, the FCC announced: 'It is the right of the public to be informed, rather than any right on the part of Government, any broadcast licensee or any individual member of the public to broadcast his own particular views on any matter which is the foundation stone of the American system of broadcasting' (*In re Editorializing*, 13 FCC 1246, 1249 (1949)).
16. 319 US 190 (1943); see also Richard W. Steele, *Propaganda in an Open Society: The Roosevelt Administration and the Media, 1933–1941* (Westport, Conn.: Greenwood Press, 1985).
17. See the 'fairness primer' of 1964, in which the Commission described the broadcaster's obligation in presenting controversial issues of public importance, indicating that where such issues are broadcast, the licensees had 'an affirmative duty generally to encourage and implement the broadcast of all sides of controversial issues over their facilities, over and beyond their obligation to make available on demand opportunities for the expression of opposing views. It is clear that any approximation of fairness in the presentation of any controversy will be difficult if not impossible of achievement unless the licensee plays a conscious and positive role in bringing about balanced presentation of the opposing viewpoints' (Public Notice of 1 July 1964, 29 Fed. Reg. 10415 (Applicability of the Fairness Doctrine in the Handling of Controversial

Issues of Public Importance), at 10423). See also *In re WLIB, Inc.* 6 Rad. Reg. 258 (P & K) (1950), where the phrase 'affirmative duty to seek out, aid, and encourage' is employed. See generally Barrow, 'The Equal Opportunities and Fairness Doctrines in Broadcasting', 447, 462.

18. Much is covered by the spate of articles by Jerome A. Barron in the mid-1960s as he sought, through the force of scholarship, to justify the constitutionality of the fairness doctrine and other similar doctrines. See e.g. Jerome A. Barron, 'Access to the Press—A New First Amendment Right', *Harvard Law Review* 80 (1976), 1641.
19. *In re Editorializing*, at 1249. There is the familiar language of trusteeship adopted by the Commission in its 1960 statement of policy on programming: 'The licensee, is, in effect, a "trustee" in the sense that his licence to operate his station imposes upon him a non-delegable duty to serve the public interest in the community he has chosen to represent as a broadcaster' (*Report and Statement of Policy re: Commission en Banc Programming Inquiry*, FCC Public Notice B, 29 July 1960; repr. in *Television Network Program Procurement, Report of the Committee on Interstate and Foreign Commerce*, HR Rep. No. 281, 88th Congress, 1st Session 157 (1963)).
20. 8 FCC at 3450 (1941). See Note: 'The Mayflower Doctrine Scuttled', *Yale Law Journal* 59 (1950), 759.
21. *Report and Statement of Policy*, 44 FCC 2303 (1960).
22. See e.g. *Primer on Ascertainment of Community Problems by Broadcast Applicants*, 27 FCC 2d 650 (1973).
23. Louis L. Jaffe, 'The Illusion of the Ideal Administration', *Harvard Law Review* 86 (1973), 1183, 1191–7. See, generally, Marver Bernstein, *Regulating Business by Independent Commission* (Princeton: Princeton University Press, 1955).
24. The US practice was considerably different from that of almost any other nation in the world because of citizen and competitor standing as a way of raising issues, as opposed to the European or Canadian approach of appointing distinguished Commissions to review issues, draw conclusions, and make recommendations. The British model could be more comprehensive, more systematic, more thorough-going, but, because of the make-up of the British Commissions, more susceptible to the charge of control.
25. *Office of Communication of the United Church of Christ* v. *FCC*, 359 F. 2d 994 (DC Cir, 1966).
26. See Sloan Commission on Cable Communications, *On the Cable: The Television of Abundance* (New York: McGraw-Hill, 1971).
27. See Monroe F. Price, 'Requiem for the Wired Nation: Cable Rulemaking at the FCC', *Virginia Law Review* 61 (1975), 541.
28. *Federal Communications Commission* v. *Pacifica Foundation*, 438 US 726 (1978). The case was not decided under the 'public-interest' standard but under a statute proscribing broadcast indecency.
29. *FCC* v. *Pacifica* 438 US at 748 (citation omitted).
30. *Trinity Methodist Church, South* v. *Federal Radio Commission*, 62 F. 2d 850 (DC Cir. 1932).
31. Mark S. Fowler and Daniel L. Brenner, 'A Marketplace Approach to Broadcast

Regulation', *Texas Law Review* 60 (1982), 207 and Ithiel de Sola Pool, *Technologies of Freedom* (Harvard, Mass.: Belknap, 1983).

32. *In the Matter of the Revision of Programming and Commercialization Policies, Ascertainment Requirements, and Program Log Requirements for Commercial Television Stations*, 98 FCC 2d 357 (1986).
33. The Television Improvement Act, dealing with violence, and the Children's Television Act, dealing with commercialization and the improvement of programming for children, were passed in 1990.
34. Kathryn C. Montgomery, *Target: Prime Time, Advocacy Groups and the Struggle over Entertainment Television* (New York, Oxford University Press, 1989), 6.
35. George Gerbner, 'Liberal Education in the Information Age', *Current Issues in Higher Education 1983–84* (1984), 14.
36. In the early 1970s, the National Citizens Committee for Broadcasting, under the leadership of the charismatic former FCC Commissioner Nicholas Johnson, established a thorough guide to violence on television and, with careful scrutiny, declared which programmes were most harmful and which companies were their major advertisers. Montgomery, *Target: Prime Time*, 108–10.
37. For a discussion of the constitutionality of boycotts of media for their editorial policies, see *Environmental Planning and Information Council* v. *Superior Court*, 680 P. 2d 1086 (Cal. 1984).
38. Patrick M. Fahey, 'Comment: Advocacy Group Boycotting of Network Television Advertisers and its Effects on Programming Content', *University of Pennsylvania Law Review* 140 (1991), 647, 704–5.
39. Ibid. 654.
40. Ibid. 654–5.
41. See Monroe E. Price, *Shattered Mirrors: Our Search for Identity and Community in the AIDS Era* (Cambridge, Mass.: Harvard University Press, 1989).

Chapter 9

1. See *Pacifica* v. *FCC*, 438 US 726 (1978); and *Shiffrin* v. *Shiffrin*, 449 US 1123 (1981).
2. See e.g. Mark G. Yudof, *When Government Speaks: Politics, Law, and Government Expression in America* (Berkeley and Los Angeles: University of California Press, 1983); and Steven Shiffrin, 'Government Speech', *UCLA Law Review* 27 (1980), 565.
3. See *National Association for the Advancement of Colored People* v. *Hunt*, 891 F. 2d 1555, 1565–6 (1990) (rejecting a claim by the NAACP that the flying of the confederate flag atop the capitol dome in Montgomery, Alabama, violates the First Amendment).
4. 'If the content of British patriotism or "Americanism" was notably ill-defined, though usually specified in commentaries associated with ritual occasions, the *practices* symbolizing it were virtually compulsory—as in standing up for the singing of the National Anthem in Britain, the flag ritual in American schools. The crucial elements seem to have been the invention of emotionally and symbolically charged signs of club membership rather than the statutes and

objects of the club. Their significance lay precisely in their undefined universality' (Eric J. Hobsbawm and Terence Ranger (eds.), *The Invention of Tradition* (New York: Cambridge University Press, 1983), 11).

5. See *United States* v. *Eichman*, 496 US 310 (1990); *Texas* v. *Johnson*, 491 US 397 (1989); Frank Michelman, 'Saving Old Glory: On Constitutional Iconography', *Stanford Law Review* 42 (1990), 1337.
6. *Minersville School District* v. *Gobitis*, 310 US 586 (1940).
7. 310 US at 596–9; Frankfurter J. invoked Balfour, *Introduction to Bagehot's English Constitution*, p. xxii, in support of the proposition that 'this country [cannot be] barred from determining the appropriateness of various means to evoke that unifying sentiment without which there can ultimately be no liberties, civil or religious'.
8. This aspect of the decision is consistent with Frankfurter's hallmark notions of judicial restraint and deferral to democratically elected legislatures. See, generally, Alexander M. Bickel, *The Least Dangerous Branch: The Supreme Court at the Bar of Politics* (New Haven: Yale University Press, 1986).
9. 310 US at 600.
10. 319 US 624 (1943).
11. Black and Douglas JJ., who had not dissented in *Gobitis*, now, three years later, had changed their view and concurred with the majority in *Barnette*.
12. 319 US at 629 n. 3. Jackson J. was quoting from James Moss, *The Flag of the United States: Its History and Symbolism* (1914), 108.
13. 319 US at 634. Stone J. dissented, on the ground that the government could not 'as a supposed education measure, and as a means of disciplining the young, compel public affirmations which violate their religious conscience'.
14. 319 US at 642.
15. 319 US at 632.
16. 310 US at 604.
17. 319 US at 641.
18. *Barnette* was decided the same year as *FCC* v. *NBC*, 319 US 239 (1943), dealing with the power of the federal government to regulate networks.
19. Here, the work of Walter Lippmann is relevant. See Walter Lippmann, *Public Opinion* (London: Allen & Unwin, 1922). Raboy characterizes Lippman's work as making a case 'for expert management of public affairs on behalf of a populace incapacitated by the complex demands of modern life' (Marc Raboy, *Missed Opportunities: The Story of Canada's Broadcasting Policy* (Buffalo, NY: McGill-Queen's, University Press, 1990), 5).
20. 319 US at 641.
21. Benedict Anderson, *Imagined Communities: Reflections on the Origin and Spread of Nationalism* (London: Verso, 1993).
22. See e.g. *Yniguez* v. *Mofford*, 730 F. Supp. 309 (D. Ariz 1990), affirmed in part, reversed in part, 939 F. 2d 727 (9th Cir. 1991), which held unconstitutional an 'English as the Official Language' amendment to the Arizona Constitution (requiring, under the court's interpretation, that all discourse by Arizona officials with the public be in English) on free-speech and equal-protection grounds. See also *Gutierrez* v. *Municipal Court of the Southeast District*, 838 F. 2d

1031 (9th Cir. 1988), *vacated*, 490 US 1016 (1989), which upheld a similar California initiative by construing it quite narrowly to allow employees to use other languages at least in personal discourse (dismissing work rules concerning employees in court system). The Supreme Court has not determined the constitutionality of these state efforts to create an official language, though incorporation of many languages into instruction in the state schools was long ago reinforced by the Court. See, generally, 'Note, "Official English": Federal Limits on Efforts to Curtail Bilingual Services in the States', *Harvard Law Review* 100 (1987), 1345.

23. Kenneth L. Karst, *Law's Promise, Law's Expression: Visions of Power in the Politics of Race, Gender, and Religion* (New Haven: Yale University Press, 1993).
24. 262 US 390 (1923).
25. 262 US 390, 402 (1923).
26. See *R.A.V.* v. *St Paul*, 112 S. Ct. 2538 (1992), and Akhil Reed Amar, 'The Case of the Missing Amendments: *R.A.V.* v. *City of St Paul*', *Harvard Law Review* 106 (November, 1992): 124.
27. See Evan G. S. Siegel, 'Comment: Closing the Campus Gates to Free Expression: The Regulation of Offensive Speech at Colleges and Universities', *Emory Law Journal* 39 (1990), 1351.
28. All these Presidential quotes are taken from the Report of the Independent Commission (Brademas Commission) (see 'Report to Congress on the National Endowment for the Arts', submitted by the Independent Commission (Washington, DC, Sept. 1990), 8–11) appointed to review the grant-making procedures of the National Endowment for the Arts and to consider 'whether the standard for publicly funded art should be different than the standard for privately funded art'.
29. See Richard Bolton (ed.), *Culture Wars: Documents from the Recent Controversies in the Arts* (New York: The New Press, 1992).
30. See 136 Cong. Rec. 517,975 (1990).
31. Bolton (ed.), *Culture Wars*, 216.
32. Edward de Grazia, *Girls Lean Back Everywhere: The Law of Obscenity and the Assault on Genius* (New York: Random House, 1992).
33. Ibid.
34. The history of the appointment process to regulatory agencies provides some, but limited guidance. Of the five members of the FCC, no more than three can be of the same political party. This could be viewed as a limitation, or rather as an invitation for brokered agreement between the two political parties. See Victor Kramer, 'What is the Public Interest? Who Represents It?', *Administrative Law Review* 26 (1974), 395.
35. The example is taken from Nat Hentoff, *Free for Me—But Not for Thee: How the American Left and Right Relentlessly Censor Each Other* (New York: HarperCollins, 1992).
36. Monroe E. Price, *Shattered Mirrors: Our Search for Identity and Community in the AIDS Era* (Cambridge Mass.: Harvard University Press, 1989).
37. Bolton (ed.), *Culture Wars*, 106–14.
38. Children's Television Act.

39. *Action for Children's TV* v. *FCC*, 11 F. 3d 170 (DC Cir. 1993) (vacated for rehearing *en banc*).
40. See Hans Gerth and C. Wright Mills, *Character and Social Structure: The Psychology of Social Institutions* (New York: Harcourt, Brace & World, 1964); Peter L. Berger and Thomas Luckmann, *The Social Construction of Reality: A Treatise in the Sociology of Knowledge* (Garden City, NY: Doubleday, 1966); Harold Robert Isaacs, *Idols of the Tribe: Group Identity and Political Change* (New York: Harper & Row, 1975); and Karst, *Law's Promise, Law's Expression.*

Chapter 10

1. See Vince Blasi, 'The Checking Value in First Amendment Theory', *American Bar Foundation Research Journal* 1977 (1977), 521.
2. This was done, until recently, through a limitation on the number of channels. Current regulations limit the reach of any common group of broadcasters to not more than 25% of US television households.
3. 436 US 775 (1978).
4. *Associate Press* v. *United States*, 326 US 1, 20 (1945).
5. The operation of the tax-incentive policy and similar efforts is traced in the following articles: Andrea L. Johnson, 'Redefining Diversity in Telecommunications: Uniform Regulatory Framework for Mass Communications', *University of California at Davis Law Review* 26 (1992), 87; Bruce R. Wilde, 'FCC Tax Certificates for Minority Ownership of Broadcast Facilities: A Critical Re-Examination of Policy', *University of Pennsylvania Law Review* 138 (1990), 979.
6. *Metro Broadcasting* v. *FCC*, 497 US 547 (1990), *rehearing denied*, 497 US 1050 (1990). In 1995, the tax incentive was scotched by Congress.
7. 'The FCC has determined that increased minority participation in broadcasting promotes programming diversity' (497 US at 569). Furthermore, 'Evidence suggest[s] that an owner's minority status influences the selection of topics for news coverage and the presentation of editorial viewpoint, especially on matters of particular concern to minorities' (ibid. 549). The majority also accepted the conclusion from several studies, cited by the FCC, that 'a minority owner is more likely to employ minorities in managerial and other important roles where they can have an impact on station policies' (ibid. 581–2).
8. R. Randall Rainey, 'The Public's Interest in Public Affairs Discourse, Democratic Governance, and Fairness in Broadcasting', *Georgetown Law Journal* 82 (1993), 269.
9. I have mentioned the historical antipathy for the FCC or Congress forcibly to alter social narratives by compelling networks, stations, and cable operators to carry works solely on the ground that they were produced by representatives of particular racial or ethnic groups. In sect. 9(*c*)(1) of the 1992 Cable Act, however, Congress provided an incentive to cable operators to dedicate channel capacity otherwise designated for leased access to a 'qualified minority programming source', defined as a programming source which 'devotes substantially all of its programming to coverage of minority viewpoints, or to

programming directed at members of minority groups' and which is over 50% minority owned. This is an extremely interesting access rule, because it has both an ownership and a content feature.

10. Technology plays odd tricks. Cable television, which is considered to be a harbinger of diversity, comes close to becoming the beneficent monopolist. While there are many more channels available to each household—50 or 70 or 500—the cable operator more or less controls the entire system. Diversity of content becomes a strategy to increase the number of subscribers to the system. Rules, now rapidly eroding, long existed to prevent owners of cable systems from owning a newspaper, telephone system, or television licence in the same community, but only in the 1992 Cable Television Consumer Protection Act has Congress encouraged competition by ensuring programme sources for new multi-channel video distributors.
11. Some studies have been cited to demonstrate that minority-owned media are more likely to feature stories about minorities or present dramas and other programmes in which minorities play significant roles. See *Metro Broadcasting*, 497 US at 583.
12. An arcane genre of access regulation provides preferred opportunities for 'independent' producers (those not linked to the major networks) to gain access to broadcast time in the periods of maximum audience viewing. This form of access is a reflection of concerns about competition among producers of programming and the power of the television networks. While the goal of the prime-time access rule was to make more broadly available a wider set of perspectives, the rule has been exploited most by such shows as *Jeopardy* and *Wheel of Fortune*. Access has led, perhaps, to debasement of taste, not a broadening of it. See Review of the Prime Time Access Rule, Notice of Proposed Rule Making, MM Docket No. 94–123 (1994).
13. For example, a common form of producer access in Europe, national quotas, is justifiable, not just on economic protection grounds, but on the theory that a pool of creators capable of using television must be fostered to maintain a healthy public sphere. The European Broadcasting Directive requires that an increasing proportion of programming be made by 'independent' producers.
14. See 47 USC sect. 315 (1994).
15. See *Miami Herald Pub. Co.* v. *Tornillo*, 418, US 21 (1974).
16. See sect. 315 of the *Communications Act of 1934*.
17. Rulings concerning debates include Henry Geller *et al.*, 54 Rad. Reg. 2d (P & F) 1246 (1983) and *Chisholm* v. *Federal Communications Commission*, 538 F. 2d 349 (DC Cir. 1976). See Thomas Blaisdell Smith, 'Reexamining the Reasonable Access and Equal Time Provisions of the Federal Communications Act: Can These Provisions Stand if the Fairness Doctrine Fails?', *Georgia Law Review* 74 (1986), 1491.
18. *Columbia Broadcasting System*, 14 Rad. Reg. (P & F) 720 (1956).
19. The statute was upheld in *CBS, Inc.* v. *FCC*, 453 US 367 (1981).
20. Rhonda Brown, 'Ad Hoc Access: The Regulation of Editorial Advertising on Television and Radio', *Yale Law and Policy Review* 6 (1988), 449.

21. These are quotations, from other opinions, used by Burger CJ in *CBS, Inc.* v. *Federal Communications Commission*, 453 US 367 (1981).
22. Ibid. 396–7.
23. *Buckley* v. *Valeo*, 424 US 1 (1976) (holding that provisions limiting expenditures by candidates on their own behalf violated the candidates' rights to freedom of speech).
24. 395 US 367 (1969).
25. 438 US 726 (1978).
26. See, generally, Steven J. Simmons, *The Fairness Doctrine and the Media* (Berkeley and Los Angeles: University of California Press, 1978), 189–228.
27. Ibid. 319.
28. See Richard R. Zaragoza, Richard J. Bodorff, and Jonathan W. Emord, 'The Public Interest Concept Transformed: The Trusteeship Model Gives Way to a Marketplace Approach', in Jon T. Powell and Wally Gair (eds.), *Public Interest and the Business of Broadcasting* (New York: Quorum Books, 1988), 27–50.
29. *Cable Communications Policy Act of 1984*, 47 USC sect. 521 (4).
30. *Missouri Knights of the Ku Klux Klan* v. *Kansas City, Missouri*, 723 F. Supp. 1347 (WD Mo. 1989).
31. Sect. 10(*a*) of the Act amended 47 USC sect. 532(*h*) of the 1984 law.
32. *The Cable Television Consumer Protection and Competition Act*, sect. 10(*a*).
33. Among the important cases is *Alliance for Community Media* v. *Federal Communications Commission*, 10 F. 3d 812 (DC Cir. 1993), vacated on granting of suggestion for rehearing *en banc*, 16 Feb. 1994, reported at 1994 US App. LEXIS 6440. See also *Altmann* v. *Television Signal Corp.*, 849 F. Supp. 1335 (ND Cal. 1994).
34. The FCC instituted this policy in 1967. See *Banzhaf* v. *FCC*, 405 F. 2d 1082 (DC Cir. 1968) (supporting the FCC requirement that broadcasters of cigarette commercials earmark a reasonable amount of time for counteradvertising).
35. These are limited to channels for public access, government, and education (the PEG channels).
36. Michael Warner, *The Letters of the Republic: Publication and the Public Sphere in Eighteenth-Century America* (Cambridge, Mass.: Harvard University Press, 1990).

Chapter 11

1. Kevin Robins, 'Reimagined Communities', *Cultural Studies* 3 (1989).
2. John Carey, *Culture as Communication* (Boston: Unwin Hyman, 1989), 2–3.
3. See my 'Comment' in Jack David and Robert B. McKay (eds.), *The Blessings of Liberty: An Enduring Constitution in a Changing World* (New York: Random House, 1989), 277–80.
4. The constitutional dimension of defamation law presents a case in point. Defamation doctrine, as developed by the Court since the 1960s, acts as a brake on state laws which would be odious to the flourishing of a national media, serving a national audience. *New York Times* v. *Sullivan*, 376 US 254 (1964). See also Elizabeth Hull, *Taking Liberties: National Barriers to the Free*

Flow of Ideas (New York: Praeger, 1990), on restrictions on information flow into the United States.

5. Dayan and Katz write about these communities glancingly in their works on great public television events. They use the term 'diasporic ceremony'. See Daniel Dayan and Elihu Katz, 'Performing Media Events' in James Curran, Anthony Smith, and Pauline Wingate (eds.), *Impacts and Influences: Essays on Media Power in the Twentieth Century* (New York, Methuen, 1987), 174–97. See also David Chaney, 'The Symbolic Form of Ritual in Mass Communications', in Peter Golding, Graham Murdock, and Philip Schlesinger (eds.), *Communicating Politics: Mass Communications and the Political Process* (New York: Holmes & Meier Publishers, 1986), 115–32. Benedict Anderson comments on the impact of diasporic groups on the politics of their homeland in Benedict Anderson, 'Exodus', *Critical Inquiry* 20 (1994), 314, 326–7: 'Many of the most uncompromising, fanatical adherents of an independent Khalistan do not live in the Punjab but have prosperous business in Melbourne and Chicago. The Tigers in Jaffna are stiffened in their violent struggles by Tamil communities in Toronto, London, and elsewhere all linked on the computer by Tamilnet.'
6. See, generally, David Morley, *Television, Audiences and Cultural Studies* (New York: Routledge, 1992), 270; Joshua Meyrowitz, 'The Generalized Elsewhere', *Critical Studies in Mass Communication* 6 (Sept. 1989), 326–34; and Joshua Meyrowitz, *No Sense of Place: The Impact of the Electronic Media on Social Behavior* (New York: Oxford University Press, 1985).
7. Meyrowitz, *No Sense of Place*, 145–7.
8. Andrew Kirby, 'A Sense of Place', *Critical Studies in Mass Communication* 6 (Sept. 1989), 322, 323 (citing Meyrowitz, *No Sense of Place*).
9. Jody Berland, 'Placing Television', *New Formations* 4 (spring 1988), 145, 147.
10. The public interest in curriculum content is illustrated by the US controversy over the 'Channel One' programme, sponsored by Whittle Communications. In 1989 Whittle Communications began to offer television equipment, including monitors, VCRs, and satellite dishes in exchange for an agreement to have students view a twelve-minute programme consisting of two minutes of advertising and a ten-minute current-events news programme. As Channel One agreements spread, so too did the public debate about the propriety of virtually compelling children to watch advertisements on a video monitor. See Cynthia Newsome, 'Note: Pay Attention: A Survey and Analysis of the Legal Battle over the Integration of Forced Television Advertising into the Public School Curriculum', *Rutgers Law Journal* 24 (1992), 281.
11. See James Atlas, *The Book Wars* (Knoxville, Tenn.: Whittle Direct Books, 1990).
12. As to libraries, see *Board of Education* v. *Pico*, 457 US 853, 869 (1982) (limiting the power of the board of education to remove books from school library). Brennan J. distinguished between the compulsory curriculum, where a school district's views may hold greater sway, and the school library, and its 'regime of voluntary inquiry'. There, 'selection of books from these libraries is entirely a matter of free choice'.
13. D. Antin, 'Fine Furs', *Critical Inquiry* 19 (1992), 151, 155.
14. Ibid. 162.

15. Michael J. Sandel, 'Post-National Democracy vs. Electronic Bonapartism', *NPQ* 9 (1992), 4.
16. *Shaw* v. *Reno*, 113 S. Ct. 2816 (1993). See also Lani Guinier, 'The Representation of Minority Interests: The Question of Single-Member Districts', *Cardozo Law Review* 14 (1993), 1135.
17. Much of the discussion here is drawn from Jeffrey Abramson, 'Democratic Designs for Electronic Town Meetings', Prepared for the Aspen Institute's Communications and Society Program, Queenstown, Maryland, 1992.
18. Ibid. 2.
19. Ibid. 3.
20. The popular right of electronic enfranchisement is, as a matter of principle, less connected to representative government than to pure democracy. For James Madison, however, 'pure Democracy' is undesirable. The Madisonian ideal places a buffer between the people and their rulers. Representative democracy is that buffer, a system in which dispassionate and reasoned decision-making might temper the desires of an otherwise unchecked popular appetite. See Ronald L. K. Collins and David M. Skover, Pissing in the Snow: A Cultural Approach to the First Amendment,' *Stanford Law Review* 45 (1993), 783, 799.
21. See e.g. Study and Report on Sports Programming Migration, Pub. L. No. 102–385, sects. 26, 28, 106 stat. 1502, 1503 (1992).
22. Anne Rawley Saldich, *Electronic Democracy: Television's Impact on the American Political Process* (New York: Praeger, 1979); and Lawrence Grossman, *The Electronic Republic: The Transformation of American Democracy* (New York: Viking, forthcoming).
23. See *Red Lion Broadcasting Co.* v. *FCC*, 395 US 367 (1969); and *Miami Herald Publishing Co.* v. *Tornillo*, 418 US 241 (1974).
24. *Turner Broadcasting System Inc.* v. *FCC*, 114 S. Ct. 2445 (1994).
25. The doctrine peered through the quagmire of scarcity in *Pacifica* v. *FCC*, 438 US 726 (1978).
26. Concern with the display of so-called pornographic publications in stores and other facilities open to the general public is a special example. See *Playboy Enterprises* v. *Meese*, 639 F. Supp. 581, 588 (DDC 1986). Billboards or advertisements in subways and buses present a useful example of the location of images in a public place that occasionally inspire public concerns.
27. See Monroe E. Price and Donald W. Hawthorne, 'Saving Public Television: The Remand of *Turner Broadcasting* and the future of Cable Regulation', *Hastings Communications and Entertainment Law Journal* 17 (1994), 65.
28. See Geoffrey Cowan, *See No Evil: The Backstage Battle over Sex and Violence on Television* (New York: Simon and Schuster, 1979).
29. *Children's Television Act of 1990*, Pub. L. No. 101–437, 104 Stat. 996 (codified at 47 USC sects. 303a–303b, 393a, 394 (Supp. III 1991)).
30. See *Stanley* v. *Georgia*, 394 US 557 (1969).
31. *Turner Broadcasting System Inc.* v. *FCC*, 114 S. Ct. 2445 (1994).
32. In *Lehman* v. *Shaker Heights*, 418 US 298, 306–7 (1974), Douglas J., concurring, wrote that, if 'we are to turn a bus or street car into either a newspaper or

a park, we take great liberties with people who, because of necessity, become commuters and, at the same time, captive viewers or listeners'. See *Erznoznik* v. *City of Jacksonville*, 422 US 205, 210–11 (1975): the court sustained a challenge to an ordinance that barred drive-in movie theatres from showing various parts of the human anatomy if the screen was visible from public streets. Powell J. wrote, 'Much that we encounter offends our aesthetic, if not our political and moral, sensibilities. . . . the burden normally falls upon the viewer to "avoid further bombardment of [his] sensibilities simply by averting [his] eyes" [citation omitted]'. See also Charles Black, 'He Cannot Choose but Hear: The Plight of the Captive Auditor', *Columbia Law Review* 53 (1953), 960.

33. *R.A.V.* v. *St Paul*, 112 S. Ct. 2538 (1992).
34. Akhil Reed Amar, 'The Case of the Missing Amendments: *R.A.V.* v. *City of St Paul*', *Harvard Law Review* 106 (1992), 124, 158.
35. See *Frisby* v. *Schultz*, 487 US 474, 485 (1988). For related cases, see e.g. *Ward* v. *Rock Against Racism*, 491 US 781 (1989); *Kovacs* v. *Cooper*, 336 US 77 (1949); *Clark* v. *Community for Creative Non-Violence*, 468 US 288 (1984) (concerning visitors who could freely leave an area). The Court seems to be limiting the 'captivity' restriction. In *Forsyth County* v. *Nationalist Movement*, 112 S. Ct. 2395, 2403 (1992), the Court held that 'listeners' reaction to speech is not a content neutral basis for regulation' (ordinance would have charged more for parade permit if hostile crowds were expected).
36. See *NAACP* v. *Alabama*, 357 US 449 (1958).
37. See *Rowan* v. *Post Office Department*, 397 US 728, 731 (1970).

Chapter 12

1. Bertrand Russell, *Portraits from Memory* (London: G. Allen & Unwin, 1956), 1.
2. Mark Yudof, *When Government Speaks: Politics, Law and Government Expression in America* (Berkeley and Los Angeles: University of California Press, 1983) 112.
3. Cass R. Sunstein, *Democracy and the Problem of Free Speech* (New York: The Free Press, 1993), 12. Sunstein likens the 1980s and 1990s debate about the regulation of speech to the pre-New Deal controversies concerning economic regulation. Then, opponents of regulation argued that the Constitution prohibited government interference 'with existing distributions of economic rights and entitlements'. The New Deal reformers 'insisted that this entire framework was built on fictions: and that the status quo was not made by nature but by human beings'. Similarly, he argues, the distribution of speech rights is a complex product of government and private action. 'Efforts to promote greater equality and diversity in broadcasting . . . seek a new and better regulatory regime, not to replace freedom with "government regulation".'
4. *Turner Broadcasting System Inc.* v. *FCC*, 114 S. Ct. 2445 (1994).
5. See James B. Twitchell, *Carnival Culture: The Trashing of Taste in America* (New York: Columbia, 1992). Twitchell adopts the carnival as the metaphor, with the idea that the gatekeeper has been replaced by the barker, calling out 'pay up and see what you want' (ibid. 2).
6. See David Morley, *Television, Audiences and Cultural Studies* (New York: Routledge, 1992), 77.

Bibliography

ABRAMSON, JEFFREY, 'Democratic Designs for Electronic Town Meetings', Prepared for the Aspen Institute Communications and Society Program, Queenstown, Md., 1992.

AKSOY, ASU, and AVCI, NABI, 'Spreading Turkish Identity', *InterMedia* 20 (Aug. 1992), 39.

—— and ROBINS, KEVIN, 'Gecekondu-Style Broadcasting in Turkey: A Confrontation of Cultural Values', *InterMedia* 21 (June 1993), 15.

ALTES, WILLEM F. KORTHALS, 'European Law: A Case Study of Changes in National Broadcasting', *Cardozo Arts and Entertainment Law Journal* 11 (1993), 313.

AMAR, AKHIL REED, 'The Case of the Missing Amendments: *R.A.V.* v. *City of St Paul*', *Harvard Law Review* 106 (1992), 124.

AMERICAN ENTERPRISE INSTITUTE'S CONFERENCE, 'The New Global Popular Culture: Is it American? Is it Good for America? Is it Good for the World?' 10 Mar. 1992, Washington, Organized by Ben Wattenberg, Senior Fellow.

ANDERSON, BENEDICT, *Imagined Communities: Reflections on the Origin and Spread of Nationalism* (London: Verso, 1983).

—— 'Exodus', *Critical Inquiry* 20 (1994), 314.

ANG, IEN, *Desperately Seeking the Audience* (New York: Routledge, 1991).

ANTIN, DAVID, 'Fine Furs', *Critical Inquiry* 19 (1992), 151.

ARROW, KENNETH JOSEPH, *Social Choice and Individual Values* (New Haven, Conn.: Yale University Press, 1963).

ASSOCIATION OF THE BAR OF THE CITY OF NEW YORK, *The Blessings of Liberty: An Enduring Constitution in a Changing World* (New York: Random House, 1989).

ATLAS, JAMES, *The Book Wars* (Knoxville, Tenn.: Whittle Direct Books, 1990).

AUDEN, W. H., 'Criticism in a Mass Society', *Mint* 2 (1948), 3.

AYLESWORTH, MERLIN H., 'Broadcasting in the Public Interest', *Annals of the American Academy of Political and Social Science* (Jan. 1935), 114.

BAKER, C. EDWIN, *Human Liberty and Freedom of Speech* (New York: Oxford University Press, 1989).

—— *Advertising and a Democratic Press* (Princeton: Princeton University Press, 1994).

BALKIN, J. M., 'Some Realism about Pluralism: Legal Realist Approaches to the First Amendment', *Duke Law Journal* 1990 (1990), 375.

Ball-Rokeach, Sandra J., and Cantor, Muriel G. (eds.), *Media, Audience and Social Structure* (London: Sage Publications, 1986).

Barendt, Eric, *Broadcasting Law: A Comparative Study* (New York: Oxford University Press, 1993).

Barnouw, Erik, *A Tower in Babel* (New York: Oxford University Press, 1966).

—— *The Golden Web* (New York: Oxford University Press, 1968).

—— *The Image Empire* (New York: Oxford University Press, 1970).

Barron, Jerome A., 'In Defense of "Fairness": A First Amendment Rationale for Broadcasting's "Fairness" Doctrine', *University of Colorado Law Review* 37 (1964), 31.

—— 'Access to the Press—A New First Amendment Right', *Harvard Law Review* 80 (1967), 1641.

Barrow, Roscoe, 'The Equal Opportunities and Fairness Doctrines in Broadcasting: Pillars in the Forum of Democracy', *University of Cincinnati Law Review* 37 (1968), 447.

Baudrillard, Jean, *The Ecstasy of Communication*, trans. Bernard and Caroline Schutze (New York: Autonomedia, 1988).

Been, Vicki, 'Exit as a Constraint on Land Use Exactions: Rethinking the Unconstitutional Conditions Doctrine', *Columbia Law Review* 91 (1991), 473.

Berger, Peter L., and Luckmann, Thomas, *The Social Construction of Reality: A Treatise in the Sociology of Knowledge* (Garden City, NY: Doubleday, 1966).

Berland, Jody, 'Placing Television', *New Formations* 4 (spring 1988), 145.

Bernstein, Marver, *Regulating Business by Independent Commission* (Princeton: Princeton University Press, 1955).

Bickel, Alexander M., *The Least Dangerous Branch: The Supreme Court at the Bar of Politics* (New Haven, Conn.: Yale University Press, 1986).

Black, Charles, 'He Cannot Choose but Hear: The Plight of the Captive Auditor', *Columbia Law Review* 53 (1953), 960.

Blasi, Vince, 'The Checking Value in First Amendment Theory', *American Bar Foundation Research Journal* 1977 (1977), 521.

Blumler, Jay G., McLeod, Jack M., and Rosengren, Karl Erik (eds.), *Comparatively Speaking: Communication and Culture Across Space and Time* (London: Sage Publications, 1992).

Bogart, Leo, *Strategy in Advertising* (New York: Harcourt, Brace & World, 1967).

Bohlen, Celestine, 'Home of First Revolution is Puzzling over This One', *New York Times*, 26 Mar. 1993.

Bollinger, Lee C., *Images of a Free Press* (Chicago: University of Chicago Press, 1991).

Bolton, Richard (ed.), *Culture Wars: Documents from the Recent Controversies in the Arts* (New York: New Press, 1992).

Bown, Matthew Cullerne, *Art under Stalin* (Oxford: Phaidon Press, 1991).

Bramsted, Ernst K., *Goebbels and National Socialist Propaganda 1925–1945* (London: Cresset Press, 1965).

BRASCH, WALTER M., and ULLOTH, DANA R., *The Press and the State* (Lanham, Md.: University Press of America, 1986).

BRIFFAULT, RICHARD, 'Our Localism: Part II—Localism and Legal Theory', *Columbia Law Review* 90 (1990), 346.

BRIGGS, ASA, *The Birth of Broadcasting* (New York: Oxford University Press, 1961).

—— *The Golden Age of Wireless* (New York: Oxford University Press, 1965).

—— *The BBC: The First Fifty Years* (Oxford: Oxford University Press, 1985).

BROWN, RHONDA, 'Ad Hoc Access: The Regulation of Editorial Advertising on Television and Radio', *Yale Law and Policy Review* 6 (1988), 449.

BROWNE, DONALD R., FIRESTONE, CHARLES M., and MICKIEWICZ, ELLEN, *Television/Radio News and Minorities* (Queenstown, Md.: Aspen Institute for Humanistic Studies, 1994).

CALHOUN, CRAIG (ed.), *Habermas and the Public Sphere* (Cambridge, Mass.: MIT Press, 1992).

CAREY, JOHN, *Communication as Culture* (Boston: Unwin Hyman, 1989).

CASSESE, ANTONIO, and CLAPHAM, ANDREW (eds.), *Transfrontier Television in Europe: The Human Rights Dimension* (Baden-Baden: Nomos Verlagsgesellschaft, 1990).

CHANEY, DAVID, 'The Symbolic Form of Ritual in Mass Communications', in Peter Golding, Graham Murdock, and Philip Schlesinger (eds.), *Communicating Politics: Mass Communications and the Political Process* (New York: Holmes & Meier Publishers, 1986), 115.

—— 'Audience Research and the BBC in the 1930s: A Mass Media Comes into Being', in James Curran, Anthony Smith, and Pauline Wingate (eds.), *Impacts and Influences: Essays on Media Power in the Twentieth Century* (New York: Methuen, 1987), 259.

CHAPMAN, ROBERT, *Selling the Sixties: The Pirates and Pop Music Radio* (London: Routledge, 1992).

CHOMSKY, NOAM, and HERMAN, EDWARD S., *Manufacturing Consent: The Political Economy of the Mass Media* (New York: Pantheon Books, 1988).

CLARKE, HILARY, 'EU Vows to "Move Forward": Consensus on Maintaining Identity Sought as AV Confab Opens', *Hollywood Reporter*, 1 July 1994.

COASE, RONALD H., *British Broadcasting: A Study in Monopoly* (London: Longmans, Green & Co., 1950).

—— 'The Federal Communications Commission', *Journal of Law and Economics* 2 (1959), 1.

—— 'The Market for Goods and the Market for Ideas', *American Economic Review, Papers and Proceedings* 64 (1974), 384.

—— 'Advertising and Free Speech', *Journal of Legal Studies* 6 (1977), 1.

COHEN, JEAN L., 'The Public Sphere, the Media, and Civil Society', in Andras Sajo and Monroe E. Price (eds.), *Rights of Media Access* (Dordrecht: Martinus Nijhoff, forthcoming).

—— and Andrew Arato, *Civil Society and Political Theory* (Cambridge, Mass.: MIT Press, 1992).

COLLINS, RICHARD, *Culture, Communication, and National Identity: The Case Study of Canadian Television* (Toronto: University of Toronto Press, 1990).

COLLINS, RONALD K. L., and SKOVER, David M., 'Pissing in the Snow: A Cultural Approach to the First Amendment', *Stanford Law Review* 45 (1993), 783.

Commission on Broadcasting to the People's Republic of China (Washington: Department of State Publication 9997, Sept. 1992).

COMMISSION ON FREEDOM OF THE PRESS, *Free and Responsible Press: A General Report on Mass Communication* (Chicago: University of Chicago Press, 1947).

COMMISSION ON RADIO AND TELEVISION POLICY, 'Report of the Working Group on Broadcaster Autonomy and the State', Prepared for the Aspen Institute Communications and Society Program (Queenstown, Md., 1994).

CONSTANTINESCU, E., '1993 Broadcasting Law in Romania', in Wolfgang Kleinwächter (ed.), *Broadcasting in Transition: The Changing Legal Framework in the Eastern Part of Europe* (Leipzig: Netcom Papers, 1993), 32.

COWAN, GEOFFREY, *See No Evil: The Backstage Battle over Sex and Violence on Television* (New York: Simon & Schuster, 1979).

DAYAN, DANIEL, and KATZ, ELIHU, 'Performing Media Events', in James Curran, Anthony Smith, and Pauline Wingate (eds.), *Impacts and Influences: Essays on Media Power in the Twentieth Century* (New York: Methuen, 1987), 174.

—— —— *Media Events: The Live Broadcasting of History* (Cambridge, Mass.: Harvard University Press, 1992).

DE GRAZIA, EDWARD, *Girls Lean Back Everywhere: The Law of Obscenity and the Assault on Genius* (New York: Random House, 1992).

DE KEERSMAEKER, Christine, 'Organization and Structure of Radio and Television Broadcasting in Belgium', *Entertainment Law Review* 3 (Sept.–Oct. 1992), 164.

DE TOCQUEVILLE, ALEXIS, *Democracy in America*, trans. Henry Reeve (London: Saunders and Otley, 1835).

DEUTSCH, KARL, *Nationalism and Social Communication* (Cambridge, Mass.: MIT Press, 1953).

DONALD, JAMES, *Sentimental Education: Schooling, Popular Culture and the Regulation of Liberty* (New York: Verso, 1992).

DOWNEY, ELIZABETH A., 'A Historical Survey of the International Regulation of Propaganda', *Michigan Yearbook of International Legal Studies* 5 (1984), 341.

DOWNS, ANTHONY, *An Economic Theory of Democracy* (New York, Harper & Brothers, 1957).

DYSON, KENNETH, and HUMPHREYS, PETER (eds.), *The Political Economy of Communications: International and European Dimensions* (New York: Routledge, 1990).

EDELMAN, M. J., *Constructing the Political Spectacle* (Chicago: University of Chicago Press, 1988).

ELDER, ROBERT E., *The United States Information Agency and American Foreign Policy* (Syracuse, NY: Syracuse University Press, 1968).

ELLUL, JACQUES, *Propaganda: The Formation of Men's Attitudes* (New York: Alfred A. Knopf, 1965).

ENTMAN, ROBERT M., *Democracy without Citizens: Media and the Decay of American Politics* (New York: Oxford University Press, 1989).

—— and WILDMAN, STEVEN S., 'Reconciling Economic and Non-Economic Perspectives on Media Policy', *Journal of Communication* 42 (winter 1992), 5.

EUGSTER, ERNEST, *Television Programming across National Boundaries: The EBU and OIRT Experience* (Dedham, Mass.: Artech House, 1983).

EWEN, STUART, *Captains of Consciousness: Advertising and the Social Roots of the Consumer Culture* (New York: McGraw-Hill, 1976).

FAHEY, PATRICK M., 'Comment: Advocacy Group Boycotting of Network Television Advertisers and its Effects on Programming Content', *University of Pennsylvania Law Review* 140 (1991), 647.

FALK, RICHARD A., 'On Regulating International Propaganda: A Plea for Moderate Aims', *Law and Contemporary Problems* 31 (1966), 622.

FEJES, FRED, *Imperialism, Media and the Good Neighbor: New Deal Foreign Policy and United States Shortwave Broadcasting to Latin America* (Norwood, NJ: Ablex Publishing Corp., 1986).

FERGUSON, MARJORIE, 'The Mythology about Globalization', *European Journal of Communications* 7 (1992), 69.

FISHKIN, JAMES S., *Democracy and Deliberation: New Directions for Democratic Reform* (New Haven, Conn.: Yale University Press, 1991).

FISKE, JOHN, *Television Culture* (London: Methuen, 1987).

FISS, OWEN M., 'Free Speech and Social Structure', *Iowa Law Review* 71 (1986), 1405.

—— 'Essays Commemorating the One Hundredth Anniversary of the Harvard Law Review: Why the State?' *Harvard Law Review* 100 (1987), 781.

—— 'State Activism and State Censorship', *Yale Law Journal* 100 (1992), 2087.

FLY, JAMES LAWRENCE, 'Regulation of Radio Broadcasting in the Public Interest', *Annals of the American Academy of Political and Social Science* (Jan. 1941), 102.

FOSTER, FRANCES H., '*Izvestiia* as a Mirror of Russian Legal Reform: Press, Law, and Crisis in the Post-Soviet Era', *Vanderbilt Journal of Transnational Law* 26 (1993), 675.

FOWLER, MARK S., and BRENNER, DANIEL L., 'A Marketplace Approach to Broadcast Regulation', *Texas Law Review* 60 (1982), 207.

GAMBRELL, JAMEY, 'Moscow: The Front Page', *New York Review of Books* 39/16 (8 Oct. 1992), 56.

GARDBAUM, STEPHEN A., 'Broadcasting, Democracy, and the Market', *Georgetown Law Journal* 82 (1993), 373.

GARNHAM, NICHOLAS, 'The Media and the Public Sphere', in Peter Golding, Graham Murdock, and Philip Schlesinger (eds.), *Communicating Politics: Mass Communications and the Political Process* (New York: Holmes & Meier, 1986).

GARNHAM, NICHOLAS, *Capitalism and Communication, Global Culture and the Economics of Information* (London: Sage Publications, 1990).

—— 'The Media and the Public Sphere', in Craig Calhoun (ed.), *Habermas and the Public Sphere* (Cambridge, Mass.: MIT Press, 1992), 359.

GELLNER, ERNEST, *Nations and Nationalism* (Oxford: Blackwell, 1983).

GERBNER, GEORGE, 'Liberal Education in the Information Age', *Current Issues in Higher Education 1983–84* (1984), 14.

GERTH, HANS, and MILLS, C. WRIGHT, *Character and Social Structure: The Psychology of Social Institutions* (New York: Harcourt, Brace & World, 1964).

GITELMAN, ZVI, 'Exiting from the Soviet Union: Emigrés or Refugees?', *Michigan Yearbook of International Legal Studies* 3 (1982), 43.

GITLIN, TODD, *The Whole World is Watching: Mass Media in the Making and Unmaking of the New Left* (Berkeley and Los Angeles: University of California Press, 1980).

GRABER, MARK A., *Transforming Free Speech: The Ambiguous Legacy of Civil Liberalism* (Berkeley and Los Angeles: University of California Press, 1991).

GREENWOOD, CHRISTOPHER, 'Free Movement of Workers under EEC Law and English Law', *New Law Journal* 133 (1983), 933.

GRIMM, HON. DIETER, 'Freedom of the Mass Media', Paper delivered at 'Rights of Access to the Media' Conference, Central European University, Budapest, Hungary, 19–21 June 1993.

GROSSMAN, LAWRENCE, *The Electronic Republic: The Transformation of American Democracy* (New York: Viking, forthcoming).

HABERMAS, JURGEN, 'The Public Sphere', *New German Critique* 1/3 (autumn 1974), 49.

—— *The Theory of Communicative Action*, trans. Thomas McCarthy (Boston: Beacon, 1984).

—— *The Structural Transformation of the Public Sphere: An Inquiry into a Category of Bourgeois Society*, trans. Thomas Burger (Cambridge, Mass.: MIT Press, 1989).

—— *Between Facts and Norms: Contributions to a Discourse Theory of Law and Democracy* (Cambridge, Mass.: MIT Press, forthcoming).

HAWTHORNE, DONALD W., and PRICE, MONROE E., 'Rewiring the First Amendment: Meaning, Content and Public Broadcasting', *Cardozo Arts and Entertainment Law Journal* 12 (1994), 499.

HEIDT, ERHARD U., *Mass Media, Cultural Tradition and National Identity* (Fort Lauderdale, Flor.: Breitenbach, 1987).

HENTOFF, NAT, *Free Speech for Me—But Not for Thee: How the American Left and Right Relentlessly Censor Each Other* (New York: HarperCollins, 1992).

HERBST, SUSAN, *Numbered Voices* (Chicago: University of Chicago Press, 1993).

HIRSCHMAN, ALBERT O., *Exit, Voice, and Loyalty: Responses to Decline in Firms, Organizations, and States* (Cambridge, Mass.: Harvard University Press, 1970).

HOBSBAWM, ERIC J., *Nations and Nationalism since 1780* (New York: Cambridge University Press, 1990).

—— and Terence Ranger (eds.), *The Invention of Tradition* (New York: Cambridge University Press, 1983).

Hull, Elizabeth, *Taking Liberties: National Barriers to the Free Flow of Ideas* (New York: Praeger, 1990).

Huntington, Samuel P., 'The Clash of Civilizations?' *Foreign Affairs* 72 (1993), 22.

Information Commission for the Study of Communication Problems (MacBride Commission), *Many Voices, One World: Towards a New More Just and More Efficient World Information and Communication Order* (London: Kogan Page, 1980).

Isaacs, Harold Robert, *Idols of the Tribe: Group Identity and Political Change* (New York: Harper & Row, 1975).

Jaffe, Louis L., 'The Illusion of the Ideal Administration', *Harvard Law Review* 86 (1973), 1191.

Jakubowicz, Karol, 'The Restructuring of Television in East-Central Europe', Paper given at the CCIS, University of Westminster, May 1992.

—— 'Study on Media Concentrations in Central and East-European Countries', *Committee of Experts on Media Concentrations and Pluralism: MM-CM (94) 17* (Strasburg: Council of Europe, 6 May 1994).

James, Caradog V., *Soviet Socialist Realism: Origins and Theory* (London: Macmillan, 1973).

Johnson, Andrea L., 'Redefining Diversity in Telecommunications: Uniform Regulatory Framework for Mass Communications', *University of California at Davis Law Review* 26 (1992), 87.

Jowett, Garth S., and O'Donnell, Victoria, *Propaganda and Persuasion* (London: Sage Publications, 1986).

Kaplan, Laurence G. C., 'The European Community's "Television Without Frontiers" Directive: Stimulating Europe to Regulate Culture', *Emory International Law Review* 8 (1994), 255.

Kapuściński, Ryszard, *Shah of Shahs*, trans. William R. Brand and Katarzyna Mroczkowska-Brand (San Diego: Harcourt Brace Jovanovich, 1985).

Karst, Kenneth L., 'Paths to Belonging: The Constitution and Cultural Identity', *North Carolina Law Review* 64 (1986), 303.

—— *Law's Promise, Law's Expression: Visions of Power in the Politics of Race, Gender, and Religion* (New Haven, Conn.: Yale University Press, 1993).

Katz, Elihu, and Wedell, George, *Broadcasting in the Third World: Promise and Performance* (Cambridge, Mass.: Harvard University Press, 1977).

Keane, John, *The Media and Democracy* (Cambridge, Mass.: Polity Press, 1991).

Kirby, Andrew, 'A Sense of Place', *Critical Studies in Mass Communication* 6 (Sept. 1989), 322.

Kleinwächter, Wolfgang, 'Out with the Cold, In with the New?', *InterMedia* 20 (May 1992), 12.

Kramer, Victor, 'What is the Public Interest? Who Represents It?', *Administrative Law Review* 26 (1974), 395.

KRISTOF, NICHOLAS D., 'Satellites Bring Information Revolution to China', *New York Times*, 11 Apr. 1993, p. 1.

KRUG, PETER, 'The Abandonment of the State Radio–Television Monopoly in the Soviet Union: The First Step Toward Broadcasting Pluralism?', *Wisconsin International Law Journal* 9 (1991), 377.

KURLAND, PHILIP, and LERNER, RALPH (eds.), *The Founders' Constitution* (Chicago: University of Chicago Press, 1987).

LABER, JERI, 'The Dictatorship Returns', *New York Review of Books*, 40/13 (15 July 1993), 40.

LAMBRECHT, BILL, 'High-Tech TV is Redefining Home Rule; Turn On, Tune In: New Technology Ushers in Age of Teledemocracy', *St Louis Post-Dispatch*, 21 Aug. 1994, p. 1B.

LEVY, LEONARD WILLIAMS, *Emergence of a Free Press* (New York: Oxford University Press, 1985).

LIEBES, TAMAR, and KATZ, ELIHU, *The Export of Meaning: Cross Cultural Readings of 'Dallas'* (New York: Oxford University Press, 1990).

LILLICH, RICHARD B. (ed.), *International Human Rights, Documentary Supplement* (Boston: Little, Brown & Company, 1991).

LIN, SUN, 'Foreign Capital and Equipment Fuel a Telecommunications Lift-off', *InterMedia* 22 (Apr. 1994), 22.

LINDBLOM, CHARLES, *Politics and Markets* (New York: Basic Books, 1977).

LIPPMANN, WALTER, *Public Opinion* (London: Allen & Unwin, 1922).

LUKE, TIMOTHY W., *Shows of Force: Power, Politics, and Ideology in Art Exhibitions* (Durham, NC: Duke University Press, 1992).

LULL, JAMES, *China Turned On: Television, Reform, and Resistance* (New York: Routledge, 1991).

LUTHAR, BREDA, 'Slovenia Struggles with the Reithian Ethos', *InterMedia* 20 (Aug. 1992), 33.

MCLEOD, JACK M., and BECKER, LEE B., 'Testing the Validity of Gratification Measures through Political Effects Analysis', in Jay G. Blumler and Elihu Katz (eds.), *The Uses of Mass Communications: Current Perspectives on Gratifications Research* (London: Sage Publications, 1974), 137.

MCNAIR, BRIAN, *Glasnost, Perestroika and the Soviet Media* (New York: Routledge, 1991).

MCNEILL, WILLIAM H., 'Fundamentalism and the World of the 1990s', in Martin E. Marty and R. Scott Appleby (eds.), *Fundamentalisms and Society: Reclaiming the Sciences, the Family, and Education* (Chicago: University of Chicago Press, 1993), 558.

MCQUAIL, DENIS, *Mass Communication Theory* (London: Sage Publications, 2nd edn., 1987).

MAINARDI, PATRICIA, *The End of the Salon: Art and the State in the Early Third Republic* (New York: Cambridge University Press, 1993).

MALEY, WILLIAM, 'Centralization and Censorship', in Colin McCabe and Olivia

Stewart (eds.), *The BBC and Public Service Broadcasting* (Manchester: Manchester University Press, 1986), 32.

MANDER, JERRY, *Four Arguments for the Elimination of Television* (New York: William Morrow & Co., 1978).

MANOFF, ROBERT K., 'Independence and Mass Media in Transition', unpublished paper, Conference on Mass Media in Transition, American University, Washington, DC, 1994.

MARTELANC, TOMO, 'Vulnerable Slovenia', *InterMedia* 20 (Aug. 1992), 34.

MARTIN, L. JOHN, *International Propaganda* (Minneapolis: University of Minnesota Press, 1958).

MATSUDA, MARI J., 'Voices of America: Accent, Antidiscrimination Law, and a Jurisprudence for the Last Reconstruction', *Yale Law Journal* 100 (1991), 1329.

MEIKLEJOHN, ALEXANDER, *Free Speech and its Relation to Self-Government* (New York: Harper, 1948).

MEYROWITZ, JOSHUA, *No Sense of Place: The Impact of the Electronic Media on Social Behavior* (New York: Oxford University Press, 1985).

—— 'The Generalized Elsewhere', *Critical Studies in Mass Communication* 6 (Sept. 1989), 326.

MICHELMAN, FRANK, 'Saving Old Glory: On Constitutional Iconography', *Stanford Law Review* 42 (1990), 1337.

MICKIEWICZ, ELLEN PROPPER, *Split Signals: Television and Politics in the Soviet Union* (New York: Oxford University Press, 1988).

—— 'Images of America', in Everette E. Dennis, George Gerbner, and Yassen N. Zassoursky (eds.), *Beyond the Cold War: Soviet and American Media Images* (London: Sage Publications, 1991).

—— and FIRESTONE, CHARLES, *Television and Elections* (Queenstown, Md.: Aspen Institute for Humanistic Studies, 1992).

MONTGOMERY, KATHRYN C., *Target: Prime Time, Advocacy Groups and the Struggle over Entertainment Television* (New York: Oxford University Press, 1989).

MORLEY, DAVID, *Television, Audiences and Cultural Studies* (New York: Routledge, 1992).

MURRAY, JOHN, *The Russian Press from Brezhnev to Yeltsin: Behind the Paper Curtain* (Aldershot: Edward Edgar Publishing Company, 1994).

NEGRINE, RALPH, and PAPATHANASSOPOULOS, STYLIANOS, *The Internationalization of Television* (New York: Pinter Publishers, 1990).

NEWSOME, CYNTHIA, 'Note: Pay Attention: A Survey and Analysis of the Legal Battle Over the Integration of Forced Television Advertising into the Public School Curriculum', *Rutgers Law Journal* 24 (1992), 281.

'Newspapers: Free to Be Bankrupt', *Post-Soviet Media Law and Policy Newsletter*, Issue 2 (17 Nov. 1993), 6.

NIEUWENHUIS, AERNOUT J., 'Media Policy in the Netherlands: Beyond the Market?' *European Journal of Communication* 7 (1992), 147.

—— 'The Crumbling Pillars of Dutch TV', *InterMedia* 20 (Aug.–Sept. 1992), 37.

NIXON, ROB, 'Keeping Television Out: The South African Story', *InterMedia* 20 (Aug.–Sept. 1992), 35.

NOAM, ELI M., *Television in Europe* (New York: Oxford University Press, 1992).

—— 'Beyond Territoriality: Economics and Politics in Telesociety', Columbia Institute for Tele-Information, Working Paper No. 690 (1994).

'Note, "Official English": Federal Limits on Efforts to Curtail Bilingual Services in the States', *Harvard Law Review* 100 (1987), 1345.

'Note: The Mayflower Doctrine Scuttled', *Yale Law Journal* 59 (1950), 759.

The NTIA Infrastructure Report: Telecommunications in the Age of Information (Washington, DC: US Department of Commerce, 1991).

O'BOYLE, MICHAEL, 'Right to Speak and Associate under Strasbourg Case-Law with Reference to Eastern and Central Europe', *Connecticut Journal of International Law* 8 (1993), 263.

O'CONNOR, JOHN J., 'Television View: Still Trapped in a Vast Wasteland', *New York Times*, 13 Dec. 1992, sect. 2, p. 1.

O'NEIL, ONORA, 'Practices of Toleration', in Judith Lichtenberg (ed.), *Democracy and the Mass Media: A Collection of Essays* (New York: Cambridge University Press, 1990).

OWEN, BRUCE M., *Economics and Freedom of Expression: Media Structure and the First Amendment* (Cambridge, Mass.: Ballinger Publishing Company, 1975).

PALETZ, DAVID L., and ENTMAN, ROBERT M., *Media Power Politics* (New York: Free Press, 1981).

PELLE, JOKE J. A., and AKKERMANS, PIET W. C., 'The Dutch Broadcasting System: A Basic Right Caught between Dutch Constitutional Law and European Community Law', *RED/ERPL* 2/1 (1990), 39.

PILDES, RICHARD H., 'The New Public Law: The Unintended Cultural Consequences of Public Policy', *Michigan Law Review* 89 (1991), 936.

PITOFSKY, ROBERT, 'The Political Content of Antitrust', *University of Pennsylvania Law Review* 127 (1979), 1051.

POCOCK, ROWLAND F., *The Early British Radio Industry* (Manchester: Manchester University Press, 1988).

POOL, ITHIEL DE SOLA, *Technologies of Freedom* (Harvard, Mass.: Belknap Press, 1983).

PORTER, VINCENT, and HASSELBACH, SUZANNE, *Pluralism, Politics and the Marketplace: The Regulation of German Broadcasting* (New York: Routledge, 1991).

POSNER, RICHARD A., 'Free Speech in an Economic Perspective', *Suffolk University Law Review* 20 (1986), 1.

Post-Soviet Media Law and Policy Newsletter, Issues 1–13 (New York: Benjamin N. Cardozo School of Law, 1993–4).

POSTMAN, NEIL, *Amusing Ourselves to Death: Public Discourse in the Age of Show Business* (New York: Viking, 1985).

PRESIDENT'S TASK FORCE ON US GOVERNMENT INTERNATIONAL BROADCASTING, *The Report of the President's Task Force on US Government International Broadcasting* (Washington, DC: Department of State Publication 9925, Dec. 1991).

PREUSS, ULRICH, 'The Constitutional Concept of the Public Sphere according to the German Basic Law', in Andras Sajo and Monroe E. Price (eds.), *Rights of Media Access* (Dordrecht: Martinus Nijhoff, forthcoming).

PRICE, MONROE E., 'Requiem for the Wired Nation: Cable Rulemaking at the FCC', *Virginia Law Review* 61 (1975), 541.

—— 'The First Amendment and Television Broadcasting by Satellite', *UCLA Law Review* 23 (1976), 879.

—— 'Taming Red Lion: The First Amendment and Structural Approaches to Media Regulation', *Federal Communications Law Journal* 31 (1979), 215.

—— 'Comment' in Jack David and Robert B. McKay (eds.), *The Blessings of Liberty: An Enduring Constitution in a Changing World* (New York: Random House, 1989), 277.

—— *Shattered Mirrors: Our Search for Identity and Community in the AIDS Era* (Cambridge, Mass.: Harvard University Press, 1989).

—— 'Congress, Free Speech, and Cable Legislation: An Introduction', *Cardozo Arts and Entertainment Law Journal* 8 (1990), 225.

—— 'Comparing Broadcast Structures: Transnational Perspectives and Post-Communist Examples', *Cardozo Arts and Entertainment Law Journal* 11 (1993), 275.

—— 'Controlling Imagery: The Fight over Using Art to Change Society', *American Art* 7 (1993), 2.

—— 'The Market for Loyalties: Electronic Media and the Global Competition for Allegiances', *Yale Law Journal* 104 (1994), 667.

—— and KRUG, PETER, 'Russia: Still Government TV, The Problem is Defining the Government', *InterMedia* 21 (1993), 21.

—— and HAWTHORNE, DONALD W., 'Saving Public Television: The Remand of *Turner Broadcasting* and the Future of Cable Regulation', *Hastings Communications and Entertainment Law Journal* 17 (1994), 65.

PRICE, ROCHELLE B., 'Jamming and the Law of International Communications', *Michigan Yearbook of International Legal Studies* 5 (1984), 391.

Quality Time? The Report of the Twentieth Century Fund Task Force on Public Television, with Background Paper by Richard Somerset-Ward (New York: Twentieth Century Fund, 1993).

RABOY, MARC, *Missed Opportunities: The Story of Canada's Broadcasting Policy* (Buffalo, NY: McGill-Queen's University Press, 1990).

—— and DAGENAIS, BERNARD (eds.), *Mass Communication and the Disruption of Social Order* (London: Sage Publications, 1992).

—— —— *Media, Crisis and Democracy: Mass Communication and the Disruption of Social Order* (London: Sage Publications, 1992).

RAINEY, R. RANDALL, 'The Public's Interest in Public Affairs Discourse, Democratic Governance, and Fairness in Broadcasting', *Georgetown Law Journal* 82 (1993), 269.

'Report to Congress on the National Endowment for the Arts', submitted by the Independent Commission (Washington, DC, Sept. 1990).

RICHTER, ANDREI, 'Newspaper: Free to be Bankrupt', *Post-Soviet Media Law and Policy Newsletter*, no. 2 (Nov. 1993), 6.

—— 'Direct Subsidies to the Press', *Post-Soviet Media Law and Policy Newsletter*, no. 4 (Jan. 1994), 2.

ROBINS, KEVIN, 'Reimagined Communities', *Cultural Studies* 3 (1989).

—— WEBSTER, FRANK, and PICKERING, MICHAEL, 'Propaganda, Information and Social Control', in Jeremy Hawthorn (ed.), *Propaganda, Persuasion and Polemic* (Baltimore, Md.: Edward Arnold, 1987), 1.

ROMANIAN LAW ON RADIO AND TELEVISION BROADCASTING, *Cardozo Arts and Entertainment Law Journal* 11 app. (1993), 609.

RUSBRIDGER, ALAN, 'The Moghul Invasion', *Guardian*, 8 Apr. 1994, p. T6.

RUSSELL, BERTRAND, *Portraits from Memory* (London: G. Allen & Unwin, 1956).

RUSSIAN FEDERATION LAW ON MASS MEDIA, *Cardozo Arts and Entertainment Law Journal* 11 app. (1993), 625.

RUTH, STEVEN, 'Comment: The Regulation of Spillover Transmissions from Direct Broadcast Satellites in Europe', *Federal Communications Law Journal* 42 (1989), 107.

RUTHERFORD, PAUL, *The Making of the Canadian Media* (Toronto: McGraw-Hill Ryerson, 1978).

SAHIN, HALUK, and AKSOY, ASU, 'Global Media and Cultural Identity in Turkey', *Journal of Communication* 43 (1992), 31.

SAJO, ANDRAS, 'Hate Speech for Hostile Hungarians', *East European Constitutional Review* 3 (1994), 82.

SALDICH, ANNE RAWLEY, *Electronic Democracy: Television's Impact on the American Political Process* (New York: Praeger, 1979).

SALECL, RENATA, *The Spoils of Freedom: Psychoanalysis and Feminism after the Fall of Socialism* (London: Routledge, 1994).

SANDEL, MICHAEL J., 'Post-National Democracy vs. Electronic Bonapartism', *NPQ* 9 (1992), 4.

SCANNELL, PADDY, 'Public Service Broadcasting and Modern Public Life', in Paddy Scannell, Philip Schlesinger, and Colin Sparks (eds.), *Culture and Power: A Media, Culture and Society Reader* (London: Sage Publications, 1992), 317.

—— and CARDIFF, D., 'Serving the Nation: Public Service Broadcasting before the War', in Bernard Waites, Tony Bennett, and Graham Martin (eds.), *Popular Culture: Past and Present* (London: Croom Helm, 1982), 161.

SCHILLER, HERBERT I., 'Fast Food, Fast Cars, Fast Political Rhetoric', *InterMedia* 20 (Aug. 1992), 21.

—— *Mass Communications and American Empire* (Boulder, Colo.: Westview Press, 1992).

SCHLESINGER, PHILIP, *Media, State and Nation: Political Violence and Collective Identities* (London: Sage Publications, 1991).
—— 'From Production to Propaganda?' in Paddy Scannell, Philip Schlesinger, and Colin Sparks (eds.), *Culture and Power: A Media, Culture and Society Reader* (London: Sage Publications, 1992).
—— 'Europe's Contradictory Communicative Space', *Daedalus* 123 (Mar. 1994), 25.
SCHUDSON, MICHAEL, *Advertising, the Uneasy Persuasion: Its Dubious Impact on American Society* (New York: Basic Books, 1984).
—— 'The "Public Sphere" and its Problems: Bringing the State (Back) In', *Notre Dame Journal of Law, Ethics and Public Policy* 8 (1994), 529.
SEN, AMARTYA KUMAR, *Poverty and Famines: An Essay on Entitlement and Deprivation* (New York: Oxford University Press, 1981).
SEPSTRUP, PREBEN, *Transnationalization of Television in Western Europe* (London: J. Libbey, 1990).
SETON-WATSON, HUGH, *Nations and States: An Inquiry into the Origins of Nations and the Politics of Nationalism* (Boulder, Colo.: Westview Press, 1977).
SHIFFRIN, STEVEN H., 'Government Speech', *UCLA Law Review* 27 (1980), 565.
—— *The First Amendment, Democracy, and Romance* (Cambridge, Mass.: Harvard University Press, 1990).
SHORT, K. R. M. (ed.), *Western Broadcasting over the Iron Curtain* (London: Croom Helm, 1986).
SHUIFU, ZHAO (Minister of Radio, Film and Television, People's Republic of China), 'Foreign Dominance of Chinese Broadcasting: Will Hearts and Minds Follow?' *InterMedia* 22 (Apr. 1994), 8.
SIEGEL, EVAN G. S., 'Comment: Closing the Campus Gates to Free Expression: The Regulation of Offensive Speech at Colleges and Universities', *Emory Law Journal* 39 (1990), 1351.
SIMMONS, STEVEN J., *The Fairness Doctrine and the Media* (Berkeley and Los Angeles: University of California Press, 1978).
SKILLEN, DAPHNE, 'Russia: TV Hovers between Independence and Propaganda', *InterMedia* 21 (June 1993), 18.
SKOVMAND, MICHAEL, and SCHRODER, KIM CHRISTIAN (eds.), *Media Cultures: Reappraising Transnational Media* (New York: Routledge, 1992).
SLOAN COMMISSION ON CABLE COMMUNICATIONS, *On the Cable: The Television of Abundance* (New York: McGraw-Hill, 1971).
SMITH, ANTHONY (ed.), *British Broadcasting* (London: Newton Abbot, 1974).
—— *Television and Political Life: Studies in Six European Countries* (London: MacMillan Press, 1979).
—— *The Geopolitics of Information: How Western Culture Dominates the World* (Boston: Faber & Faber, 1980).
—— 'Licences and Liberty', in Colin McCabe and Olivia Stewart (eds.), *The BBC and Public Service Broadcasting* (Manchester: Manchester University Press, 1986), 233.

SMITH, ANTHONY D., *National Identity* (New York: Penguin Books, 1991).

SMITH, THOMAS BLAISDELL, 'Reexamining the Reasonable Access and Equal Time Provisions of the Federal Communications Act: Can These Provisions Stand if the Fairness Doctrine Fails?', *Georgia Law Review* 74 (1986), 1491.

STEELE, RICHARD W., *Propaganda in an Open Society: The Roosevelt Administration and the Media, 1933–1941* (Westport, Conn.: Greenwood Press, 1985).

STEIN, ERIC, 'History against Free Speech: The New German Law Against the "Auschwitz"—and other—"Lies" ', *Michigan Law Review* 85 (1986), 277.

STERN, PAUL G., 'Note: A Pluralistic Reading of the First Amendment and its Relation to Public Discourse', *Yale Law Journal* 99 (1990), 925.

STONE, GEOFFREY R., 'Content Regulation and the First Amendment', *William and Mary Law Review* 25 (1983), 189.

—— 'Hate Speech and the US Constitution', *East European Constitutional Review* 3 (1994), 78.

STRAUSS, DAVID A., 'Persuasion, Autonomy, and Freedom of Expression', *Columbia Law Review* 91 (1991), 334.

SUNSTEIN, CASS R., *Democracy and the Problem of Free Speech* (New York: The Free Press, 1993).

Sykes Committee Report, United Kingdom Committee of Enquiry (London: King's Printer, 1923), 6.

TICHI, CECILIA, *Electronic Hearth: Creating an American Television Culture* (New York: Oxford University Press, 1991).

TIEBOUT, CHARLES A., 'A Pure Theory of Local Expenditures', *Journal of Political Economics* 64 (1956), 416.

TOMLINSON, ALAN (ed.), *Consumption, Identity, and Style: Marketing, Meanings, and the Packaging of Pleasure* (New York: Routledge, 1990).

TUNSTALL, JEREMY, *The Media are American* (New York: Columbia University Press, 1977).

TWITCHELL, JAMES B., *Carnival Culture: The Trashing of Taste in America* (New York: Columbia University Press, 1992).

UDOVICKI, KAROLINA, 'Letter to the New Yorker', *New Yorker* (23 May 1994), 9.

US DEPARTMENT OF COMMERCE, NATIONAL TELECOMMUNICATIONS AND INFORMATION ADMINISTRATION, *Globalization of the Mass Media* (Washington: NTIA Special Publication 93–290, Jan. 1993).

VACHNADZE, G. N., *Secrets of Journalism in Russia: Mass Media under Gorbachev and Yeltsin* (New York: Nova Science Publishers, 1992).

VAN LOON, AD 'Pluralism, Concentration and Competition in the Media Sector', *CDMM (92) 8 Vol. I* (Strasburg: Council of Europe, 1991).

—— 'National Media Policies under EEC Law Taking into Account Fundamental Rights', *Media Law and Practice* 14 (1993), 17.

WARNER, MICHAEL, *The Letters of the Republic: Publication and the Public Sphere in Eighteenth-Century America* (Cambridge, Mass.: Harvard University Press, 1990).

WEINBERG, JONATHAN, 'Broadcasting and Speech', *California Law Review* 81 (1993), 1103.

WHITE, HOWARD A., 'Fine Tuning the Federal Government's Role in Public Broadcasting', *Federal Communications Law Journal* 46 (1994), 491.

WILDE, BRUCE R., 'FCC Tax Certificates for Minority Ownership of Broadcast Facilities: A Critical Re-Examination of Policy', *University of Pennsylvania Law Review* 138 (1990), 979.

YASSKY, DAVID, 'Eras of the First Amendment', *Columbia Law Review* 91 (1991), 1699.

YUDOF, MARK G., 'When Governments Speak: Toward a Theory of Government Expression and the First Amendment', *Texas Law Review* 57 (1979), 863.

—— *When Government Speaks: Politics, Law, and Government Expression in America* (Berkeley and Los Angeles: University of California Press, 1983).

ZARAGOZA, RICHARD R., BODORFF, RICHARD J., and EMORD, JONATHAN W., 'The Public Interest Concept Transformed: The Trusteeship Model Gives Way to a Marketplace Approach', in Jon T. Powell and Wally Gair (eds.), *Public Interest and the Business of Broadcasting* (New York: Quorum Books, 1988), 31.

ZEIDENBERG, LEONARD, 'President Pushes TV Marti; ITU Pushes Back', *Broadcasting* 118 (9 Apr. 1990), 37.

ZHEN, ZUO LIU, 'Broadcasting for the People, To the People', *InterMedia* 22 (Apr. 1994), 10.

Index